PROTEST AND PARTNERSHIP

Global Indigenous Issues Series

Series Editor: Roberta Rice, Associate Professor, Department of Political Science, University of Calgary

ISSN 2561-3057 (Print) ISSN 2561-3065 (Online)

The Global Indigenous Issues series explores Indigenous peoples' cultural, political, social, economic and environmental struggles in para-colonial and post-colonial societies. The series includes original research on local, regional, national, and transnational experiences.

UNIVERSITY OF CALGARY
Press

PROTEST AND PARTNERSHIP

Case Studies of Indigenous Peoples, Consultation and
Engagement, and Resource Development in Canada

EDITED BY

Jennifer Winter and Brendan Boyd

Global Indigenous Issues Series
ISSN 2561-3057 (Print) ISSN 2561-3065 (Online)

University of Calgary Press
2500 University Drive NW
Calgary, Alberta
Canada T2N 1N4
press.ucalgary.ca

LIBRARY AND ARCHIVES CANADA CATALOGUING IN PUBLICATION

Title: Protest and partnership : case studies of Indigenous peoples, consultation and engagement, and resource development in Canada / edited by Jennifer Winter and Brendan Boyd.
Names: Winter, Jennifer, editor. | Boyd, Brendan, editor.
Series: Global indigenous issues series ; no. 3.
Description: Series statement: Global indigenous issues series ; 3 | Includes bibliographical references and index.
Identifiers: Canadiana (print) 20230623999 | Canadiana (ebook) 20230624197 | ISBN 9781773852034 (hardcover) | ISBN 9781773852041 (softcover) | ISBN 9781773852058 (open access PDF) | ISBN 9781773852065 (PDF) | ISBN 9781773852072 (EPUB)
Subjects: LCSH: Economic development—Canada. | LCSH: Sustainable development—Canada. | LCSH: Indigenous peoples—Canada—Economic conditions. | LCSH: Indigenous peoples—Legal status, laws, etc.—Canada. | LCSH: Indigenous peoples—Land tenure—Canada. | LCSH: Indigenous peoples—Canada—Politics and government.
Classification: LCC HC120.E5 P76 2024 | DDC 338.90089/97071—dc23

The University of Calgary Press acknowledges the support of the Government of Alberta through the Alberta Media Fund for our publications. We acknowledge the financial support of the Government of Canada. We acknowledge the financial support of the Canada Council for the Arts for our publishing program.

Alberta Government   Canadä   Canada Council   Conseil des Arts
                                        for the Arts   du Canada

Printed and bound in Canada by Imprimerie Gauvin Ltée
♻ This book is printed on Enviro book paper

Copyediting by Peter Midgley
Cover image: Colourbox 58754138
Cover design, page design, and typesetting by Melina Cusano

We wish to express our gratitude to the contributors to this volume and the Indigenous communities that have shared their stories.

To our contributors, thank you for your perseverance in this project. We appreciate your dedication.

To the communities who partnered with researchers in this volume, we acknowledge and pay tribute to your willingness to trust us with your experiences and expertise.

Table of Contents

Foreword

The genesis of *Protest and Partnership: Case Studies of Indigenous Communities, Consultation and Engagement, and Resource Development in Canada* was a workshop in December 2014 and a conference in November 2016, both hosted by the University of Calgary's School of Public Policy.

The workshop brought together nine Canadian academics with expertise in community-based research, natural resource development, and its effects on Indigenous communities. The purpose of the workshop was to identify potential case studies of successes and failures in consultation and engagement processes for further exploration and research and eventual publication as independent articles. An informal collaboration followed, with the School of Public Policy providing small funding support to engage research assistants for participants pursuing the case studies as independent research projects.

The purpose of the conference was "to share knowledge and stories about policy issues critical to Indigenous Peoples in Canada,"[1] including preliminary results from the case studies. The conference included a keynote address by Chief Jim Boucher of Fort McKay First Nation on the story of the Nation's economic successes; a panel on business and entrepreneurship in Indigenous communities; a panel with case studies of Indigenous communities' experience with resource development; and a panel on improving consultation and engagement processes.

Several of the book contributors—Boyd, McMillan, Rodon, and Slowey—presented work in progress at the conference, and we felt pursuing a book to share the experiences of Indigenous communities with consultation, engagement, and resource development, based on contributors' pre-existing research relationships would be valuable. We felt a collection of case studies, in a book where we could contrast different types of resource development activities where Indigenous Peoples had a variety of critical roles ranging from partners to protestors, would be more powerful than individual articles. Following the conference, Boyd and Winter began the process of developing a book prospectus and securing additional contributions.

The chapter contributors had pre-existing relationships with Indigenous communities, and case study topics were chosen with these in mind. We targeted breadth in Canadian jurisdiction and resource development activities to highlight differences in provincial and territorial Crown-Indigenous relations and show how the type of resource extraction may influence protest or partnership. Our focus is to understand the mechanisms and processes for successful and mutually beneficial resource governance relationships, and to assess what factors contribute to Indigenous Peoples' protest and legal challenge of resource projects. Where possible, we include Indigenous voices. For example, chapter 4 is written with Indigenous community members, and chapter 6 was written at the request of Meadow Lake First Nation.

We hope that these case studies offer important insights into the role of Indigenous Peoples in resource development in Canada—an issue of critical importance to Indigenous Peoples, governments in Canada, and all Canadians.

NOTE

1   S. Lorefice, B. Boyd and Gaétan Caron. 2017. "Indigenous Policy Conference Summary Report: Beyond Reconciliation." *The School of Public Policy Publications* 10, SPP Summary Paper. https://doi.org/10.11575/sppp.v10i0.43131.

Introduction

Brendan Boyd and Jennifer Winter

Indigenous[1] Peoples have become important participants in natural resource development across the globe. The 2007 United Nations Declaration on the Rights of Indigenous Peoples (UNDRIP), which calls for the free, prior, and informed consent (FPIC) of Indigenous Peoples in decisions that involve or affect them, reflects and solidifies this role. While Canada was one of only four countries that dissented at the time of adoption, Prime Minister Justin Trudeau's Liberal government fully endorsed the declaration in 2016 and enshrined it in legislation in 2021. Part of the reason Canada was initially reticent to sign was because it was unclear how the principles of FPIC sit with Canadian constitutional recognition of Aboriginal Rights (Coates and Favel 2016a, b). In the mid-2000s, a handful of decisions by the Canadian courts established that to maintain the honour of the Crown in its relations with Indigenous Peoples, governments in Canada have a fiduciary duty to consult and accommodate Indigenous Peoples' concerns in decisions or activities that could affect their rights or territories. Constitutional scholar Peter Hogg states that "no area of Canadian law has been so transformed in such a short period of time as the law of aboriginal rights" (Hogg 2009). Gallagher (2011) argues that Indigenous People are being empowered in decision-making to the point where he refers to them as the new "resource rulers" in Canada. Some go further, arguing that resource development provides a means to address the lack of opportunity Indigenous Peoples experience in Canada, and that this opportunity can include improvements in health, social, and cultural conditions (Slowey 2009; Coates and Crowley 2013; Coates 2015, 2018; Coates and Favel 2016b).

Yet many scholars argue that there has been little change for Indigenous Peoples, as court decisions have either been ignored, poorly implemented, or

1

resisted by governments and non-Indigenous society (Alfred 2001; Borrows 2015; Palmater 2020). Some argue that Indigenous Peoples must work within frameworks and processes established by governments and industry that maintain existing power imbalances (Palmater 2015; Borrows 2016). They suggest these activities demonstrate an assimilationist intent by increasing the presence of the Canadian state and businesses on Indigenous lands and society. Alfred (2001) notes that the state retains the ultimate power to expropriate Indigenous lands, while Palmater (2018a) highlights that Indigenous Peoples do not have control over the means, such as police or military, to deny the state or industry access to their land. Relatedly, governments' preference for policy over formal legislation when it comes to Indigenous rights (e.g., the Inherent Rights Policy) "severely limits Indigenous groups' ability to seek enforcement and accountability through the courts" (Metallic 2017, 18).

Both approaches take a high-level view of court decisions and legal rights, as well as of the broader relationship between Indigenous Peoples, the Canadian state, and society. The purpose of this edited volume is to explore, in detail, the process and institutions used to engage Indigenous Peoples in resource development to understand whether these processes lead to greater involvement and control in decision-making. The contributors to this book ask what determines whether attempts at engagement and involvement lead to the empowerment for Indigenous Peoples in resource development decisions by investigating a cross-section of resource development projects in Canada in which Indigenous Peoples have a critical role. Our goal is to advance understanding of the mechanisms and processes for successful establishment of mutually beneficial resource governance relationships, with attention to factors that contribute to Indigenous protests and legal challenges. While the chapters address a variety of influences, the primary focus is on the institutions, mechanisms, and processes used to consult and engage Indigenous communities as these are important factors to consider in assessing whether these communities are empowered in resource development decisions. This fine-grained analysis of institutions and processes through case studies addresses an important gap in the literature discussing Indigenous Peoples and resource development in Canada. The weakness of this approach is that by peering too closely at the processes used for engagement, one can ignore the broader societal context, including historical and current power and socio-economic imbalances. As we discuss below, the second chapter of this book formally addresses the different perspectives that Indigenous groups, government, and industry have on engagement processes. Furthermore, each of the chapter authors is a community-based researcher who has made concerted effort to capture and incorporate the perspectives of Indigenous communities and leaders. Indeed, this is the purpose of the case studies and this volume. For example, chapter 4—by McMillan, Maloney, and Gaudet—is co-authored with two members of the Kwilmu'kw Maw-klusuaqn Negotiation Office (KMKNO).

In this introduction, we have two purposes. First, we provide a brief review of the context relevant to Indigenous Peoples and resource development in Canada. We discuss the political and legal developments in Canada and internationally that have purportedly empowered Indigenous communities and allowed them a greater say in decision-making. Slow and uneven progress in developing equitable and mutually acceptable relationships and outcomes among Indigenous communities, resource development companies, and government necessitates a better understanding of *what works* in these relationships. Thus, the second goal of this introduction is to identify and discuss the different mechanisms used to involve Indigenous communities in resource development decisions and activities. This provides a broad framework in which we situate the subsequent chapters of this volume. Establishing a better understanding of how industry and governments consult and engage with Indigenous communities, and of the relationships that exist among these groups, is essential to creating solutions to what often seems like an intractable problem.

Processes

Historically, Indigenous Peoples have been excluded from decisions about resource development. This has led many to posit a fundamentally exploitative relationship between local Indigenous communities that live close to resources and wealthy governments and corporations that desire to develop those resources (Abele 1997; Green 2003; Howlett et al. 2011). This approach tends to view Indigenous Peoples solely as the victims of resource development. For example, the Berger (1978) report, which reviewed the impacts of a proposed pipeline in the McKenzie Valley in Northwest Territories, is widely seen as ground-breaking for recognizing the adverse impacts of resource development on Indigenous communities. However, the report was largely silent on Indigenous perspectives of the project, relegating them to the role of passive receivers of the impacts of development rather than seeing them as active participants with control over the future of their people and culture (Angell and Parkins 2011).

Over time, several mechanisms or processes have emerged through which the interests, aspirations and perspectives of Indigenous Peoples and communities can be incorporated into the planning and implementation of projects that could affect them. These include the government's duty to consult, which is often conducted through environmental assessment or other regulatory processes; agreements signed between Indigenous communities and private companies; and shared governance and management arrangements that could include Indigenous communities, government, and industry. These processes occur within broader institutional contexts—most notably, different governance and legal regimes in different provinces and different treaty relationships, including modern treaties, historic treaties, and instances where no treaty exists.

Importantly, we do not assume that either development in all cases or no development in any case is the end goal or most desirable outcome. In some cases, Indigenous communities have worked to stop or dramatically alter resource development activities that would take place on their traditional territories, while in others, they have been keen to participate in projects to improve their situation. We do argue that whatever the outcome, processes should seek to empower Indigenous communities in decision-making while increasing the legitimacy of decisions among all actors. Chataway describes the importance of how decisions are made:

> The importance of process, in addition to good structures, is often overlooked. However, a brief reflection on one's own experiences with decision making indicates that the same outcome, depending upon how it is arrived at, can alienate, divide and anger us, or it can empower and reassure us. This sense of procedural justice, the sense that one has had a voice and been treated respectfully, is so important that it has been found to predict our level of trust in our political representatives, independent of whether decisions are made in our favour or not. For instance, the almost universally opposed White Paper that proposed in 1969 to terminate the Indian Act, may have been largely acceptable to Aboriginal People if it had been developed through a

broad-based decision-making process with Aboriginal People"
(Chataway 2002, 79).

As noted earlier, Indigenous Peoples are often coerced into working with the frameworks and processes established by the state and industry (Palmater 2015). Indigenous Peoples are compelled to adopt fundamentally different worldviews, values, and norms. As Nadasdy states: "First Nations peoples have to learn completely new and uncharacteristic ways of speaking and thinking" (2003, 2). It is therefore essential to consider the interplay between ideas, including worldviews, values, norms, and institutions in assessing the empowerment of Indigenous Peoples. This is not to say that outcomes are unimportant. Indeed, there has been significant debate about whether procedural justice can be separated from substantive justice, meaning the extent to which decisions protect Indigenous rights, minimize harms, and maximize benefits to Indigenous communities (Sossin 2010), given weak policy and legislative protection of Indigenous self-determination (Borrows 2016). However, substantive justice can be difficult to determine; a project can be seen as beneficial or harmful to Indigenous communities depending on its specific characteristics, such as the nature of the activity and the relationship with the community and the role of the state (Anderson 1999, 2002; Slowey 2009; Palmater 2015). In addition, different parties may have different assessments. Chapter 1 of this volume examines how Indigenous Peoples, governments, and industry view and discuss consultation and engagement, highlighting their different approaches and perspectives. In chapter 5, Bikowski and Slowey engage this debate in the context of unconventional energy extraction in Alberta and New Brunswick. They explore whether the design and implementation of consultation and engagement contributes to Indigenous Peoples' perception of a project, compared to more substantive outcomes like the effect on the standard of living in the community and past relations with the Crown. In chapter 4, McMillan, Maloney, and Gaudet explore this issue via the strategies of the Mi'kmaq of Nova Scotia in regaining control of treaty-protected resources. The Mi'kmaq story highlights internal tensions and the challenges of "uneven, competitive, inadequate, and often unpredictable approaches to consultation and negotiation" by Crown and corporate actors.

Duty to Consult

While the duty is consult is founded in the Canadian constitution and its emergence in case law can be traced back to the 1970s, a series of court decisions in the 2000s greatly increased its importance in resource development decisions. The *Haida Nation v. British Columbia* (2004) and *Taku River Tlingit First Nation v. British Columbia* (2004) decisions established the duty to consult in cases where Indigenous groups had a claim to the land in question.[2] The *Haida Nation* case involved the transfer and replacement of a logging licence by the BC government in the traditional territory of the Haida Nation on the Queen Charlotte Islands. The courts ruled that the Haida Nation had a strong claim to the land and the provincial government's actions could affect this. Therefore, to maintain honourable relations with Indigenous Peoples, the government had a duty to consult with them and attempt to address any impacts the decision might have before moving forward. The *Haida* decision highlights the importance of process by indicating that consultation must be meaningful. Although there are no criteria set out for what specifically constitutes meaningful consultation, the decision indicates that it must affect reconciliation between Aboriginal People and the Crown. The *Taku River Tlingit* case involved a mine access road that would cross Taku River Tlingit First Nation (TRTFN) traditional territory. In this instance, the Supreme Court found BC had fulfilled its obligation to meaningfully consult, as TRTFN participated in the lengthy (3.5-year) environmental assessment of the mine. This decision places limits on the Crown's duty, finding "there is no ultimate duty to reach agreement" and "accommodation requires that Aboriginal concerns be balanced reasonably with the potential impact of the particular decision on those concerns and with competing societal concerns" (*Taku River Tlingit First Nation v. British Columbia*, 2004, para. 555).

Mikisew Cree First Nation (MCFN) v. Canada (2005) extends the duty to consult to instances where Treaty Rights were already established. In this case, the court found that the Government of Canada had to consult with the MCFN regarding a new winter road that could affect their hunting and trapping rights designated under Treaty 8.[3] In 2010, *Beckman v. Little Salmon/Carmacks First Nation* confirmed that even when modern treaties have been signed and contain provisions for negotiation,[4] the duty to consult remains and serves as a constitutional protection or safety net in the relationship. At issue in the case was the transfer of land from the Yukon government to a private citizen, where Indigenous hunting and fishing rights had already been established through a modern land claims process. Further decisions, such as *Clyde River (Hamlet) v. Petroleum Geo-Services Inc.* (2017) and *Chippewas of the Thames First Nation v. Enbridge Pipelines Inc.* (2017) have continued to refine and provide guidance on how the duty to consult should be implemented.[5] Of particular importance is the subsequent 2018 *Mikisew Cree First Nation v. Canada (Governor General in Council)* decision, which affirmed that the duty to consult does not apply to legislative processes. Palmater (2018b) asserts this ruling undermines the very concept and spirit of the duty to consult. The case law continues to develop at a rapid pace. For example, decisions in 2021 addressed the consideration of the cumulative effects of development (*Yahey v. British Columbia*, 2021), the nature of the Crown's fiduciary duty, and how Indigenous Peoples are compensated when it is breached (*Southwind v. Canada*, 2021), and the extension of the duty to consult to economic rights (*Ermineskin Cree Nation v. Canada*, 2021).

Indigenous Peoples have also been pursuing claims of land ownership or title. This would provide direct control over the land and decision-making authority on activities conducted within it. In 2014, the first judicial recognition of Aboriginal land title was in *Tsilhqot'in v. British Columbia*. The decision was the result of a series of court cases over several decades that established the concept of Aboriginal title and establish a test that had to be met to prove ownership of a specified piece of land. While there has been much speculation among experts, and concern by governments and industry, about the effect on resource development projects' approval and implementation, there are limitations to the decision's broader application. These limitations come from the high level of evidence required to prove ownership, the amount of territory over which claims can be made, and the powers that ownership grants (Coates and Newman 2014). Indeed, Manuel (2017) notes that Indigenous Peoples only control 0.2% of Canada's land base. Furthermore, Borrows (2015) criticizes *Tsilhqot'in*, arguing that decision actually legitimizes the myth of *terra nullius*, the notion that a land is unoccupied and can be claimed by a state beginning to occupy it.

Despite legal rulings that the federal government alone can fulfill the duty to consult, it has delegated some aspects of the process to provinces, industry, and arms-length administrative organizations. The predominant instance where duty to consult is delegated is the environmental review process. Bodies that conduct the duty to consult on behalf of the Crown include federal or provincial environmental assessment agencies, the Canada Energy Regulator (formerly the National Energy Board), and the Canadian Nuclear Safety Commission. Combining Indigenous consultation with existing regulatory bodies and processes makes sense on the surface because they both inform government decision-making (Lambrecht 2013). However, Indigenous leaders and scholars have argued that existing processes have not lived up to expectations in terms of creating meaningful input for Indigenous groups (Wismer 1996; Noble and Udofia 2015). Many have argued that because the only processes available are defined and controlled by the state, whether Indigenous Peoples feel they are fair or not is moot, because there are no other options, and they have no power to change them (Alfred 2001; Palmater 2015; Borrows 2016; Simpson 2017). Other shortcomings of the process identified in the academic literature include insufficient time; asymmetry in capacity between Indigenous communities and government or industry; exclusion of traditional Indigenous knowledge; ambiguity around who, or what part of an institution, is responsible for the duty to consult (Promislow 2013; Ritchie 2013); a focus on individual projects in isolation rather than the cumulative impact of development (Ritchie 2013); and a lack of clarity over when accommodation is required and what form it should take (Mullan 2011).

In addition to the above, there are other issues or complications with implementation of the duty to consult. For example, Gardner, Kirchhoff, and Tsuji (2015) studied a proposed hydroelectricity dam in Ontario where the local Indigenous group was a proponent. The authors found that other Indigenous communities located upstream from the project were affected and were not sufficiently consulted. There is also the question of who should be consulted in cases where more than one group or actor claims to speak for a single community. This issue has arisen when communities have different positions than national or regional Indigenous organizations (Peach 2016). Multiple consultations can affect Indigenous groups in a way that goes beyond those from a single project, as psychological and cultural effects can arise when Indigenous communities are continually required to make their case and explain their concerns (Booth and Skelton 2006). This is particularly true when the consultation process is perceived to be a rubber stamp rather than meaningful engagement and does not empower these groups in development decisions.

The extant research and analysis on the duty to consult shows a process that is still working out flaws and that can result in unintended consequences.

Accordingly, it is essential to understand more about how the consultation process is functioning and what it looks like in practice. Governments in Canada have produced a plethora of guidance documents for public officials that outline what consultation entails and how it should be undertaken (Aboriginal Affairs and Northern Development Canada 2011; Government of Newfoundland and Labrador 2013; Government of Saskatchewan 2013). But this provides only a narrow window into the process. In their chapter comparing two mining projects, one in Nunavut and one in Nunatsiavut, Rodon, Therrien, and Bouchard (chapter 3) address this dilemma by examining whether assessment processes can contribute to meaningful consultation.

IBAs and Economic Development

The most common way industry has engaged and negotiated with Indigenous groups is through impact benefit agreements (IBAs). IBAs are private agreements signed between industry and an Indigenous community that outline the expected impacts if a project moves forward and the benefits the community receives. Some view the emergence of IBAs as a negative development for Indigenous Peoples, while others see them in a more positive light.

Cameron and Levitan (2014) argue that IBAs essentially turn the duty to consult over to private companies and limit Indigenous communities' access to legal and political channels to voice their concerns. Similarly, O'Faircheallaigh (2010) argues that IBAs cannot be separated from political processes and community planning. While they may provide economic benefits, they can also affect Indigenous groups' ability to oppose the project and their access to judicial and regulatory recourse. Dylan, Smallboy, and Lightman (2013) echo this sentiment by suggesting that Indigenous communities have little power when signing IBAs because they do not have the ability to veto development. The project could still go ahead without their involvement, leaving them with little leverage in negotiations. In addition, Indigenous communities have limited tools to address poverty and poor social conditions. This makes them more likely to accept an agreement that does not maximize their benefits because it is the only opportunity to improve their situation.

Fidler and Hitch (2007) question whether the benefits of IBAs are shared fairly and equally within and across communities. In addition, there can be asymmetry of information in negotiations and Indigenous communities do not necessarily have the capacity to be involved as equals in the process. IBAs are usually private documents, preventing Indigenous communities from learning and gaining expertise in this area. To ensure that Indigenous communities see economic benefits from development, Shanks (2006) argues that revenue sharing should be negotiated between governments and Indigenous groups rather than through IBAs with industry.

The benefits of IBAs are often tied to a specific project, which makes the benefits localized and short term. Coates and Crowley (2013) suggest a regional approach to skill development that allows workers to be mobile and find new jobs in other communities. They also propose an IBA renewal system that ensures benefits will be long-term and is flexible enough to adapt to changes in economic circumstances. One of the shortcomings of IBAs is that they tend to focus on economic goals rather than community or social outcomes. This is often referred to as development in the community versus development of the community (Beckley et al. 2008). While many IBAs now contain provisions for community development (Sosa and Keenan 2001), others argue that to avoid a piecemeal approach, agreements addressing social programs should be negotiated with government rather than industry (Knotsh and Warda 2009). There is evidence to suggest that social development and cohesion within a community are actually prerequisites to economic development (Chataway 2002).

Other scholars have taken a more positive view of IBAs and view them as complementary to government's duty to consult. According to Fidler (2010), IBAs can be mutually beneficial: the proponent increases the certainty that the project will go ahead and be on schedule while Indigenous groups have a voice in development and receive benefits from the project. Prno, Bradshaw, and Lapierre (2010) study three communities that signed IBAs and find that they are all seeing benefits, although not all the benefits that were outlined in the agreements. Gibson MacDonald, Zoe, and Satterfield (2014) argue it is possible to link IBAs to traditional values of reciprocity and mutual exchange in some Indigenous communities. They suggest these agreements mirror early relations between Indigenous Peoples and European settlers and provide the means for this to be restored to some extent. In this volume, Wyatt and Dumoe examine the linkages between governance, community engagement, and economic development in their chapter on the Meadow Lake model of forestry. Similarly, McMillan, Maloney, and Gaudet demonstrate how community engagement within Mi'kmaq communities led to participatory decision-making around allowable development and created community-driven consultation and negotiation processes.

Treacy, Campbell, and Dickson (2007) provide a list of activities involved in consultation, including providing accurate and timely information, providing financial contributions for expert assistance to these groups, soliciting and confirming Indigenous interests and concerns, offering to work together and share benefits, and fully documenting and sharing with government all interactions. There is evidence to suggest that communities that have control and play an important decision-making role in development decisions experience the best outcomes in terms of community and social development (Rodon and Lévesque 2015). This theme is taken up by Rodon, Therrien, and Bouchard in this volume as they seek to understand if and how IBAs contribute to meaningful consultation of the Indigenous communities that are involved.

Modern Treaties and Co-management

The modern land claims process, also referred to as comprehensive agreements or modern treaties, have been championed as an example of a new era in Indigenous-state relations based on a nation-to-nation relationship and the goal of Indigenous self-governance (Martin and Hoffman 2008; White 2020). This process seeks to address Indigenous rights that have not been established or upheld and address grievances existing treaties have not fulfilled. Since the 1970s, negotiations between the federal government and Indigenous Peoples have led to thirty agreements that provide protection of rights, transfer of land and capital, participation in resource development environmental management, and in some cases provisions for self-governance (Crown-Indigenous Relations and Northern Affairs Canada 2023a, b).

There are serious questions as to whether modern treaties have led to substantive changes for Indigenous Peoples. Some have asserted that the modern treaty process requires the surrender of inherent and traditional rights due to, for example, the inclusion of explicit extinguishment clauses (Diabo 2013; Manuel and Derrickson 2017; Venne 2017). Venne (2017) rejects the modern treaty-making process as illegitimate, as it assumes the Crown remains the assumptive title holder of all lands and Indigenous Peoples are required to assert and prove their claims against this assumption. Rynard (2000) compares two modern treaties—the 1975 James Bay and North Quebec Agreement and the 1999 Nisga'a Final Agreement—and finds that both bear similarities to historic treaties that extinguished fundamental Indigenous rights. Saku (2002) finds that communities that had signed modern treaties did not display better socio-economic outcomes than other communities. Saku concludes that by themselves, modern treaties do not lead to economic development. Dana, Anderson, and Meis-Mason (2009), focusing on the Dene people in NWT, find that concerns about the effects of resource development on environmental, cultural, and social conditions remain in these communities. Slowey (2007) argues that because the process of negotiation is still set solely by the state, recent agreements such as Paix des Braves have not fundamentally altered the institution of Canadian federalism or empowered Indigenous Peoples. She argues there has not been a movement toward a nation-to-nation relationship or treaty federalism. Alfred (2001) makes a similar observation, noting that the state dictates the terms of treaty negotiation, imposes its own definitions of democratic participation and decision-making, and denies the validity of Indigenous forms of consultation and political representation. In this volume, Cameron, Martin, and Sharpe (chapter 2) examine the history of land claims agreements in Yukon and argue that their presence is a primary reason that there have been few protests among Indigenous communities over resource development. Rodon, Therrien, and Bouchard (chapter 3) also address this debate by examining whether a land claims agreement facilitates Indigenous empowerment in decision-making in the two cases they study. McMillan, Maloney, and Gaudet (chapter 4) look outside the land claims process to the unique experience of the Mi'kmaq people, through the history of the Mi'kmaq Rights Initiative and the KMKNO.

Within modern treaties, smaller-scale collaborative arrangements regarding resource development are possible. O'Faircheallaigh (2007) proposes that Indigenous groups should be involved in ongoing environmental monitoring and management—monitoring projects' environmental impacts and implementation of environmental regulations. One of the issues with Indigenous engagement is that it only occurs as a project is under review. A concern regarding environmental assessment processes is that monitoring and ensuring compliance with standards is often weak. Therefore, there is an opportunity to create a system where Indigenous communities have a role in ongoing environmental monitoring. O'Faircheallaigh (2007) notes there would have to be provisions for inclusion and utilization of traditional ecological knowledge.

As Indigenous Peoples have an important role in the development of resources in Canada, it is essential to understand how their cultures and perspectives influence resource management. The knowledge and perspectives that Indigenous Peoples have acquired throughout their long history living on the land are often referred to as traditional ecological knowledge (TEK). TEK can be distinguished from the processes of inquiry and knowledge-generation that conform to western-based notions of the scientific method and typically inform resource management decisions. In chapter 1, Boyd, Lorefice, and Winter examine Indigenous Peoples' views of evidence and knowledge, how they differ from those of government and industry, and how these factors are incorporated into decision-making. Insight and information gathered through traditional methods first emerged as a way for Indigenous groups to demonstrate their ownership or rights to the land. The recognition and inclusion of TEK in decision-making has been a controversial issue, as Indigenous groups have sought to ensure the knowledge they possess is given equal weight to scientific analysis performed by industry and government.

Indigenous perspectives and knowledge can contribute to the management of resources in Canada. Indigenous involvement in resource development projects and regulatory processes, and the use of TEK, can increase the sustainability of development (Hill et al. 2012). For example, Innu and Inuit communities contributed to the inclusion of sustainable development as a criterion in the environmental assessment of a mining project located at Voisey's Bay, Newfoundland and Labrador (Gibson et al. 2005). However, the extent to which Indigenous involvement will strengthen the quality and durability of resource development decisions will be determined by the process that is used (Reed 2008). The process must fully engage Indigenous groups in a meaningful way to ensure resource development and management incorporates local knowledge. Not only will this increase the legitimacy of the process, but it will also improve the quality of environmental outcomes that are produced.

Indigenous perspectives and TEK have been particularly influential in the study of the forestry sector as they provide a different definition of sustainable forestry compared to that of industry (Karjala, Sherry and Dewhurst 2004). Indigenous approaches to sustainable forestry are place-based and are not connected to a human presence. In contrast, industry's approach is resource-based which focuses on the utility of forests to humans. Parsons and Prest (2003, 779) go further, arguing that Aboriginal forestry is a distinct approach to resource development that "combines current forest management models with traditional cultural Aboriginal forest practice." The authors argue that this approach is becoming more common with increasing participation of Indigenous communities in forestry.

Wyatt (2008) reviews the history of First Nations involvement in Canadian forestry, finding a spectrum of types of involvement. These include forestry by First Nations, forestry for First Nations, forestry with First Nations, and Aboriginal forestry. Wyatt finds that forestry by First Nations is the most common: Indigenous Peoples are involved but have little decision-making authority in forest management practices. He suggests the first three types of involvement could lead to better representation of Indigenous Peoples, but the term "Aboriginal forestry" should only refer to a situation where practices and values have been informed by Indigenous perspectives in a meaningful way.

Several lessons emerged from the study of Indigenous involvement in resource management: each project has unique features and a one-size-fits-all approach to management will not work; TEK is not just about documentation or recording of knowledge, it is about respecting the relationship between knowledge and knowledge holders; co-management is a social learning process for managing human use of resources, not just an institution for managing the resources; and economic development is a sustainable process toward community goals not just about jobs and business revenue (Wyatt et al. 2010). However, Wellstead and Stedman (2008) are pessimistic about the likelihood that government policy and programming will shift to reflect these lessons and move toward a model of forestry led by First Nations.

The lessons provided by the literature are critical to ensuring that TEK and Indigenous perspectives are not included perfunctorily in decision-making but instead have a real influence on the outcomes of resource management. Once again, there is a need to study how consultation and engagement is conducted to ascertain the role TEK and Indigenous perspectives play in the process and what influence they have on decision-making. For example, are certain consultation practices more amendable to the inclusion of TEK than others? What barriers currently exist to a more equitable weighting of different forms of knowledge in the consultation process? These questions are an important gap in the literature that needs to be addressed.

The Structure of the Book

The chapters in this book present a series of case studies that cover a range of resource development sectors, including oil and gas, renewable energy, mining, and forestry. Indigenous communities in all regions of the country, including the Maritimes, the North, Central, and Western Canada are represented. In chapter 1, Boyd, Lorefice, and Winter examine policy statements and guideline documents on consultation and engagement produced by Indigenous groups, government, and industry to provide context for the later case studies. Recognizing criticisms that the Canadian state imposes legal and policy framework on Indigenous Peoples (Alfred 2001; Nadasdy 2003; Palmater 2015), the purpose is to provide insight into how Indigenous Peoples' perspective differ from the other actors involved in these processes. These differences should set the stage for the case studies and be kept in mind throughout the course of this volume. In chapter 2, Cameron, Martin, and Sharpe describe the development of modern treaties in Yukon, and how this has influenced resource governance in the territory. In chapter 3, Rodon, Therrien, and Bouchard examine the role of land claim agreements, impact assessment processes, and IBAs in contributing to meaningful consultation for mining projects on Inuit territory. In chapter 4, McMillan, Maloney, and Gaudet review the history of the Mi'kmaq Rights Initiative and the KMKNO in establishing the Mi'kmaq consultation and negotiation methods. Bikowski and Slowey (chapter 5) explore what elements influence Indigenous communities' support or rejection of oil and gas projects by comparing oil sands development in Alberta to shale development in New Brunswick. Lastly, in chapter 6, Wyatt and Dumoe describe the governance structure, community engagement, and economic development arising from the Meadow Lake model of forest development.

Finally, and perhaps most importantly, the Indigenous communities included in the case studies have played a variety of roles in the projects that have been proposed or developed on or near their land. For example, as outlined by Bikowski and Slowey, the Fort McKay First Nation in Alberta has developed many business partnerships with the oil sands companies operating on their traditional territory and, although disputes have occurred, they have largely worked with industry as partners. This situation is similar for Meadow Lake and its relationship with the forestry industry, who partnered with Wyatt and Dumoe in their chapter. In contrast, the Elsipogtog First Nation has protested against proposed shale gas development in New Brunswick, leading to acrimonious relations with the proponent and government. In other cases, such as the Inuit located near the Mary River mine and Mi'kmaq communities involved in the KMNKO process, divisions emerged between the broader organization representing Indigenous interests and the local communities.[6] Studying these cases, and the others included in the book, will provide a better understanding of the agreements, organizations, and mechanisms used to consult and engage Indigenous Peoples and their impact on their empowerment in resource development. It will also create insights and lessons that can improve the design and implementation of those processes and institutions.

NOTES

1   We note that Canadian governments have recently switched to using the word "Indigenous," though the term "Aboriginal" has a specific legal meaning and includes First Nations, Inuit, and Métis. We use the term Indigenous as it is the most inclusive collective noun, as recommended by First Nations and Indigenous Studies, University of British Columbia on the Indigenous Foundations website (2017) and Indigenous Corporation Training blog (2016). Our use of alternative terms reflects the use of those terms in works cited in order to maintain scholarly accuracy and the intent of the original work.

2   A claim could involve actual ownership or title to the land or specific rights of use such as hunting or fishing.

3   Treaty 8 is one of the eleven Numbered Treaties signed between the Government of Canada and Indigenous people between 1871 and 1921. It encompasses parts of northern Saskatchewan, Alberta and BC and part of Northwest Territories.

4   Modern treaties are comprehensive land claim agreements signed starting in 1975 between the Government of Canada, provincial and territorial governments, and Indigenous Peoples (Crown-Indigenous Relations and Northern Affairs Canada 2023a, b). These agreements define Indigenous rights and title and often establish greater self-governance among Indigenous communities.

5   For a history of the duty to consult, see Newman (2017).

6   These communities collaborated on the chapters with Rodon, Therrien, and Bouchard and McMillan, Maloney, and Gaudet, respectively.

References

Abele, F. 1997. "Understanding what happened here." In *Understanding Canada: Building on the new Canadian political economy*, ed. by W. Clement. Montreal-Kingston: McGill-Queen's University Press, 118–40.

Aboriginal Affairs and Northern Development Canada. 2011. *Aboriginal Consultation and Accommodation—Updated Guidelines for Federal Officials to Fulfill the Duty to Consult*. Ottawa: Government of Canada. https://www.rcaanc-cirnac.gc.ca/eng/110 0100014664/1609421824729.

Alfred, Taiaiake. 2001. "Deconstructing the British Columbia Treaty Process." *Balayi: Culture, Law and Colonialism* 3: 37–65.

Anderson, R. B. 1999. *Economic Development Among the Aboriginal Peoples in Canada: The Hope for the Future*. Concord, ON: Captus Press.

———. 2002. "Entrepreneurship and Aboriginal Canadians." *Journal of Development Entrepreneurship* 7, no. 1: 45–65.

Angell, A. and J. Parkins. 2011. "Resource Development and Aboriginal Culture in the Canadian North." *Polar Record* 47, no. 240: 69–79.

Beckley, T. M., D. Martz, S. Nadeau, E. Wall, and B. Reimer. 2008. "Multiple Capacities, Multiple Outcomes: Delving Deeply into the Meaning of Community Capacity." *Journal of Rural and Community Development* 3, no. 3: 56–75.

Beckman v. Little Salmon/Carmacks First Nation, 2010 SCC 53, [2010] 3 S.C.R. 103.

Berger, Thomas R. 1978. "The McKenzie Valley Pipeline Inquiry." *Osgoode Hall Law Journal* 16, no. 3: 639–47. http://digitalcommons.osgoode.yorku.ca/ohlj/vol16/iss3/5.

Booth, A., and N. Skelton. 2006. "'You Spoil Everything!' Indigenous Peoples and the Consequences of Industrial Development in British Columbia," *Environment, Development and Sustainability* 8, no. 3: 685–702.

Borrows, John. 2015. "The Durability of Terra Nullius: *Tsihlqot'in Nation v. British Columbia*." *UBC Law Review* 48, no. 3: 701–42.

———. 2016. *Freedom and Indigenous Constitutionalism*. Toronto: University of Toronto Press.

Cameron, E. and T. Levitan. 2014. "Impact Benefit Agreements and the Neoliberalization of Resource Governance and Indigenous-state Relations in Northern Canada." *Studies in Political Economy* 93: 25–52.

Chataway, C. 2002. "Successful Development in Aboriginal Communities: Does it Depend upon a Particular Process." *The Journal of Aboriginal Economic Development* 3, no. 1: 76–88. https://emedia.captus.com/epub/ebook/JAED-OpenAccess/v3n1/76/

Chippewas of the Thames First Nation v. Enbridge Pipelines Inc., [2017] 1 SCR 1099, 2017 SCC 41.

Clyde River (Hamlet) v. Petroleum Geo-Services Inc., [2017] 1 SCR 1069, 2017 SCC 40.

Coates, K. 2018. *Catching the Next Wave: How BC First Nations Can Benefit from Another LNG Boom*. Ottawa: MacDonald-Laurier Institute. https://macdonaldlaurier.ca/mli-files/pdf/MLI_LNGBoom_Final_web.pdf.

Coates, K. and B. L. Crowley. 2013. *The Way Out: New thinking about Aboriginal Engagement and Energy Infrastructure to the West Coast*. Ottawa: MacDonald-Laurier Institute. http://www.macdonaldlaurier.ca/files/pdf/2013.05.30-MLI-3NorthernGateway-WebReady-vFinal.pdf.

Coates, K. and B. Favel. 2016a. *Understanding FPIC: From Assertion and Assumption on 'Free, Prior and Informed Consent' to a New Model for Indigenous Engagement on Resource Development*. Ottawa: MacDonald-Laurier Institute. https://macdonaldlaurier.ca/mli-files/pdf/MLINumber9-FPICCoates-Flavel04-29-WebReady.pdf.

——. 2016b. *Understanding UNDRIP: Choosing Action on Priorities over Sweeping Claims about the United Nations Declaration on the Rights of Indigenous Peoples*, Ottawa: MacDonald-Laurier Institute. https://macdonaldlaurier.ca/mli-files/pdf/MLI-10-UNDRIPCoates-Flavel05-16-WebReadyV4.pdf.

Coates, K. and D. Newman. 2014. *The End is Not Nigh: Reason over Alarmism in Analysing the Tsilhqo'in Decision*. Ottawa: MacDonald-Laurier Institute. http://www.macdonaldlaurier.ca/files/pdf/MLITheEndIsNotNigh.pdf.

Coates, K. S. 2015. *Sharing The Wealth: How Resource Revenue Agreements Can Honour Treaties, Improve Communities, and Facilitate Canadian Development*. Ottawa: MacDonald-Laurier Institute. https://macdonaldlaurier.ca/mli-files/pdf/MLIresourcerevenuesharingweb.pdf

Crown-Indigenous Relations and Northern Affairs Canada. 2023a. "Modern Treaties." Government of Canada. Last modified February 28, 2023. https://www.rcaanc-cirnac.gc.ca/eng/1677073191939/1677073214344.

——. 2023b. "Treaties and agreements." Government of Canada. Last modified April 11, 2023. https://www.rcaanc-cirnac.gc.ca/eng/1100100028574/1529354437231.

Dana, L. P., R. B. Anderson, and A. Meis-Mason. 2009. "A Study of the Impact of Oil and Gas Development on the Dene First Nations of the Sahtu (Great Bear Lake) Region of the Canadian Northwest Territories (NWT)." *Journal of Enterprising Communities* 3, no. 1: 94–117.

Diabo, Russell. 2013. "Harper Launches Major First Nations Termination Plan." Socialist Project. Accessed January 10, 2013. https://socialistproject.ca/2013/01/b756/.

Dylan, A., B. Smallboy, and E. Lightman. 2013. "Saying No to Resource Development Is not an Option: Economic Development in Moose Cree First Nation." *Journal of Canadian Studies* 1: 59–90.

Ermineskin Cree Nation v. Canada (Environment and Climate Change), 2021 FC 758. https://decisions.fct-cf.gc.ca/fc-cf/decisions/en/item/500449/index.do.

Fidler, C. 2010. "Increasing the Sustainability of a Resource Development: Aboriginal Engagement and Negotiated Agreements." *Environmental Development and Sustainability* 12: 233–44.

Fidler, C., and M. Hitch. 2007. "Impact and Benefit Agreements: A Contentious Issue for Environmental and Aboriginal Justice." *Environments Journal* 35, no. 2: 49–69.

First Nations and Indigenous Studies, University of British Columbia. 2017. "Terminology," University of British Columbia. Indigenous Foundations. Accessed August 2017. http://indigenousfoundations.arts.ubc.ca/terminology/

Gallagher, B. 2011. *Resource Rulers: Fortune and Folly on Canada's Road to Resources*. n.p.: Bill Gallagher.

Gardner, H. L., D. Kirchhoff, and L. J. Tsuju. 2015. "The Streamlining of the Kabinakagami River Hydroelectricity Project Environmental Assessment: What Is the 'Duty to Consult' with other Impacted Aboriginal Communities when the Co-proponent of the Project is an Aboriginal Community?" *The International Indigenous Policy Journal* 6, no. 3. https://doi.org/10.18584/iipj.2015.6.3.4

Gibson MacDonald, G., J. B. Zoe, and T. Satterfield. 2014. "Reciprocity in the Canadian Dene Diamond Mining Economy." In *Natural Resource Extraction and Indigenous Livelihoods*, ed. Emma Gilberthorpe and Gavin Hilson (London: Routledge), 57–74.

Gibson, R. B., S. Holtz, J. Tansey, G. Whitelaw, and S. Hassan. 2005. *Sustainability Assessment: Criteria, Process and Applications*. London: Routledge.

Government of Newfoundland and Labrador. 2013. *The Government of Newfoundland and Labrador's Aboriginal Consultation Policy on Land and Resource Development Decisions ("The Policy")*. https://www.gov.nl.ca/exec/iar/files/aboriginal_consultation.pdf https://www.gov.nl.ca/iias/wp-content/uploads/aboriginal_consultation.pdf.

Government of Saskatchewan. 2013. *Proponent Handbook Voluntary Engagement with First Nations and Métis Communities to Inform Government's Duty to Consult Process*. Regina: Ministry of Government Relations. http://publications.gov.sk.ca/documents/313/94455-Proponent_Handbook.pdf.

Green, J. 2003. "Decolonization and recolonization in Canada." In *Changing Canada: Political Economy as Transformation*, ed. W. Clement and L. F. Vosko (Montreal-Kingston: McGill-Queen's University Press), 51–78.

Haida Nation v. British Columbia (Minister of Forests) [2004] 3 SCR 511, 2004 SCC 73.

Hill, R., C. Grant, M. George, C. Robinson, S. Jackson, and N. Abel. 2012. "A Typology of Indigenous Engagement in Australian Environmental Management: Implications for Knowledge Integration and Social-ecological System Sustainability." *Ecology and Society* 17, no. 1: 23.

Hogg, P. 2009. "The Constitutional Basis of Aboriginal Rights." In *Aboriginal Law Since Delgamuukw*, ed. by M. Morellato (Aurora, ON: Canada Law Book), 3–16.

Howlett, C., M. Seini, D. McCallum, and N. Osborne. 2011. "Neoliberalism, Mineral Development and Indigenous People: A Framework for Analysis." *Australian Geographer* 42, no. 3: 309–23.

Indigenous Corporation Training Inc. 2016. "Indigenous or Aboriginal: Which Is Correct?" *Working Effectively with Indigenous Peoples* (blog), January 5, 2016. https://www.ictinc.ca/blog/indigenous-or-aboriginal-which-is-correct.

Karjala, M., E. Sherry. and S. Dewhurst. 2004. "Criteria and Indicators for Sustainable Forest Planning: A Framework for Recording Aboriginal Resource and Social Values." *Forest Policy and Economics* 6, no. 2: 95–110.

Knotsh, C. and J. Warda. 2009. *Impact Benefits Agreements: A Tool for Healthy Inuit Communities.* Ottawa: National Aboriginal Health Organization.

Lambrecht, K. 2013. *Aboriginal Consultation, Environmental Assessment and Regulatory Review in Canada.* Regina: University of Regina Press.

Manuel, Alfred. 2017. "From Dispossession to Dependency." In *Whose Land is it Anyway? A Manual for Decolonization*, ed. Peter McFarlance and Nicole Shabus (Vancouver: Federation of Post-Secondary Educators of BC) , 18–21.

Manuel, Arthur and Ronald Derrickson (Grand Chief). 2017. *The Reconciliation Manifesto: Recovering the Land, Rebuilding the Economy.* Toronto: James Lorimer & Company.

Martin, T. and S. Hoffman, S., eds. 2008. *Power Struggles: Hydro Development and First Nations in Manitoba and Quebec.* Winnipeg: University of Manitoba Press.

Metallic, Naiomi. 2017. "The Relationship Between Canada and Indigenous People: Where Are We?" Irwin Law Special Series, Special Lecture 2017—Canada at 150: The Charter and the Constitution. Accessed via https://papers.ssrn.com/sol3/papers.cfm?abstract_id=3089051.

Mikisew Cree First Nation v. Canada (Governor General in Council), [2018] 2 SCR 765, 2018 SCC 40.

Mullan, D. 2011. "The Supreme Court and the Duty to Consult Aboriginal Peoples: A Lifting of the Fog." *Canadian Journal of Administrative Law and Practice* 24, no. 3: 233–60.

Nadasdy, P. 2003. *Hunters and Bureaucrats: Power, Knowledge, and Aboriginal-state Relations in the Southwest Yukon.* Vancouver: UBC Press.

Newman, D. 2017. "The Section 35 Duty to Consult." In *The Oxford Handbook of the Canadian Constitution*, ed. P. Oliver, P. Macklem and N. Des Rosiers (New York: Oxford University Press) , 349–66.

Noble, B., and A. Udofia. 2015. *Protectors of the Land: Toward an EA Process that Works for Aboriginal Communities and Developers.* Ottawa: MacDonald-Laurier Institute. http://www.macdonaldlaurier.ca/files/pdf/Noble-eAs-Final.pdf.

O'Faircheallaigh, C. 2007. "Environmental Agreements, EIA Follow-up and Aboriginal Participation in Environmental Management: The Canadian Experience." *Environmental Impact Assessment Review* 27, no. 4: 319–42.

———. 2010. "Aboriginal-mining Company Contractual Agreements in Australia and Canada: Implications for Political Autonomy and Community Development." *Canadian Journal of Development Studies* 30, nos. 1–2: 69–86.

Palmater, P. 2015. *Indigenous Nationhood: Empowering Grassroots Citizens.* Halifax: Fernwood Publishing.

———. 2018a. "True Test of Reconciliation: Respect the Indigenous Right to Say No." Canadian Dimension. Accessed May 15, 2018. https://canadiandimension.com/articles/view/true-test-of-reconciliation-respect-the-indigenous-right-to-say-no.

———. 2018b. "The Supreme Court Has Just Gutted the Crown's Duty to Consult First Nations." *Maclean's.* October 11, 2018. https://www.macleans.ca/opinion/the-supreme-court-has-just-gutted-the-crowns-duty-to-consult-first-nations/.

———. 2020. "Mi'kmaw Treaty Rights, Reconciliation and the 'Rule of Law'." Canadian Dimension. Accessed September 22, 2020. https://canadiandimension.com/articles/view/mikmaw-treaty-rights-reconciliation-and-the-rule-of-law.

Parsons, R. and G. Prest. 2003. "Aboriginal Forestry and Canada." *The Forestry Chronicle* 79, no. 4: 779–84.

Peach, I. 2016. "Who Speaks for Whom? Implementing the Crown's Duty to Consult in the Case of Divided Aboriginal Political Structures." *Canadian Public Administration* 59, no. 1: 95–112.

Prno, J., B. Bradshaw, and D. Lapierre. 2010. *Impact and Benefit Agreements: Are They Working?* N.p.: Canada Institute of Mining, Metallurgy and Petroleum.

Promislow, J. 2013. "Irreconcilable? The Duty to Consult and Administrative Decision Makers." *Constitutional Forum* 22, no. 1: 63–78.

Reed, Mark S. 2008. "Stakeholder Participation for Environmental Management: A Literature Review." *Biological Conservation* 141, no. 10: 2417–431.

Ritchie, K. 2013. "Issues Associated with the Implementation of the Duty to Consult and Accommodate Aboriginal Peoples: Threatening the Goals of Reconciliation and Meaningful Consultation." *UBC Law Review* 46, no. 2: 397–438.

Rodon, T. and F. Lévesque. 2015. "Understanding the Social and Economic Impacts of Mining Development in Inuit Communities: Experiences with Past and Present Mines in Inuit Nunangat." *The Northern Review* 41: 13–39.

Rynard, P. 2000. "Welcome In, but Check your Rights at the Door: The James Bay and Nisga'a Agreements in Canada." *Canadian Journal of Political Science* 33, no. 2: 211–43.

Saku, J. 2002. "Modern Land Claim Agreements and Northern Canadian Aboriginal Communities." *World Development* 30, no. 1: 141–51.

Shanks, G. 2006. *Sharing in the Benefits of Resource Development: A Study of First Nations-industry Impact Benefits Agreements.* Ottawa: Public Policy Forum.

Simpson, Leanne Betasamosake. 2017. *As We Have Always Done: Indigenous Freedom Through Radical Resistance.* Minneapolis: University of Minnesota Press.

Slowey, G. 2007. "Federalism and First Nations: In Search of Space." In *Constructing Tomorrow's Federalism: New Perspectives on Canadian Governance*, ed. I. Peach (Winnipeg: University of Manitoba Press), 157–70.

————. 2009. "A fine balance." In *First Nations, First Thoughts*, ed. A. Timpson (Vancouver: UBC Press), 229–50.

Sosa, I. and K. Keenan. 2001. *Impact Benefit Agreements Between Aboriginal Communities and Mining Companies: Their Use in Canada*. Canadian Environmental Law Association. http://www.cela.ca/sites/cela.ca/files/uploads/IBAeng.pdf.

Sossin, L. 2010. "The Duty to Consult and Accommodate: Procedural Justice as Aboriginal Rights." *Canadian Journal of Administrative Law and Practice* 23: 93–113.

Southwind v. Canada, 2021 SCC 28. https://decisions.scc-csc.ca/scc-csc/scc-csc/en/item/18955/index.do.

Taku River Tlingit First Nation v. British Columbia (Project Assessment Director), [2004] 3 S.C.R. 550, 2004 SCC 74.

Treacy, Heather L., Tara L. Campbell, and Jamie D. Dickson. 2007. "The Current State of the Law in Canada on Crown Obligations to Consult and Accommodate Aboriginal Interests in Resource Development." *Alberta Law Review* 44, no. 3: 571–618.

Tsilhqot'in Nation v. British Columbia, 2014 SCC 44, [2014] 2 S.C.R. 256.

Venne, Sharon. 2017. "Crown Title: A Legal Lie." In *Whose Land Is It Anyway? A Manual for Decolonization*, ed. Peter McFarlance and Nicole Shabus (Vancouver: Federation of Post-Secondary Educators of BC) , 14–17.

Wellstead, A., and R. Stedman. 2008. "Integration and Intersection of First Nations in the Canadian Forestry Sector: Implications for Economic Development." *Journal of Aboriginal Economic Development* 6, no. 1: 30–43.

White, Graham. 2020. *Indigenous Empowerment through Co-management: Land Claims Boards, Wildlife Management, and Environmental Regulation*. Vancouver: UBC Press.

Wismer, S. 1996. "The Nasty Game: How Environmental Assessment is Failing Aboriginal Communities in Canada's North." *Alternatives Journal* 22, no. 4: 10–17.

Wyatt, S. 2008. "First Nations, Forest Lands, and 'Aboriginal Forestry' in Canada: From Exclusion to Comanagement and Beyond." *Canadian Journal of Forestry Resources* 38: 171–80.

Wyatt, S., J-F. Fortier, G. Greskiw, M. Hébert, S. Nadeau, D. Natcher, P. Smith, and R. Trosper. 2010. *Collaboration between Aboriginal Peoples and the Canadian Forestry Industry: A Dynamic Relationship*. Edmonton: Sustainable Forestry Management Network.

Yahey v. British Columbia, 2021 BCSC 1287. https://www.bccourts.ca/jdb-txt/sc/21/12/2021BCSC1287.htm.

Indigenous, Industry and Government Perspectives on Consultation and Engagement in Resource Development[1]

Brendan Boyd, Sophie Lorefice, Jennifer Winter

Proposed resource development projects in Canada are frequently on or near the traditional territories of Indigenous[2] Peoples, which affects the rights of Indigenous Peoples and triggers the Crown's fiduciary duty to consult. In many instances, projects are subject to protests and court challenges from Indigenous communities or groups. Recent examples include the Trans Mountain and Coastal Gaslink pipelines in BC; hydraulic fracturing for oil and gas exploration in New Brunswick and Nova Scotia; seismic testing in Canada's north near Clyde River; lobster fisheries in Atlantic Canada; and hydroelectric and mining projects in BC and Nunavut. While these cases represent a small portion of the total incidences where the duty to consult is triggered, they often become the subject of intense political and public debate.

As discussed in the introduction to this volume, many scholars argue that the institutions and processes used to engage Indigenous Peoples in re-source development cannot lead to empowerment because they are defined and determined by the state and industry, while Indigenous People have no control over these processes and their legal and governance traditions are not represented (Alfred 2001; Palmater 2015; Borrows 2016). Specifically, weak policy and legislative support for Indigenous self-determination leaves Indigenous communities with little power to make decisions about natur-al resource development (Borrows 2016). Others argue that the dichotomy posed for Indigenous communities between economic development and the preservation of rights and traditional practices is overdrawn (Notzke 1995; Anderson 1999, 2002; Slowey 2009; Angell and Parkins 2011). They suggest Indigenous Peoples are not just passive recipients of the impacts of resource development. For example, Slowey (2009) argues that participating in re-source development has the potential to empower Indigenous groups and give them greater capacity to navigate and manage these changes, while preserving their rights and identity. However, criminal prosecution of indi-viduals and communities who exercise their rights outside of formal agree-ments and processes undermines the capacity of Indigenous communities to engage in self-determined resource development (Palmater 2015). We argue that, in either case, it is essential to consider how Indigenous Peoples perceive and understand the institutions and processes through which they are cur-rently involved in resource development. Several scholars argue that a shared vision between Indigenous groups and proponents of resource development projects does not exist (Borrows 2016; Manuel 2017; Simpson 2017). Manuel and Derrickson (2017) note that the Auditor General of Canada has indicated that all parties must share a common vision of their relationship for treaty ne-gotiations to be successful. They argue that this does not currently exist in the BC treaty process, and that promises of reconciliation have become entangled in the modern treaty process wherein reconciliation becomes a tool of disen-franchisement and a means of severing Indigenous Peoples from their lands. It is therefore essential to examine how Indigenous Peoples' ideas about these institutions and processes differ from those of government and industry.

In this chapter, we analyze policy statements and guideline documents related to consultation[3] and engagement to understand how Indigenous Peoples view and understand key concepts associated with consultation and engagement processes and compare their perceptions to those of govern-ment and industry. Bridging the differences between frames or worldviews is an important first step in improving consultation and engagement with Indigenous groups in resource development decisions and developing a shared vision (Borrows 2016; Manuel 2017; Simpson 2017; Boyd and Lorefice 2018). Gallagher (2011) argues that, given the historical success of legal chal-lenges, unless relations with industry and government improve, Indigenous groups will continue to use the legal system to defend their rights. The legal system is a time-consuming and financially costly avenue for dispute resolu-tion and its adversarial nature is not conducive to the development of positive relations. Moreover, legal standing does not translate into practical change when Canadian governments fail to uphold those rights (Palmater 2020). The courts are also a powerful tool for government and industry to dismiss or resist Indigenous claims, as project proponents are able to secure injunctions in response to Indigenous resistance (Manuel and Derrickson 2017). Thus, finding common ground amongst Indigenous Peoples, governments, and industry on engagement and consultation practices is imperative to upholding Indigenous rights, the future of resource development, the Canadian economy, and ultimately to the reconciliation of the relationship between Indigenous Peoples and the rest of Canada.

The remainder of the chapter proceeds as follows. First, we present a short outline of the research approach and methodology. Most of the chapter is a discussion of the results of our analysis. We provide a detailed review of policy documents, comparing the use and frequency of identified keywords, such as *consultation, reconciliation, veto* and *consent*. Following our review, we conclude with a summary of our results and identify some areas of future research based on our analysis.

Research Approach and Methodology

The documents used in the analysis are policy statements or guidelines, designed to inform and guide individuals and organizations in implementing the duty to consult or in engaging with Indigenous communities. Between 2016 and 2018, we gathered policies and guidance documents through an extensive online search and separated them into the three categories: Indigenous groups, industry, and government. The search produced 61 documents: 17 from industry, 22 from Indigenous groups and 21 from government; the appendix reports the full list. The industry documents include documents from companies and industry associations. Documents from Indigenous groups include documents from First Nations, Indigenous political institutions, and Indigenous associations. The number of documents from each group is not the same; however, exact symmetry is difficult to achieve and not necessarily valuable because every document varies in length.

Using NVivo software, which allows systematic coding and organization of textual data, we conducted a quantitative content analysis, counting the instances of a reference (Viasmoradi, Turunen, and Bondas 2013). We assessed and compared the frequency of occurrence of keywords in the documents in each category (Indigenous groups, government, and industry). This provides an indication of the level of importance placed upon central concepts by each of the actors. Each word search included stemmed words. For example, counts of the term *sustainable* included the word *sustainability*, and searches of the term *relationship* also included its plural, *relationships*. To ensure that differences in word counts are not related to differences in the number and length of documents, we report and analyze the number of mentions per every 10,000 words.

The documents include Indigenous groups in different regions of the country; all provinces, the federal government, and the Government of Northwest Territories[4]; and a cross-section of resource industries. However, caution should be exercised when generalizing about how each actor understands consultation or how they believe it should be implemented. This is particularly true for Indigenous groups. In many Indigenous cultures, knowledge and history is shared and passed down orally rather than in written form. Thus, many of the protocols and guidelines that Indigenous groups have regarding consultation may not be captured in a review of publicly available documents. Given that there are hundreds of First Nation, Inuit, and Métis communities in Canada, it is difficult to make conclusive generalizations about a common approach to consultation and engagement. Finally, we do not intend to speak for the Indigenous Peoples, groups, and communities whose documents have been included in this chapter. The final source of information and interpretation of these documents is, of course, the communities and organizations who created them. Nevertheless, these publicly available documents provide a window into the understandings, motivations, and issues that Indigenous groups, along with government and industry, have regarding consultation processes.

Detailed Review of Policy Documents

Drawing on the approach of Boyd and Lorefice (2018), we examine several areas where differing views among Indigenous groups, industry, and governments may create barriers to the meaningful involvement of Indigenous Peoples in resources development. These include the terms used to describe Indigenous Peoples' involvement in resource development; the connection to reconciliation; and whether the duty to consult provides a veto to or requires consent from Indigenous Peoples. We also compare these groups' perspectives on key issues associated with the process of consultation and engagement, including delegation of the duty to consult to third parties; provision of capacity supports; the time allotted for discussion and debate; information-sharing and transparency from project proponents; and the inclusion of traditional knowledge in decision-making.

Consultation, Engagement and Accommodation

As discussed above and elsewhere in this book, Canadian courts prescribe and shape the definition and practice of the duty to consult. Legal definitions notwithstanding, different terms are used to describe Indigenous Peoples' involvement in resource development. The terms consultation and engagement are often used in concert or even synonymously. However, consultation refers more to the Crown's legal obligation to meaningfully consult with Indigenous Peoples prior to making a decision or taking a course of action that may affect their rights and privileges, in accordance with Section 35 of the Constitution Act and the many subsequent Supreme Court, Federal Court of Appeal, and subnational courts' rulings in this matter. Engagement refers to a range of actions taken by private companies as they interact with Indigenous Peoples to find common ground on a proposed project. Engagement activities can support the Crown fulfilling its legal obligations but is a broader term, which means that we would expect industry to use the term engagement more than government and Indigenous groups that are involved directly in the duty to consult. Often engagement is viewed as a deeper form of involvement that allows for a back-and-forth dialogue and greater participation by the group being engaged. Consultation is a narrower process where feedback is received from a stakeholder on a decision or plan that is almost fully formed. Comparing the incidence of these two terms gives us insight into how each group views the involvement of Indigenous Peoples in resource development decisions.

A key component of the duty to consult, explicitly stated by the courts, is that Indigenous Peoples must be accommodated when it is found that a project infringes upon their rights. But Indigenous groups indicate that there is too much focus on the initial consultation procedures and whether the duty to consult is being conducted fairly, compared to the time spent on ensuring the processes lead to substantive outcomes through accommodation, including amendments to a project, revenue sharing, economic development opportunities, access to resources, and capacity building (Hupacasath First Nation 2006; First Nations Leadership Council 2013). We would expect Indigenous groups to use the term accommodation more than government and industry.

To assess how often the terms *consultation, engagement* and *accommodation* were used, we compared their frequency across each actor's documents. Figure 1 shows that industry used the term *engagement* the most of all three actors. However, all three used the term less frequently than *consultation*. Both *consultation* and *accommodation* appear more in government documents than those of Indigenous groups and industry. However, the difference between the frequencies of use of each term is greatest among government documents. It is also worth noting that the frequency of use for both terms is the highest amongst any other term examined.[5]

Governments tend to view accommodation more as a process of seeking compromise in an attempt to harmonize conflicting interests and stress that a commitment to the process does not require a duty to agree (Gouvernement du Québec 2008; Government of British Columbia 2014; Government of Nova Scotia 2015). Industry does not make frequent mention of accommodation, though the Association for Mining Exploration British Columbia (2015) takes a similar approach as government in highlighting that consultation does not necessarily mean reaching agreement but provides a forum for discussion.

As discussed above and in other chapters, the duty to consult is prescribed and shaped by the Canadian courts. However, notwithstanding the legal definition, the general concept of consultation may be used with different meanings. For example, there are several definitions of consultation in the documents we examined. The Government of British Columbia (2010) states that "consultation in its least technical definition is talking together for mutual understanding." From industry, the Association for Mining Exploration British Columbia (2015) states "consultation and engagement are about sharing information, listening to and respecting concerns raised, and looking for ways to address those concerns in a manner that is reasonable and commensurate with the nature, scope and duration of the exploration activities being carried out." The Assembly of First Nations of Quebec and Labrador (2005) suggests "consultations are an excellent opportunity for First Nations to exercise their jurisdiction over, and their social and economic interest in, lands and natural resources." These definitions display differences in how each group approaches consultation. For Indigenous groups, it is about political and legal empowerment. This contrasts with the other definitions, which use language oriented to strengthening existing relationships and processes.

Canadian court cases have also emphasized that consultation must be meaningful. However, as with consultation, definitions and interpretations

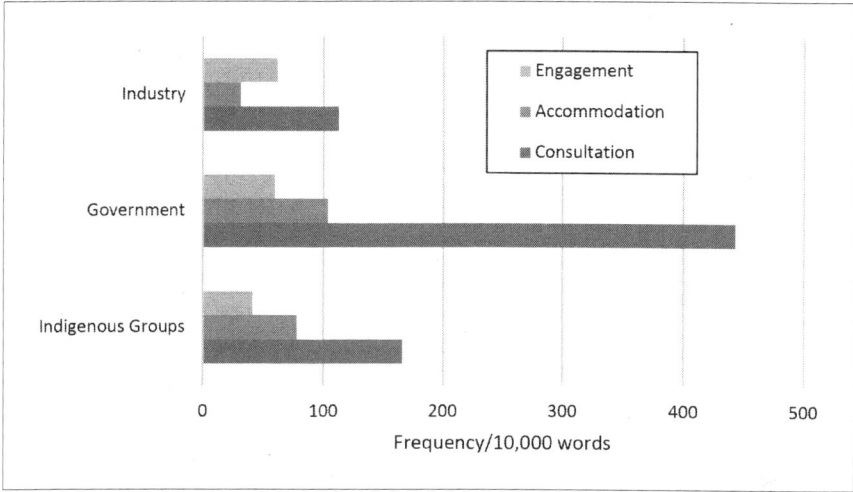

Figure 1.1: Frequency of Use of "Consultation," "Engagement," and "Accommodation

may differ. Indigenous groups that addressed meaningful consultation suggested that it required being engaged early, allowing sufficient time for input to be prepared and considered, and having a say in strategic planning decisions (Kluane First Nation 2012; Meyers Norris Penny 2009; Sam n.d.). AANDC[6] (2011) states "a meaningful consultation process is characterized by good faith and an attempt by parties to understand each other's concerns, and move to address them." This means consultation is "carried out in a timely, efficient and responsive manner; transparent and predictable; accessible, reasonable, flexible and fair; founded in the principles of good faith, respect and reciprocal responsibility; respectful of the uniqueness of First Nation, Métis and Inuit communities; and, includes accommodation (e.g. changing of timelines, project parameters),.where appropriate" (AADNC 2011). Governments also recognize that meaningful consultation is an iterative process rather than a single action or event (Fisheries and Oceans Canada 2006; AANDC 2011; Nova Scotia 2015). For example, AANDC (2011) indicates that departments and agencies are encouraged to develop long-term working relationships and processes rather than working together only on an ad hoc or case-by-case basis. Industry documents did not provide a clear definition of meaningful consultation. The Calgary Chamber of Commerce (2015) indicates the need for a clear definition but does not offer one. Several industry documents did note the importance of involving Indigenous Peoples in determining the process itself and ensuring it is acceptable and informed by the interests of Indigenous communities (Canadian Association of Petroleum Producers 2006; Association for Mining Exploration British Columbia 2015; Canadian Wind Energy Association n.d.).

The 1996 Report of the Royal Commission of Aboriginal Peoples highlighted the need for a nation-to-nation relationship between Indigenous Peoples and the Canadian state (Dussault et al. 1996). While the phrase has become popular in recent years, it has yet to occur in a meaningful way. Palmater (2011) and Manuel and Derrickson (2017) suggest that there has been no desire on the part of elected governments to implement or support mechanisms that would achieve self-governance. Court rulings have not necessitated or facilitated a nation-to-nation relationship. For example, Palmater (2018a) argues the *Mikisew Cree First Nation v. Canada* decision, which ruled that the duty to consult did not apply to the legislative branch of government, means there is no duty on the part of the Canadian state to engage Indigenous Peoples at the highest levels of lawmaking. Alfred (2001) states that a nation-to-nation relationship is not possible as long as Canadian laws and institutions are dominant and apply on Indigenous lands. The documents examined in this chapter outline that consultation should be driven by the political will to establish a nation-to-nation relationship (Assembly of First Nations of Quebec and Labrador 2005; Federation of Saskatchewan Indian Nations n.d.; National Centre for First Nations Governance n.d). Government documents tend to view the purpose of the duty to consult as fulfilling legal requirements (e.g., AANDC 2011; Government of Alberta 2014). The Government of Alberta (2014) states that the purpose of its policy is "to be consistent with case law and demonstrate a practical approach to meeting the requirements established by the courts." There are a few exceptions; notably, the Government of British Columbia (n.d.) and the Government of Nova Scotia (2015). The BC policy on consultation emphasizes the need for "government-to-government relationships where First Nations are rights-holders not stakeholders" (Government of British Columbia, n.d.). Industry documents stress mitigating uncertainty faced by resource companies, which affects their operations and ability to raise capital, through effective relationships (Alberta Chamber of Resources 2006; Canadian Association of Petroleum Producers 2006; Association for Mining Exploration British Columbia 2015; Canadian Wind Energy Association n.d.). The Alberta Chamber of Resources (2006) states "corporate image and reputation have become important in marketing goods and services, and even in the ability to access certain markets. A positive image with respect to Aboriginal relations can be a significant competitive advantage in the marketplace."

Perspectives on Reconciliation

In the reason for decision of the *Clyde River* case, Justices Karakatsanis and Brown state, "this court has on several occasions affirmed the role of the duty to consult in fostering reconciliation" (*Clyde River (Hamlet) v. Petroleum Geo-Services Inc.*, 2017, s. 1). Thus, reconciliation could be an important purpose or motivator for engaging in consultation. The principle of reconciliation refers to "establishing and maintaining a mutually respectful relationship between Aboriginal and non-Aboriginal peoples in this country" (Sinclair 2015). However, many scholars have argued that the phrase has become symbolic, meaningless, or worse, a means to assimilate Indigenous Peoples and continue resource development on their land (Alfred 2001, 2009, 2017; Manuel and Derrickson 2017; Palmater 2017, 2018b, 2021). To assess how important reconciliation was to each group, we compared the frequency with which each used the terms *reconciliation, relationship, respect,* and *trust* (figure 2). Documents from Indigenous groups referenced reconciliation 18 times per 10,000 words. This was twice as frequent as government, and six times more frequently than industry. Trust was mentioned seven times per 10,000 words by industry, three times by Indigenous groups and one time by governments. Of note is the importance all three groups placed on the word *relationship*, with equal occurrences in Indigenous and industry documents (40 per 10,000), and higher frequency than respect.

Approximately half of the government documents accounted for the references to reconciliation. As an example of the language used, AANDC's consultation policy states "the Crown's efforts to consult and, where appropriate, accommodate Aboriginal groups whose potential or established Aboriginal or Treaty Rights may be adversely affected should be consistent with the overarching objectives of reconciliation" (AANDC 2011). Just under half of Indigenous groups' documents mentioned reconciliation at least once. The National Centre for First Nations Governance (2009) states that "the consultation and accommodation process is driven by the primary purpose of reconciliation." Less than a quarter of industry documents mentioned reconciliation as part of the process of consultation and engagement.

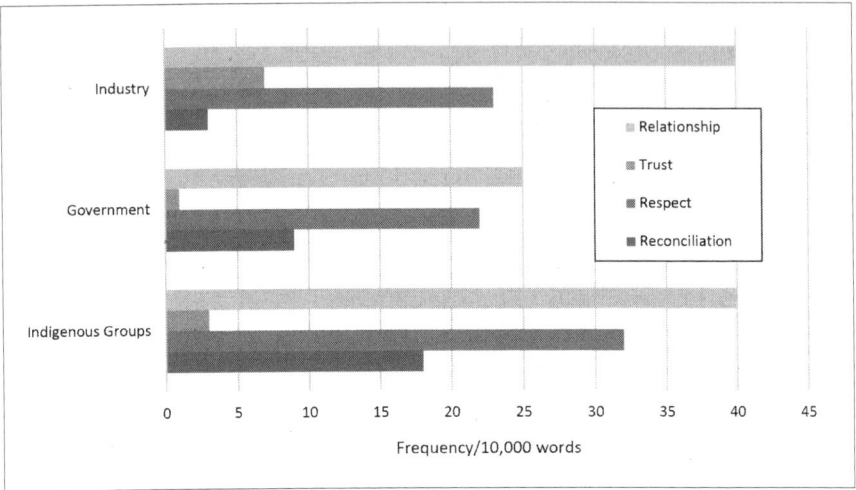

Figure 1.2: Frequency of Use of "Relationship," "Trust," "Respect," and "Reconciliation"

One document, from the First Nations Leadership Council, indicated that it does not see a good faith attempt at reconciliation through consultation by government: "rather than building the relationships, trust and momentum required for the transformational change that reconciliation requires, the Crown's approaches to consultation and accommodation are fueling growing impatience, frustration, and conflict" (First Nations Leadership Council 2013). The First Nations Leadership Council argues that the number of court challenges against government decisions, such as approvals of major resource projects or pipelines, highlights that the duty to consult has not been implemented in a way that advances reconciliation.

Differing Perspectives on Consent Versus Veto

Whether Indigenous communities or nations have a veto—and whether consent is the same as a veto—when resource development infringes upon their rights remains an unsettled question that is slowly being resolved through the court system. The use of the terms *consent* and *veto* in the documents examined sheds light on the perspectives of the three actors and how they interpret the rights of Indigenous Peoples.

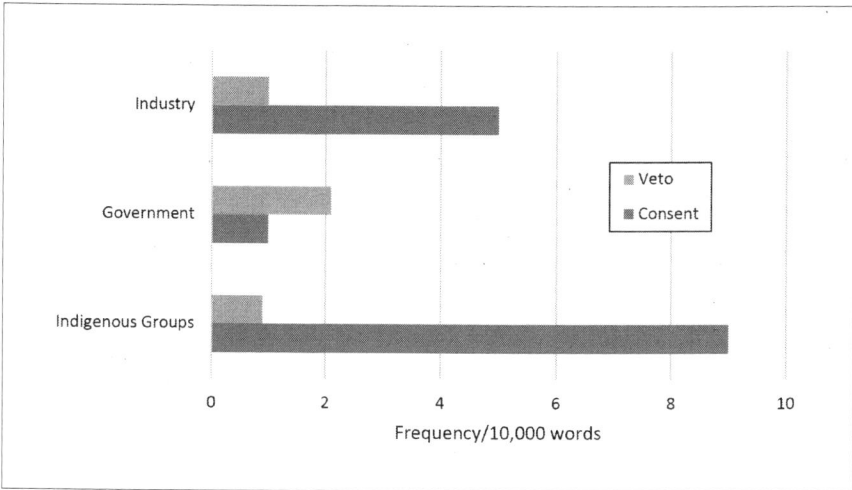

Figure 1.3: Frequency of Use of "Veto" and "Consent"

Figure 3 compares the frequency with which Indigenous groups, government, and industry used the terms *veto* and *consent*. Indigenous groups mentioned consent nine times per 10,000 words, while industry and government referenced the term four times and once per 10,000 words respectively. Conversely, government used the term veto 2.1 times per 10,000 words, approximately twice as frequently as Indigenous groups and industry. Perhaps not surprisingly, the documents produced by Indigenous groups highlight the language used by the courts, which indicates that consent is required (Hupacasath First Nation 2006; Kluane First Nation 2012; Sam n.d.). Government and industry documents focus on the courts' assertion that the duty to consult does not grant Indigenous Peoples a veto on projects (AANDC 2011; Government of Alberta 2013; Association for Mining Exploration British Columbia 2015; Mining Association of Manitoba 2016). The First Nations Leadership Council (2013) provides an interesting perspective in arguing that no actor has a veto if true reconciliation is the goal. The First Nations Leadership Council suggests that this reflects the tradition of many Indigenous groups of consensus-based decision-making, where deliberation continues until all parties agree on a decision. Further, the document indicates that, while Indigenous groups may not desire to completely stop a project on their own, the notion that it would move forward without their agreement demonstrates a lack of respect for their concerns and rights.

Delegation of Procedural Aspects of Consultation

Canadian governments can delegate procedural aspects of the duty to consult to third parties (*Chippewas of the Thames First Nation v. Enbridge Pipelines Inc.*). We examined the frequency of use for the terms *delegation* and *procedural aspects* to compare how important this concern was for each group. As figure 4 shows, governments discuss delegation and procedural aspects of the duty to consult much more frequently than Indigenous groups or industry. Government documents state that procedural aspects involve meeting with Indigenous communities, sharing and discussing information, identifying project impacts, and implementing mitigation measures (Government of Alberta 2013; Government of British Columbia 2014; Government of Nova Scotia 2015).

The rationale for delegation identified in the documents is that proponents are generally in a better position to fulfill this role because they have intimate knowledge of the project (for example, Government of British Columbia 2014). This was seen by some Indigenous groups as the Crown shirking its responsibility and not promoting positive relations. For example, the First Nations Leadership Council (2013) indicates that just because delegation is legally permissible does not mean it is appropriate, acceptable, desirable, or meaningful. Industry's primary concern is having clarity on their responsibilities and a smooth transition to government consultation when issues are outside their authority, such as a royalty-sharing agreement (for example, Canadian Chamber of Commerce 2016).

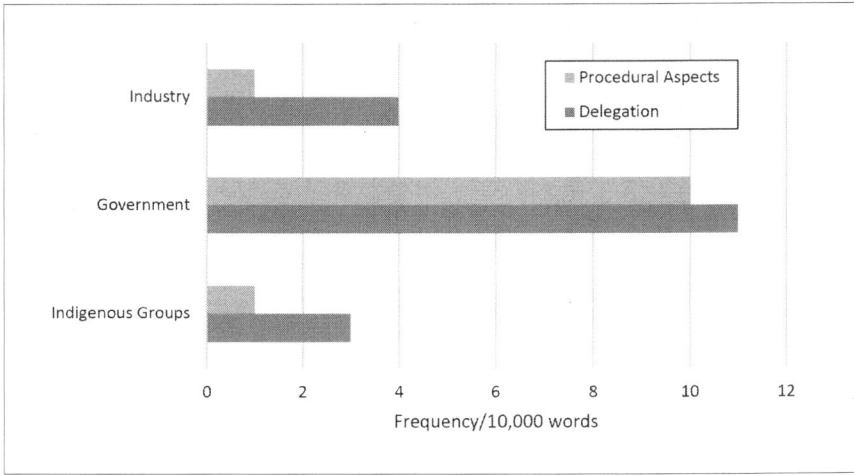

Figure 1.4: Frequency of Use of "Procedural Aspects" and "Delegation"

Timing of Consultation

An important concern for Indigenous groups was that consultation processes are often rushed, and that insufficient time is dedicated to establishing
trusting relationships and allowing for respectful and meaningful consultation (for example, Assembly of First Nations of Quebec and Labrador 2005;
First Nations Leadership Council 2013). Indeed, the Federal Court of Appeal
ruled that federal government consultation on the Northern Gateway pipeline was "brief, hurried and inadequate" (*Gitxaala Nation v. Canada*, at sec.
325). However, one industry document expressed concerns about timeline
extensions delaying a project and increasing uncertainty (Calgary Chamber
of Commerce 2015). Government documents discuss timing of consultation
relative to statutory requirements, but the Government of Saskatchewan
(2013) also stressed the importance of voluntary engagement prior to formal
processes. This document highlighted the potential for early engagement
to address problems before they arise and build working relationships with
Indigenous communities. The document indicated that early engagement is
important when determining the level of capacity funding necessary to ensure
that members of Indigenous communities can adequately participate in consultation processes. The Assembly of First Nations of Quebec and Labrador

(2005) suggested that seasonal customs and traditions of Indigenous Peoples should also factor into timing, thus creating a need for flexibility in terms of government and industry consultation processes.

Capacity Building

Capacity building refers to attempts to increase revenue, skills, infrastructure, etc., in Indigenous communities to address asymmetries in wealth, power, and knowledge that can limit effective implementation of the duty to consult and engagement. The issue was important to all actors, but potentially most important to industry, which mentioned the term *capacity* twice as frequently as government, with mentions by Indigenous groups falling about midway between the other two (figure 5).

Governments recognize their responsibility and are generally amenable to providing capacity support (e.g., Government of Manitoba 2009 and AANDC 2011). Of particular interest is a Government of Alberta program, the First Nations Consultation Capacity Investment Fund, which provides ongoing support for communities to participate in consultation processes and is funded by industry (Government of Alberta 2013). As noted previously, project proponents are not legally obliged to provide supports through the duty to consult.[7] However, Indigenous groups, government, and industry all note that it can help build relationships and trust (e.g., Kluane First Nation [2012], Government of Saskatchewan [2013], and Association for Mining Exploration British Columbia [2015]). The Association for Mining Exploration British Columbia (2015) raises concerns about support provision, including their ability to fund supports, ensuring funding is commensurate to the level of consultation, and ensuring that it benefits the entire community, not just a few individuals. Capacity issues can be exacerbated by the high number of consultations facing many communities and the potential for fatigue in communities (Government of Northwest Territories 2012). One community has called on government and industry to look for more creative ways, beyond monetary support, to ensure the full involvement of Indigenous Peoples in consultation processes (Hupacasath First Nation 2006).

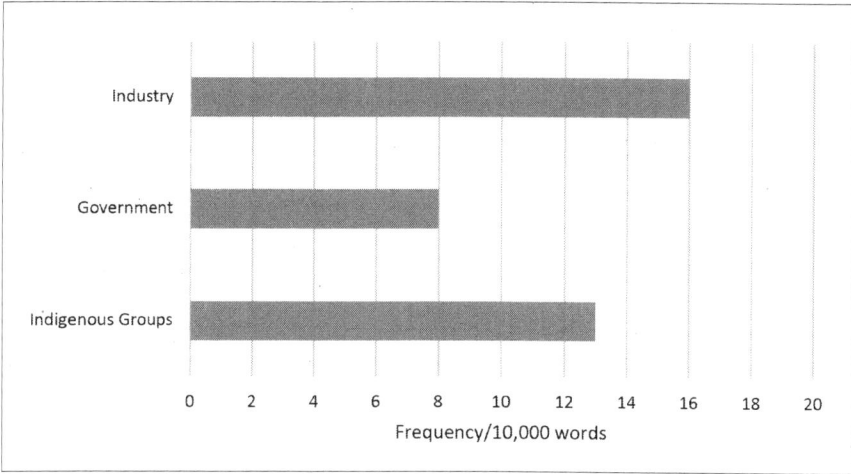

Figure 1.5: Frequency of Use of "Capacity"

Economic and Community Development

A key point raised by the BC First Nations Energy and Mining Council (2008) is that communities should benefit from resource development on their traditional territories, not just be compensated or accommodated for the impacts of development. Industry tends to think of these benefits as directly related to the project (Alberta Chamber of Resources 2006; Cameco 2014; BluEarth Renewables 2015). This includes job opportunities and skills training, opportunities for local businesses to provide services and revenue sharing or partnership agreements. Increasingly, Indigenous communities are thinking beyond immediate job opportunities to revenue sharing, partnerships, equity, and other agreements, which provide more direct involvement in projects and contribute to community development (Hupacasath First Nation 2006; BC First Nations Energy and Mining Council 2008; National Centre for First Nations Governance 2009).

However, we found that even though industry mentioned economic development more than community development, they referenced both more than Indigenous groups. The Prospectors and Developers Association of Canada (2014) states that "industry can view this situation as a 'double tax,'

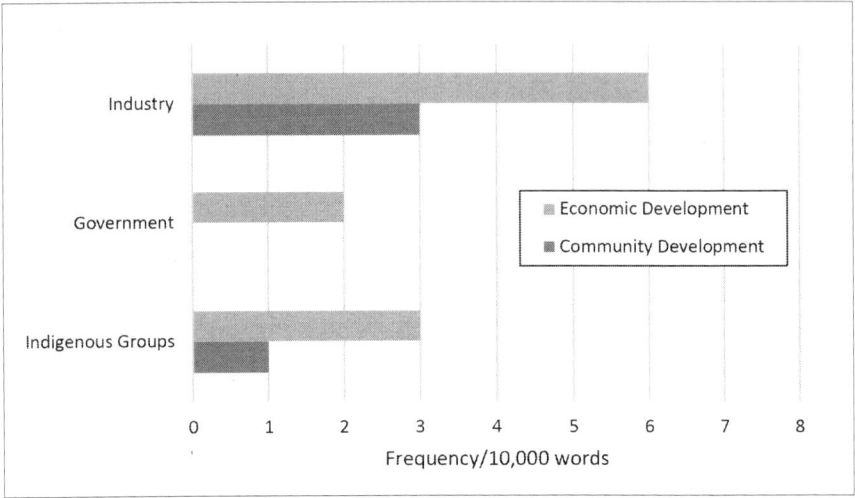

Figure 1.6: Frequency of Use of "Community Development," and "Economic Development"

given that companies pay fees, taxes and royalties to federal, provincial and territorial governments, as well as contribute funds to Aboriginal communities through commercial arrangements." It is also important to note that discussion of training and education often focused on trades, rather than employment at the management and executive level (Alberta Chamber of Resources 2006; Forest Products Sector Council 2011; Cameco 2014). The Forest Products Sector Council document also notes that more opportunities need to be created for Indigenous women.

Information-Sharing and Transparency

Lack of information-sharing and transparency in consultation and engagement processes was a common barrier referenced by all groups. Figure 7 demonstrates Indigenous groups and government discussed the issue more frequently than industry. Government policies stress the importance of documenting all activities and materials that are undertaken related to consultation to demonstrate to the courts how it has fulfilled its legal obligations (Fisheries and Oceans Canada 2006; AANDC 2011; Government of Newfoundland and Labrador 2013). This includes events, telephone calls, emails, site visits, and notifications about activities. Governments encourage project proponents to record all engagement activities as well, and share them with government, as they can contribute toward the Crown's responsibility. For Indigenous groups, the issue is the transparency and communication of project information and government decision-making (Cragg and Siebenmorgen 2011; National Centre for First Nations Governance n.d.).

Government and industry warn that essentially no conversations should be off the record because this information may be required to prove to the courts that consultation occurred (AANDC 2011; Government of Saskatchewan 2013). However, this can potentially impede the establishment of good relationships. The First Nations Leadership Council (2013) states that "no relationship, whether Crown-Aboriginal, federal-provincial, spouses, or otherwise can be enlivened if every contact or engagement is on the record." The Federation of Saskatchewan Indian Nations (n.d.) indicates "First Nations need to approach all discussions cautiously and with a view that all discussions with the Crown may ultimately be presented as evidence in a court to determine whether the Crown is justified in infringing a First Nation's Treaty or First Nation rights or First Nation title and document, confirm and retain all dialogue." Indeed, we found that Indigenous groups reference the terms *document(s)* and *documentation* significantly less than industry and government.

An important concern for governments was co-ordinating information among departments and agencies to improve communication and decision-making within government (Government of Alberta 2014; Government of Nova Scotia 2015). This included formal processes (e.g., centralized record keeping), and informal avenues (e.g., meeting and discussions among departments). For industry, a priority was having face-to-face meetings with communities, rather than by phone or email, to establish relationships (BluEarth Renewables 2015; Calgary Chamber of Commerce 2015). All actors noted the importance of providing information in an accessible and culturally appropriate format, rather than long technical reports (for example, Canadian Energy Pipeline Association [2014], Government of Saskatchewan [2013]; Assembly of First Nations of Quebec and Labrador [2015]; Suncor [2016]). This was an important component of the *Clyde River* decision, where the proponents provided what the courts referred to as a "practically inaccessible document dump" where "only a fraction of this enormous document was translated into Inuktitut" ([2017] SCC 40: sec. 49).

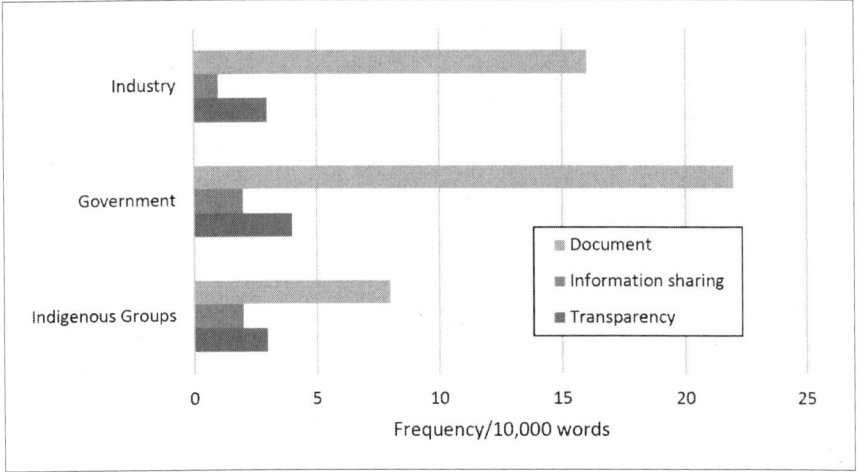

Figure 1.7: Frequency of Use of "Document," "Information-Sharing," and "Transparency"
Note: The "document" frequency count includes the sum of "document" and "documentation."

Traditional Knowledge

As mentioned above, the lack of inclusion of traditional knowledge in decision-making processes has been a barrier to effective consultation in the past. This theme was discussed in the documents of all actors; however, Indigenous groups and industry mentioned traditional knowledge twice as frequently as government (figure 8). There is an acknowledgement within government and industry that efforts should be made to understand and consider this when consulting and engaging. For example, the Alberta Chamber of Resources (2006) states "the first step is to understand cultural differences; the next step is to bridge them—not to change them." Some industry documents suggest the inclusion of traditional knowledge can improve project development, in addition to defining Indigenous rights and providing more fulsome participation in decision-making (Association for Mining Exploration British Columbia 2015; Mining Association of Manitoba 2016). This is in line with scholars who have noted that Indigenous knowledge can improve decision-making and should be incorporated into environmental assessment processes (O'Faircheallaigh 2007; Lambrecht 2013). Indeed, discussion of sustainability originates primarily from Indigenous groups and industry. The main themes include concerns regarding the protection of traditional land,

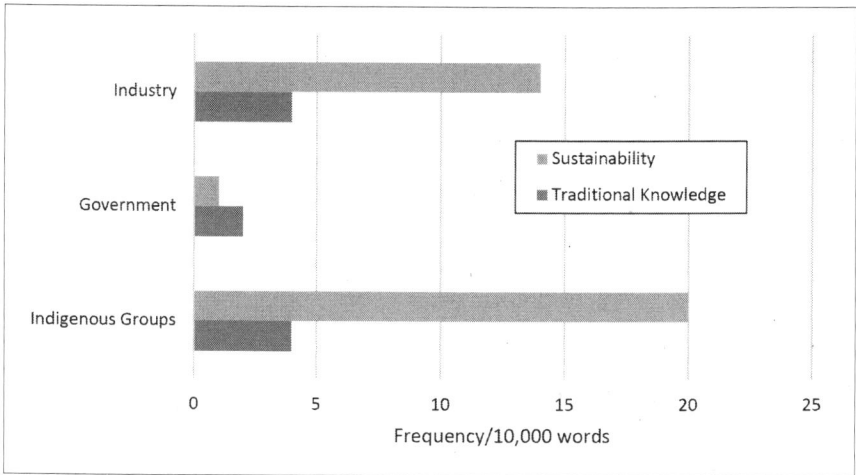

Figure 1.8: Frequency of Use of "Sustainability" and "Traditional Knowledge"

Note: The "traditional knowledge" frequency count includes the sum of "traditional knowledge," "traditional ecological knowledge," "Indigenous knowledge," "Aboriginal knowledge," and "local knowledge."

the benefits of self-monitoring of approved projects, the provision of land use guidelines to project proponents, and the importance of negotiating long-term employment. The Government of British Columbia's (n.d.) consultation guideline is one of the few government documents that encourages the use of Indigenous knowledge of the land as a means of preserving the environment.

Working toward the inclusion of Indigenous knowledge in a meaningful way is difficult and requires more than simply reading a report or viewing information without someone to explain it. For example, the First Nations Leadership Council (2013) stresses the need to have Elders or knowledge holders present during the decision-making process to interpret and communicate traditional knowledge, rather than simply making maps or charting important sites. The importance of Elders and other informal leaders in preserving, protecting, and promoting culture and tradition was an important theme emerging from our analysis. Industry and government frequently identified the need to connect and develop relationships with these individuals (Government of Saskatchewan 2013; Association for Mining Exploration British Columbia 2015). This is not just to involve these individuals, as it was noted the involvement can also improve the project. The Government of

British Columbia (n.d.), in a document for proponents on building relationships with First Nations, states "First Nations hold a wealth of knowledge about the diversity and interactions among plant and animal species, landforms, watercourses and other biophysical features. Companies may benefit from this knowledge in order to build new practices for protecting and conserving resources, including heritage resources individuals, in addition to formal band or tribal leadership."

Summary and Conclusions

The goal of this chapter was to provide a quantitative analysis of policy statements and guideline documents related to consultation and engagement produced by Indigenous groups, government, and industry to assess their understandings of key issues and concepts. Our research has uncovered several key conclusions that should be considered in the design of consultation and engagement processes.

The term *consultation* was the most common way Indigenous groups, government, and industry talked about Indigenous involvement in resource development. Discussion of broader engagement and substantive accommodation was less common. Somewhat surprisingly this was the case for industry, even though they are not directly responsible for fulfilling the legal duty to consult. However, the government used the term *consultation* substantially more, in comparison to the two other terms. This suggests that governments may be more concerned with fulfilling the formal requirements of consultation rather than the broader spectrum of activities that could fall under engagement. It also supports the hypothesis that government is less concerned with the substantive accommodation than the procedural requirements of consultation.

Indigenous groups' documents revealed that resource development is often thought of in the context of reconciliation. This concept is much less prominent in industry and government documents. The perspective provided by Indigenous groups is that resource development cannot be approached as a regular business or government transaction—it is a distinct and unique relationship. The primary reason for this is that Indigenous communities and nations are rights holders, not stakeholders. While the concepts of reconciliation and respect are much less frequently referenced by government and industry documents, the term *relationship* was used with the same frequency in industry documents as Indigenous groups' documents (40 per 10,000), indicating an attitude more in line with the concept of reconciliation than might otherwise be inferred.

In terms of the concept of *accommodation*, there was relatively similar frequency of use by Indigenous groups (78) and government (104). However, our textual analysis reveals different viewpoints. Indigenous groups' language reflects substantive components of accommodation, such as changes to projects and compensation. In contrast, the government documents discussed accommodation as part of reaching compromise and focused on procedural aspects.

One instance where perspectives and objectives differed was around the timing of consultation. An important concern for Indigenous groups was that consultation processes are often rushed, and that insufficient time is dedicated to establishing trusting relationships and allowing for respectful and meaningful consultation. There is a clear tension between the time required for meaningful consultation and business risk due to delays, increasing costs, and lost windows of opportunity. Interests are not aligned in this case, and documents offered little in the way of solutions to this conundrum.

Our analysis revealed that the capacity of Indigenous communities to fully participate in consultation and engagement was recognized as a challenge by all three groups. As a corollary, effectively addressing the challenge through capacity building and the provision of supports was also recognized as an issue. Industry documents also noted financial concerns associated with industry-provided support for capacity building and community and economic development.

Another point of alignment amongst the three actors was the concept of information-sharing and transparency. While the concepts were not very important in terms of frequency of use, all groups agreed that transparency is a positive element of relationship-building. On the negative side, however, is government's focus on documentation and the procedural aspect of information-sharing, something that was often viewed negatively in the documents of Indigenous groups.

The lack of inclusion of traditional knowledge in decision-making processes was a theme discussed in the documents of all groups and was acknowledged as a barrier to effective consultation. Indigenous groups and industry documents were more focused on the concept of sustainability. Some industry documents suggest the inclusion of traditional knowledge can improve project development, in addition to defining Indigenous rights and providing more fulsome participation in decision-making.

Scholars have highlighted many issues with the institutions and processes used to engage Indigenous Peoples, including issues with delegation, asymmetries in information about projects and funding for gathering that information, and the cumulative effect of consultation on Indigenous communities (Booth and Skelton 2006; Ritchie 2013). Particularly concerning are projects—such as the Site C Dam and Trans Mountain Pipeline—where Indigenous groups have asserted that the duty to consult had not been meaningfully implemented but projects were allowed to proceed. These instances suggest that the duty to consult may be used as a minimum procedural necessity rather than as a mechanism of authentic engagement (Manuel and Derrickson 2017). This chapter contributes to this line of inquiry by examining how Indigenous Peoples view and understand key concepts related to consultation and engagement processes and compare them to those of government and industry. The limitation of our work is that we examine policy documents and it is not feasible in the scope of this project to determine how closely these guidelines and statements are followed in practice. Clearly, more work is needed in this area to understand how Indigenous Peoples view consultation and engagement processes. The case studies of specific processes and communities in this volume are a starting point for better understanding.

Several Indigenous groups' documents suggest that existing processes, such as environmental assessments, are unlikely to satisfy the duty to consult unless they are particularly robust (Assembly of First Nations of Quebec and Labrador 2005; First Nations Leadership Council 2013). In addition, a common theme from our analysis is that meaningful consultation requires involving Indigenous Peoples in the design of the consultation process itself. This supports the argument that institutions and processes are still defined and controlled by the state, which limits the extent to which they will empower Indigenous People in decision-making (Alfred 2001; Borrows 2016; Palmater 2016; Simpson 2017). Therefore, future work should examine what processes, mechanisms and tools are seen by Indigenous Peoples as representing their interests, cultures, and traditions and what new institutions can be developed with Indigenous People to replace those that do not. The other chapters in this book are a start in this direction.

Third, as argued by Sossin (2010), Borrows (2016), and Simpson (2017), while the duty to consult aims at achieving procedural fairness for Indigenous

Peoples and respect for their constitutional rights, it is not yet clear whether it will lead to substantive outcomes. There is an opportunity for more research on the link between consultation and engagement activities and the outcomes of development in communities. There are several reasons why this is the case. The most commonly cited issues are the difficulty in measuring social, cultural, and emotional benefits, which are less easily specified than economic benefits, and the relationship between these broad categories of benefits (North Slave Métis Alliance 1999; Tsetta et al. 2005; Campbell 2007; Westman and Joly 2019; Zurba and Bullock 2020). It takes a long time to collect the longitudinal data necessary to assess the impact of development (North Slave Métis Alliance 1999; Angell and Parkins 2011; Papillon and Rodon 2017). Finally, work on how the benefits of development are distributed within communities, including gendered analysis, is only beginning to emerge (Amnesty International 2016; Nightingale et al. 2017; Manning et al. 2018). Thus, determining whether the institutions and processes used to involve Indigenous Peoples in decision-making has led to substantive improvements in community socio-economic status is difficult at best. The other chapters in this volume focus largely on whether institutions and processes increase power in decision-making, although Wyatt and Dumoe (chapter 6) in this book provide some evidence on community benefits in their case study of Meadow Lake Reserve.

NOTES

1   We thank the Social Sciences and Humanities Research Council for funding this research, and Kiran Gurm, Kristy Peterson, and Brittney Whittaker for their excellent research assistance. We thank Emily Galley for very helpful comments on our draft.

2   We note that only recently Canadian governments switched to using the word "Indigenous"; instead, the term "Aboriginal" is used in the context of Canada's constitution and includes First Nations, Inuit, and Métis. We choose to use the term Indigenous as the most inclusive collective noun, as recommended by First Nations and Indigenous Studies, University of British Columbia on the Indigenous Foundations website and Indigenous Corporation Training (2016). Our use of alternative terms reflects the use of those terms in works cited in order to maintain scholarly accuracy and the intent of the original work.

3   Consultation refers to the Crown's obligation to meaningfully consult with Indigenous Peoples prior to the Crown making a decision or taking a course of action that may affect their rights and privileges, in accordance with Section 35 of the Constitution Act and the many subsequent provincial court, Supreme Court, and Federal Court of Appeal rulings on this matter. Project proponents are frequently required to engage

with Indigenous communities in support of the Crown fulfilling its obligations. Engagement refers to a broad range of actions taken by companies and government departments as they interact with Indigenous Peoples to find common ground when the relevant authorities are assessing a proposed project.

4   Yukon and Nunavut are excluded, as they did not have publicly accessible policy documents at the time of analysis.

5   The exception is "accommodation," which has a frequency of only 31 per 10,000 words in industry documents.

6   Canada's Indigenous relations ministry has undergone several transformations. Originally the Department of Indian Affairs and Northern Development (the legal title), its applied title changed to Aboriginal Affairs and Northern Development Canada (AANDC) in 2011, and then to Indigenous and Northern Affairs Canada in 2015 (Derworiz and Albers 2018). It dissolved into two ministries in 2017: Crown-Indigenous Relations and Northern Affairs Canada and Indigenous Services Canada. In 2018, Crown-Indigenous Relations and Northern Affairs Canada became Crown-Indigenous Relations and the northern affairs portfolio moved to a new ministry of Intergovernmental and Northern Affairs and Internal Trade. Throughout this chapter, we refer to the documents produced by the ministry as published at the time.

7   However, the Government of Newfoundland and Labrador (2013) indicates that "since Aboriginal consultation is included as part of the project assessment, proponents are required to provide reasonably necessary capacity funding to facilitate the provision by Aboriginal organizations of pertinent information on potential impacts of project specific activities on asserted Aboriginal rights and any required financial compensation."

Appendix: List of Documents in Detailed Review

In this appendix we list the documents we collected between 2016 and 2018, and which form the data for our analysis.

Government

Environmental Assessment Office, Government of British Columbia. 2013. *Guide to Involving Proponents when Consulting First Nations in the Environmental Assessment Process*. Victoria: Government of British Columbia. http://www2.gov. bc.ca/assets/gov/environment/natural-resource-stewardship/consulting-with-first-nations/first-nations/proponents_guide_fn_consultation_environmental_assessment_process_dec2013.pdf.

Gouvernement du Québec. 2008. *Interim Guide for Consulting the Aboriginal Communities*. Québec: Secrétariat aux affaires autochtones. https://web.archive. org/web/20200926140950/https://www.autochtones.gouv.qc.ca/publications_documentation/publications/guide_inter_2008_en.pdf.

Government of Alberta. 2013. *The Government of Alberta's Policy on Consultation with First Nations on Land and Natural Resource Management, 2013*. Edmonton: Government of Alberta. https://open.alberta.ca/publications/6713979

———. 2014. *The Government of Alberta's Guidelines on Consultation with First Nations on Land and Natural Resource Management, 2014*. Edmonton: Government of Alberta. https://open.alberta.ca/dataset/f1eb5282-5784-45f7-a35a-f03bf206de0e/resource/263300f3-5ca9-4477-98d4-d30d505aa694/download/3775118-2014-guidelines-consultation-first-nations-land-natural-resource-management.pdf.

Government of British Columbia. 2010. *Updated Procedures for Meeting Legal Obligations when Consulting First Nations (Interim)*. Victoria: Government of British Columbia. https://www2.gov.bc.ca/assets/gov/environment/natural-resource-stewardship/consulting-with-first-nations/first-nations/legal_obligations_when_consulting_with_first_nations.pd.

———. 2014. *Guide to Involving Proponents when Consulting First Nations*. Victoria: Government of British Columbia. https://www2.gov.bc.ca/assets/gov/environment/natural-resource-stewardship/consulting-with-first-nations/first-nations/involving_proponents_guide_when_consulting_with_first_nations.pdf.

———. n.d. *Building Relationships with First Nations: Respecting Rights and Doing Good Business*. Victoria: Ministry of Aboriginal Relations and Reconciliation. https://www2.gov.bc.ca/assets/gov/environment/natural-resource-stewardship/consulting-with-first-nations/first-nations/building_relationships_with_first_nations__english.pdf.

Government of Canada, AANDC (Aboriginal Affairs and Northern Development Canada). 2011. *Aboriginal Consultation and Accommodation: Updated Guidelines for Federal Officials to Fulfill the Duty to Consult*. Ottawa: Minister of the Department of Aboriginal Affairs and Northern Development Canada. https://www.rcaanc-cirnac.gc.ca/eng/1100100014664/1609421824729.

Government of Canada, Fisheries and Oceans Canada. 2006. *Consultation with First Nations: Best Practices.* http://www.dfo-mpo.gc.ca/Library/329385.pdf.

Government of Manitoba. 2009. *Interim Provincial Policy for Crown Consultations with First Nations, Métis Communities and Other Aboriginal Communities.* https://www.gov.mb.ca/imr/ir/resources/pubs/interim%20prov%20policy%20for%20crown%20consultation%20-%202009.pdf.

Government of New Brunswick. 2011. *Government of New Brunswick Duty to Consult Policy.* Fredericton: Aboriginal Affairs Secretariat. https://web.archive.org/web/20211023062047/http://www2.gnb.ca/content/dam/gnb/Departments/aas-saa/pdf/en/DutytoConsultPolicy.pdf.

Government of Newfoundland and Labrador. 2013. *The Government of Newfoundland and Labrador's Aboriginal Consultation Policy on Land and Resource Development Decisions ("The Policy").* https://www.gov.nl.ca/exec/iar/files/aboriginal_consultation.pdf.

Government of Northwest Territories. 2007. *The Government of the Northwest Territories' Approach to Consultation with Aboriginal Governments and Organizations.* Government Aboriginal Affairs and Government Relations. https://www.eia.gov.nt.ca/sites/eia/files/aboriginal_consultation_approach.pdf.

———. 2012. *Respect, Recognition, Responsibility: Government of the Northwest Territories' Approach to Engaging with Aboriginal Governments.* Yellowknife: Government of the Northwest Territories. http://www.assembly.gov.nt.ca/sites/default/files/12-06-08td23-173.pdf.

Government of Nova Scotia, Office of Aboriginal Affairs. 2012. *Proponents' Guide: The Role of Proponents in Crown Consultation with the Mi'kmaq of Nova Scotia.* Accessed via https://novascotia.ca/nse/ea/docs/ea-proponents-guide-to-mikmaq-consultation.pdf.

Government of Nova Scotia. 2015. *Government of Nova Scotia Policies and Guidelines: Consultation with the Mi'kmaq of Nova Scotia.* Accessed via https://novascotia.ca/abor/docs/April%202015_GNS%20Mi'kmaq%20Consultation%20Policy%20and%20Guidelines%20FINAL.pdf.

Government of Ontario. 2016. Environmental Assessments: Consulting Indigenous Communities (website). Accessed February 11, 2017. https://www.ontario.ca/page/environmental-assessments-consulting-aboriginal-communities.

Government of Ontario. 2017. Draft guidelines for ministries on consultation with Aboriginal peoples related to Aboriginal rights and treaty rights (website). Accessed July 2, 2023 via https://web.archive.org/web/20180614002502/https://www.ontario.ca/page/draft-guidelines-ministries-consultation-aboriginal-peoples-related-aboriginal-rights-and-treaty.

Government of Prince Edward Island. 2014. *Government of Prince Edward Island Provincial Policy on Consultation with the Mi'kmaq.* Charlottetown: Government of Prince Edward Island. https://web.archive.org/web/20170827003753/http://www.gov.pe.ca/photos/sites/aboriginalaffairs/file/Provincial%20Policy%20

on%20Consultation%20with%20the%20Mikmaq%20-%20Revised%20March%20
3%2C%202014.pdf.

Government of Saskatchewan. 2010. *First Nation and Métis Consultation Policy Framework*. Regina: Government of Saskatchewan. http://publications.gov.sk.ca/documents/313/98187-Consultation%20Policy%20Framework.pdf.

———. 2013. *Proponent Handbook: Voluntary Engagement with First Nations and Métis Communities to Inform Government's Duty to Consult Process*. Regina: Government of Saskatchewan. http://publications.gov.sk.ca/documents/313/94455-Proponent_Handbook.pdf.

Indigenous Groups

Assembly of First Nations. 2011. *Environmental Assessments and Major Projects Policy Considerations*. https://web.archive.org/web/20220128172735/http://afn.ca/uploads/files/environmental_assessments_&_major_projects_policy_considerations.pdf.

Assembly of First Nations of Quebec and Labrador Sustainable Development Institute. 2005. *Consultations Protocol of First Nations of Quebec and Labrador*. Wendake (Québec): Assembly of First Nations of Quebec and Labrador. http://fnqlsdi.ca/wp-content/uploads/2013/05/protocole_consultation_2005_en.pdf.

BC First Nations Energy and Mining Council. 2008. *Mining and Mineral Exploration Plan*. Vancouver: BC First Nations Energy & Mining Council. https://fnemc.ca/wp-content/uploads/2015/07/Mining-Action-Plan.pdf.

———. 2010. *Sharing the Wealth: First Nation Resource Participation Models*. Vancouver: BC First Nations Energy & Mining Council. https://fnemc.ca/wp-content/uploads/2015/07/Sharing-the-Wealth-2010.pdf

Canadian Council for Aboriginal Business. n.d. *Progressive Aboriginal Relations*. Toronto: Canadian Council for Aboriginal Business. https://www.ccab.com/wp-content/uploads/2016/08/PAR-Overview.pdf.

Federation of Saskatchewan Indian Nations. n.d. *Federation of Saskatchewan Indian Nations Consultation Policy*. http://caid.ca/FSINConPol.pdf.

First Nations Leadership Council. 2013. *Advancing an Indigenous Framework for Consultation and Accommodation in BC*. Vancouver: First Nations Leadership Council. http://fns.bc.ca/wp-content/uploads/2016/10/319_UBCIC_IndigActionBook-Text_loresSpreads.pdf.

Hupacasath First Nation. 2006. *Hupacasath Land Use Plan Phase 2*. https://web.archive.org/web/20200104001248/http://hupacasath.ca/wp-content/uploads/2016/03/LUP-Phase2-2006.pdf.

International Institute for Sustainable Development. 2001. *Integrating Aboriginal Values into Land-Use and Resource Management*. https://web.archive.org/web/20200103234552/https://www.iisd.org/pdf/skownan_final_nopics.pdf.

————. 2004. *Out of Respect: The Tahltan, Mining, and the Seven Questions to Sustainability*. Winnipeg: International Institute for Sustainable Development. https://www.iisd.org/system/files/publications/natres_out_of_respect.pdf.

Kluane First Nation. 2012. *Proponents Engagement Guide*. Burwash Landing, Yukon: Kluane First Nation.

Meyers Norris Penny LLP. 2009. *Best Practices for Consultation and Accommodation*, prepared for New Relationship Trust. Accessed via https://web.archive.org/web/20171031104203/https://newrelationshiptrust.ca/wp-content/uploads/2017/04/consultation-and-accomodation-report.pdf.

National Centre for First Nations Governance. 2009. *Crown Consultation Policies and Practices Across Canada*. Accessed via https://web.archive.org/web/20170623055618/http://fngovernance.org/publication_docs/NCFNG_Crown_Consultation_Practices.pdf.

————. n.d. *Consultation Fact Sheet 2: Consultation Procedures/Steps*. https://fngovernance.org/wp-content/uploads/2020/06/Consultation_Steps_Factsheet.pdf.

————. n.d. *Consultation Fact Sheet 4: Accommodation*. https://fngovernance.org/wp-content/uploads/2020/06/First_Nation_Accommodation_FactSheet.pdf.

Sam, Fred. n.d. *Nak'azdli Nation Stewardship Policy*. Fort St. James, BC: Nak'azdli Band Council. https://nakazdli.files.wordpress.com/2015/05/stewardship-policy1.pdf.

Tahltan Nation. 2013. *Tahltan-BC Government Shared Decision-Making Agreement 2013*. https://www2.gov.bc.ca/assets/gov/zzzz-to-be-moved/9efbd86da302a0712e6559bdb2c7f9dd/9efbd86da302a0712e6559bdb2c7f9dd/agreements/sdm_tahltan.pdf.

Terms of Reference for a Mi'kmaq-Nova Scotia-Canada Consultation Process n.d. https://novascotia.ca/abor/docs/MK_NS_CAN_Consultation_TOR_Sept2010_English.pdf.

Wet'suwet'en First Nation. n.d. Natural Resource Project Development Protocol (website). Accessed May 10, 2023. http://www.wetsuweten.com/territory/mining/.

Industry

Alberta Chamber of Resources. 2006. *Learning from Experience: Aboriginal Programs in the Resource Industries*. Edmonton: Alberta Chamber of Resources.

Association for Mining Exploration British Columbia. 2015. *Aboriginal Engagement Guidebook: A Practical and Principled Approach for Mineral Explorers*. Vancouver: AMEBC. http://amebc.ca/wp-content/uploads/2017/04/aboriginal-engagement-guidebook-revised-may-2015.pdf.

BluEarth Renewables Inc. 2015. *Aboriginal Relations Policy*. https://web.archive.org/web/20170705035232/http://www.bluearthrenewables.com/wp-content/uploads/2014/12/BluEarth_ARPolicy_12Jan2015_Final.pdf.

Calgary Chamber of Commerce. 2015. *The Consultation Conundrum: Examining Aboriginal Consultation in Alberta*. https://web.archive.org/web/20160811020054/

http://www.calgarychamber.com/sites/default/files/Calgary%20Chamber%20-%20 Aboriginal%20Consultation%20Report.pdf.

Cameco Corporation. 2014. "Aboriginal Peoples Engagement." Strength in Depth Sustainable Development Report. Accessed May 10, 2023. https://www.cameco. com/sustainable_development/2014/supportive-communities/aboriginal-peoples-engagement/.

Canadian Association of Petroleum Producers. 2006. *Developing Effective Working Relationships with Aboriginal Communities*. Calgary: CAPP. https://web.archive. org/web/20181121182014/http://www.capp.ca/publications-and-statistics/ publications/100984..

Canadian Chamber of Commerce. 2016. *Seizing Six Opportunities for More Clarity in the Duty to Consult and Accommodate Process.* https://web.archive.org/ web/20200806101509/http:/www.chamber.ca/media/blog/160914-seizing-six-opportunities-for-more-clarity-in-the-duty-to-consult-and-accommodate-process/.

Canadian Energy Pipeline Association. 2014. *CEPA Consultation Framework: Principles, Objectives and Guidelines.* https://web.archive.org/web/20141114225928/ http://www.cepa.com/wp-content/uploads/2011/06/CEPA-Consultation-Framework-20131.pdf

Canadian Wind Energy Association. n.d. *Best Practices for Community Engagement and Public Consultation.* Original document removed from the internet—a revised version can be accessed at https://renewablesassociation.ca/community-engagement/.

Forest Products Sector Council. 2011. *Conversation and Collaboration: Building the Future Canadian Forest Products Sector with Aboriginal Talent.* Ottawa: Forest Products Sector Council. http://www.fpac.ca/publications/FPSC-CSPF-Final-English-Report-Conversation-and-Collaboration.pdf.

Imperial Oil. n.d. *Indigenous Relations Guiding Principles and Guidelines.* http://cdn. imperialoil.ca/~/media/imperial/files/community/indigenous_relations_gp_and_ guidelines.pdf.

International Council on Mining and Metals. 2013. *Indigenous Peoples and Mining: Position Statement.* London, UK: ICMM. https://www.icmm.com/en-gb/members/ member-commitments/position-statements/indigenous-peoples-and-mining-position-statement.

Mining Association of Canada. 2008. *Towards Sustainable Mining Framework: Mining and Aboriginal Peoples.* https://web.archive.org/web/20170215101717/http://mining.ca/ sites/default/files/documents/TSMAboriginalandCommunityOutreachFramework. pdf.

———. 2015. *TSM Assessment Protocol: A Tool for Assessing Aboriginal and Community Outreach Performance.* https://web.archive.org/web/20170831072531/http:// mining.ca/sites/default/files/documents/TSM-Aboriginal-and-Community-Outreach-Protocol-2015.pdf

Mining Association of Manitoba. 2016. *2016 Aboriginal Engagement Handbook: A Handbook for Proponents of Mineral Exploration and Mining in Manitoba.* Winnipeg: Mining Association of Manitoba. https://www.mines.ca/wcm-docs/docs/publications/aboriginal_engagement_handbook_final.pdf.

Prospectors and Developers Association of Canada. 2014. *Government Resource Revenue Sharing with Aboriginal Communities: A Jurisdictional Review.* Ottawa: PDAC. http://www.pdac.ca/pdf-viewer?doc=/docs/default-source/default-document-library/pdac-grrs-report-2014.pdf.

Suncor. 2016. *Policy Statement: Canadian Aboriginal Relations.* Calgary: Suncor. https://web.archive.org/web/20161205141417/http://www.suncor.com/sustainability/community-consultation/aboriginal-relations.

References

Alberta Chamber of Resources. 2006. *Learning from Experience: Aboriginal Programs in the Resource Industries.* Edmonton: Alberta Chamber of Resources.

Alfred, Taiaiake. 2001. "Deconstructing the British Columbia Treaty Process." *Balayi: Culture, Law and Colonialism* 3: 37–65.

———. 2009. *Peace, Power, Righteousness: An Indigenous Manifesto.* 2nd ed. Oxford University Press.

———. 2017. "It's All About the Land." In *Whose Land is it Anyway? A Manual for Decolonization,* ed. Peter McFarlance and Nicole Shabus (Vancouver: Federation of Post-Secondary Educators of BC), 10–13. https://fpse.ca/decolonization-manual#:~:text=Manual%20for%20Decolonization-,Whose%20Land%20Is%20It%20Anyway%3F,the%20path%20forward%20to%20reconciliation

Amnesty International. 2016. *Out of Sight, Out of Mind: Gender, Indigenous Rights, and Energy Development in Northeast British Columbia, Canada.* London: Amnesty International Ltd.

Anderson, R. 1999. *Economic Development Among the Aboriginal Peoples in Canada: The Hope for the Future.* Concord, ON: Captus Press.

———. 2002. "Entrepreneurship and Aboriginal Canadians." *Journal of Development Entrepreneurship* 7, no. 1: 45–65.

Angell, A. and Parkins, J. 2011. "Resource Development and Aboriginal Culture in the Canadian North." *Polar Record* 47, no. 240: 69–79.

Assembly of First Nations of Quebec and Labrador Sustainable Development Institute. 2005. *Consultations Protocol of First Nations of Quebec and Labrador.* Wendake (Québec): Assembly of First Nations of Quebec and Labrador. http://fnqlsdi.ca/wp-content/uploads/2013/05/protocole_consultation_2005_en.pdf.

Association for Mining Exploration British Columbia. 2015. *Aboriginal Engagement Guidebook: A Practical and Principled Approach for Mineral Explorers.* Vancouver: AMEBC. http://amebc.ca/wp-content/uploads/2017/04/aboriginal-engagement-guidebook-revised-may-2015.pdf

BC First Nations Energy and Mining Council. 2008. *Mining and Mineral Exploration Plan.* Vancouver: BC First Nations Energy & Mining Council. https://fnemc.ca/wp-content/uploads/2015/07/Mining-Action-Plan.pdf

BluEarth Renewables Inc. 2015. *Aboriginal Relations Policy.* https://web.archive.org/web/20170705035232/http://www.bluearthrenewables.com/wp-content/uploads/2014/12/BluEarth_ARPolicy_12Jan2015_Final.pdf

Booth, A., and N. Skelton. 2006. "'You Spoil Everything!' Indigenous Peoples and the Consequences of Industrial Development in British Columbia." *Environment, Development and Sustainability* 8, no. 3: 685–702.

Borrows, John. 2016. *Freedom and Indigenous Constitutionalism.* Toronto: University of Toronto Press.

Calgary Chamber of Commerce. 2015. *The Consultation Conundrum: Examining Aboriginal Consultation in Alberta.* https://web.archive.org/web/20160811020054/http://www.calgarychamber.com/sites/default/files/Calgary%20Chamber%20-%20Aboriginal%20Consultation%20Report.pdf.

Cameco Corporation. 2014. "Aboriginal Peoples Engagement." Strength in Depth Sustainable Development Report. Accessed May 10, 2023. https://www.cameco.com/sustainable_development/2014/supportive-communities/aboriginal-peoples-engagement/.

Campbell, Kathryn M. 2007. "'What Was It They Lost?' The Impact of Resource Development on Family Violence in a Northern Aboriginal Community." *Journal of Ethnicity in Criminal Justice* 5, no. 1: 57–80.

Canadian Association of Petroleum Producers. 2006. *Developing Effective Working Relationships with Aboriginal Communities.* Ottawa: The Canadian Chamber of Commerce. Accessed via https://canadacommons.ca/artifacts/1214937/seizing-six-opportunities-for-more-clarity-in-the-duty-to-consult-and-accommodate-process/1768035/.

Canadian Chamber of Commerce. 2016. *Seizing Six Opportunities for More Clarity in the Duty to Consult and Accommodate Process.* https://canadacommons.ca/artifacts/1214937/seizing-six-opportunities-for-more-clarity-in-the-duty-to-consult-and-accommodate-process/1768035/

Canadian Energy Pipeline Association. 2014. *CEPA Consultation Framework: Principles, Objectives and Guidelines.* https://web.archive.org/web/20141114225928/http://www.cepa.com/wp-content/uploads/2011/06/CEPA-Consultation-Framework-20131.pdf

Canadian Wind Energy Association. n.d. *Best Practices for Community Engagement and Public Consultation.* Original document removed from internet—a current version is available at https://renewablesassociation.ca/community-engagement/.

Chippewas of the Thames First Nation v. Enbridge Pipelines Inc., [2017] 1 SCR 1099, 2017 SCC 41. https://scc-csc.lexum.com/scc-csc/scc-csc/en/item/16744/index.do.

Clyde River (Hamlet) v. Petroleum Geo-Services Inc., [2017] 1 SCR 1069, 2017 SCC 40. https://scc-csc.lexum.com/scc-csc/scc-csc/en/item/16743/index.do.

Cragg, Wesley and Peter Siebenmorgen. 2011. *CBERN-NNK Knowledge Needs Research Summary: Report to the CBERN/Naskapi Steering Committee and the Naskapi Community*, accessed via https://yorkspace.library.yorku.ca/xmlui/bitstream/handle/10315/37130/Nov%202011%20CBERN-NNK-Report-English-Final.compressed%20%281%29.pdf?sequence=1.

Dussault, René, Georges Erasmus, Paul L. A. H. Chartrand, J. Peter Meekison, Viola Robinson, Mary Sillett, and Bertha Wilson. 1996. *Report of the Royal Commission on Aboriginal Peoples*. 5 vols. Canada: Royal Commission on Aboriginal Peoples. https://www.bac-lac.gc.ca/eng/discover/aboriginal-heritage/royal-commission-aboriginal-peoples/Pages/final-report.aspx.

Federation of Saskatchewan Indian Nations. n.d. *Federation of Saskatchewan Indian Nations Consultation Policy*. http://caid.ca/FSINConPol.pdf.

First Nations and Indigenous Studies, University of British Columbia. 2017. "Terminology." University of British Columbia. Indigenous Foundations. Accessed August 2017. http://indigenousfoundations.arts.ubc.ca/terminology/

First Nations Leadership Council. 2013. *Advancing an Indigenous Framework for Consultation and Accommodation in BC*. Vancouver: First Nations Leadership Council. http://fns.bc.ca/wp-content/uploads/2016/10/319_UBCIC_IndigActionBook-Text_loresSpreads.pdf.

Forest Products Sector Council. 2011. *Conversation and Collaboration: Building the Future Canadian Forest Products Sector with Aboriginal Talent*. Ottawa: Forest Products Sector Council. http://www.fpac.ca/publications/FPSC-CSPF-Final-English-Report-Conversation-and-Collaboration.pdf.

Gallagher, B. 2011. *Resource Rulers: Fortune and Folly on Canada's Road to Resources*. n.p.: Bill Gallagher.

Gitxaala Nation v. Canada, 2016 FCA 187. https://decisions.fca-caf.gc.ca/fca-caf/decisions/en/item/145744/index.do.

Gouvernement du Québec. 2008. *Interim Guide for Consulting the Aboriginal Communities*. Québec: Secrétariat aux affaires autochtones. https://cdn-contenu.quebec.ca/cdn-contenu/adm/min/conseil-executif/publications-adm/srpni/administratives/orientations/en/guide_inter_2008_en.pdf

Government of Alberta. 2013. *The Government of Alberta's Policy on Consultation with First Nations on Land and Natural Resource Management, 2013*. Edmonton: Government of Alberta. https://open.alberta.ca/publications/6713979.

———. 2014. *The Government of Alberta's Guidelines on Consultation with First Nations on Land and Natural Resource Management, 2014*. Edmonton: Government of Alberta. https://open.alberta.ca/dataset/f1eb5282-5784-45f7-a35a-f03bf206de0e/resource/263300f3-5ca9-4477-98d4-d30d505aa694/download/3775118-2014-guidelines-consultation-first-nations-land-natural-resource-management.pdf.

Government of British Columbia. 2010. *Updated Procedures for Meeting Legal Obligations when Consulting First Nations (Interim)*. Victoria: Government of British Columbia. https://www2.gov.bc.ca/assets/gov/environment/natural-resource-stewardship/consulting-with-first-nations/first-nations/legal_obligations_when_consulting_with_first_nations.pdf

———. 2014. *Guide to Involving Proponents when Consulting First Nations.* Victoria: Government of British Columbia. https://www2.gov.bc.ca/assets/gov/environment/ natural-resource-stewardship/consulting-with-first-nations/first-nations/ involving_proponents_guide_when_consulting_with_first_nations.pdf.

———. n.d. *Building Relationships with First Nations: Respecting Rights and Doing Good Business.* Victoria: Ministry of Aboriginal Relations and Reconciliation. https://www2.gov.bc.ca/assets/gov/environment/natural-resource-stewardship/ consulting-with-first-nations/first-nations/building_relationships_with_first_ nations__english.pdf

Government of Canada, AANDC (Aboriginal Affairs and Northern Development Canada). 2011. *Aboriginal Consultation and Accommodation: Updated Guidelines for Federal Officials to Fulfill the Duty to Consult.* Ottawa: Minister of the Department of Aboriginal Affairs and Northern Development Canada. https:// www.rcaanc-cirnac.gc.ca/eng/1100100014664/1609421824729.

Government of Canada, Fisheries and Oceans Canada. 2006. *Consultation with First Nations: Best Practices.* Ottawa: Fisheries and Oceans Canada. https://waves-vagues.dfo-mpo.gc.ca/library-bibliotheque/329385.pdf.

Government of Manitoba. 2009. *Interim Provincial Policy for Crown Consultations with First Nations, Métis Communities and Other Aboriginal Communities.* https://www. gov.mb.ca/imr/ir/resources/pubs/interim%20prov%20policy%20for%20crown%20 consultation%20-%202009.pdf.

Government of Newfoundland and Labrador. 2013. *The Government of Newfoundland and Labrador's Aboriginal Consultation Policy on Land and Resource Development Decisions ("The Policy").* https://www.gov.nl.ca/exec/iar/files/aboriginal_ consultation.pdf.

Government of Northwest Territories. 2012. *Respect, Recognition, Responsibility: Government of the Northwest Territories' Approach to Engaging with Aboriginal Governments.* Yellowknife: Government of the Northwest Territories. http://www. assembly.gov.nt.ca/sites/default/files/12-06-08td23-173.pdf.

Government of Nova Scotia. 2015. *Government of Nova Scotia Policies and Guidelines: Consultation with the Mi'kmaq of Nova Scotia.* Accessed via https://novascotia. ca/abor/docs/April%202015_GNS%20Mi'kmaq%20Consultation%20Policy%20 and%20Guidelines%20FINAL.pdf.

Government of Saskatchewan. 2013. *Proponent Handbook: Voluntary Engagement with First Nations and Métis Communities to Inform Government's Duty to Consult Process.* Regina: Government of Saskatchewan. http://publications.gov.sk.ca/ documents/313/94455-Proponent_Handbook.pdf.

Hupacasath First Nation. 2006. *Hupacasath Land Use Plan Phase 2.* Port Alberni: Husacasath First Nation. https://web.archive.org/web/20200104001248/http:// hupacasath.ca/wp-content/uploads/2016/03/LUP-Phase2-2006.pdf..

Indigenous Corporation Training Inc. 2016. "Indigenous or Aboriginal: Which Is Correct?" *Working Effectively with Indigenous Peoples* (blog), January 5, 2016. https://www.ictinc.ca/blog/indigenous-or-aboriginal-which-is-correct.

Kluane First Nation. 2012. *Proponents Engagement Guide.* Burwash Landing, Yukon: Kluane First Nation.

Lambrecht, K. 2013. *Aboriginal Consultation, Environmental Assessment and Regulatory Review in Canada.* Regina: University of Regina Press.

Manning, Susan, Patricia Nash, Leah Levac, Deborah Stienstra & Jane Stinson. 2018. *Strengthening Impact Assessments for Indigenous Women.* Ottawa: Canadian Environmental Assessment Agency.

Manuel, Alfred. 2017. "From Dispossession to Dependency." In *Whose Land is it Anyway? A Manual for Decolonization,* ed. Peter McFarlance and Nicole Shabus (Vancouver: Federation of Post-Secondary Educators of BC), 18–21.

Manuel, Arthur and Ronald Derrickson (Grand Chief). 2017. *The Reconciliation Manifesto: Recovering the Land, Rebuilding the Economy.* Toronto: James Lorimer & Company.

Meyers Norris Penny LLP. 2009. *Best Practices for Consultation and Accommodation,* prepared for New Relationship Trust, accessed via https://web.archive.org/web/20171031104203/https://newrelationshiptrust.ca/wp-content/uploads/2017/04/consultation-and-accomodation-report.pdf.

Mining Association of Manitoba. 2016. *2016 Aboriginal Engagement Handbook.* https://www.mines.ca/wcm-docs/docs/publications/aboriginal_engagement_handbook_final.pdf

Nightingale, Elana, Karina Czyzewski, Frank Tester & Nadia Aaruaq. 2017. "The Effects of Resource Extraction on Inuit Women and Their Families: Evidence from Canada." *Gender & Development* 25, no. 3: 367–85.

National Centre for First Nations Governance. 2009. *Crown Consultation Policies and Practices Across Canada.* Vancouver: National Centre for First Nations Governance. https://caid.ca/NCFNG-CroConPol2009.pdf

———. n.d. *Consultation Fact Sheet 2: Consultation Procedures/Steps.* https://fngovernance.org/wp-content/uploads/2020/06/Consultation_Steps_Factsheet.pdf.

North Slave Métis Alliance. 1999. *Can't Live Without Work: North Slave Metis Alliance Environmental, Social, Economic and Cultural Concerns: A Companion to the Comprehensive Study Report on the Diavik Diamonds Project.* Yellowknife: North Slave Métis Alliance.

Notzke, C. 1995. "A New Perspective in Aboriginal Natural Resource Management: Co-management," *Geoforum* 26, no. 2: 187–209.

O'Faircheallaigh, C. 2007. "Environmental Agreements, EIA Follow-up and Aboriginal Participation in Environmental Management: The Canadian Experience." *Environmental Impact Assessment Review* 27, no. 4: 319–42.

Palmater, P. 2015. *Indigenous Nationhood: Empowering Grassroots Citizens.* Halifax: Fernwood Publishing.

———. 2016. "Trudeau's empty budget promises on the nation-to-nation relationship." 2016. *Policy Options*, March 23, 2016. https://policyoptions.irpp.org/2016/03/23/trudeaus-empty-budget-promises-on-the-nation-to-nation-relationship/.

———. 2018a. "True Test of Reconciliation: Respect the Indigenous Right to Say No." Canadian Dimension. Accessed May 15, 2018. https://canadiandimension.com/articles/view/true-test-of-reconciliation-respect-the-indigenous-right-to-say-no.

———. 2018b. "The Supreme Court Has Just Gutted the Crown's Duty to Consult First Nations." *Maclean's*. October 11, 2018. https://www.macleans.ca/opinion/the-supreme-court-has-just-gutted-the-crowns-duty-to-consult-first-nations/.

———. 2020. "Mi'kmaw Treaty Rights, Reconciliation and the 'Rule of Law'." Canadian Dimension. Accessed September 22, 2020. https://canadiandimension.com/articles/view/mikmaw-treaty-rights-reconciliation-and-the-rule-of-law.

———. 2021. "'At every turn, Canada chooses the path of injustice toward Indigenous peoples.'" *Maclean's*. January 29. https://macleans.ca/opinion/at-every-turn-canada-chooses-the-path-of-injustice-toward-indigenous-peoples/.

Palmater, Pamela D. 2011. "Stretched Beyond Human Limits: Death by Poverty in First Nations." *Canadian Review of Social Policy* 65/66: 112–27.

Papillon, M. and T. Rodon. 2017. "Proponent-Indigenous Agreements and the Implementation of the Right to Free, Prior and Informed Consent in Canada." *Environmental Impact Assessment* 62: 216–24.

Prospectors and Developers Association of Canada. 2014. *Government Resource Revenue Sharing with Aboriginal Communities: A Jurisdictional Review*. Ottawa: PDAC. http://www.pdac.ca/pdf-viewer?doc=/docs/default-source/default-document-library/pdac-grrs-report-2014.pdf.

Ritchie, K. 2013. "Issues Associated with the Implementation of the Duty to Consult and Accommodate Aboriginal Peoples: Threatening the Goals of Reconciliation and Meaningful Consultation." *UBC Law Review* 46, no. 2: 397–438.

Sam, Fred. n.d. *Nak'azdli Nation Stewardship Policy*. Fort St. James, BC: Nak'azdli Band Council. https://nakazdli.files.wordpress.com/2015/05/stewardship-policy1.pdf.

Simpson, Leanne Betasamosake. 2017. *As We Have Always Done: Indigenous Freedom Through Radical Resistance*. Minneapolis: University of Minnesota Press.

Sinclair, Murray. *Honouring the Truth, Reconciling for the Future Summary of the Final Report of the Truth and Reconciliation Commission of Canada*. Winnipeg: Truth and Reconciliation Commission of Canada. McGill-Queen's University Press, for the Truth and Reconciliation Commission of Canada. https://ehprnh2mwo3.exactdn.com/wp-content/uploads/2021/01/Executive_Summary_English_Web.pdf

Slowey, G. 2009. "A fine balance." In *First Nations, First Thoughts*, ed. A. Timpson (Vancouver: UBC Press), 229–50.

Sossin, L. 2010. "The Duty to Consult and Accommodate: Procedural Justice as Aboriginal Rights." *Canadian Journal of Administrative Law and Practice* 23: 93–113.

Suncor. 2016. *Policy Statement: Canadian Aboriginal Relations.* Calgary: Suncor. https://web.archive.org/web/20161205141417/http://www.suncor.com/sustainability/community-consultation/aboriginal-relations.

Tsetta, Shirley, Ginger Gibson, Linda McDevitt, and Sarah Plotner. 2005. "Telling a Story of Change the Dene Way: Indicators for Monitoring in Diamond Impacted Communities." *Pimatisiwin: A Journal of Aboriginal and Indigenous Community Health* 3, no. 1: 59–69.

Westman, Clinton N. and Tara L. Joly. 2019. "Oil Sands Extraction in Alberta, Canada: A Review of Impacts and Processes Concerning Indigenous Peoples." *Human Ecology* 47: 233–43.

Zurba, Melanie and Ryan Bullock. 2020. "Bioenergy Development and the Implications for the Social Wellbeing of Indigenous Peoples in Canada." *Ambio* 49, 299–309.

Honouring Modern Treaty Relationships: Intent and Implementation of Partnerships in Yukon

Kirk Cameron, Emily Martin, and Cody Sharpe

Yukon is home to fourteen First Nations, eleven of which have signed Final Agreements (modern treaties) and Self-Government Agreements (SGAs) with the Government of Canada and the Government of Yukon. These agreements, protected by the Canadian constitution, have created a guaranteed role for First Nations in lands and resources governance in the territory. We argue that the institutionalization and evolving implementation of co-management has significantly impacted the role of mass public opposition to resource development projects. We also suggest that the meaningful implementation of these institutions, and the treaty relationships from which they stem, depend very much on the leaders of the day. Although a thorough evaluation of the success of co-management in Yukon is beyond the scope of this paper (Clark and Joe-Strack 2017), Yukon's experience as an early leader in gradually defining and implementing co-management of lands and resources through land claim settlements may be of practical value to other jurisdictions.

Across Canada, restarting the relationship between Indigenous and non-Indigenous (or public) governments is both a critical task and an unavoidable obligation of each party. John Borrows and Michael Coyle, two of the nation's leading experts on Aboriginal and Indigenous law, argue that "Canadians must come to grips with the reality that treaty-making was more focused on building relationships and much less concerned with cataloging rights.... Treaties first and foremost are concerned with right relations between First Peoples and settler governments" (Borrows and Coyle 2017, 13).

Publicly, it has been the vision of Yukon's First Nations since the early 1970s to develop a new relationship. This vision drove the development of modern treaties with the territorial and federal governments, and it is the institutionalization of this vision that explains why there have been relatively few incidences of First Nation-exclusive protest over resource development in Yukon. The term co-management has been defined and redefined many times, but generally it describes a relationship where some degree of decision-making power is shared between governments, rights holders, and/or resource/land users to govern specific resources or landscape at a regional scale (Berkes 1991; Natcher and Hickey 2005; Armitage et al. 2011; Clark and Joe-Strack 2017) with the intention to achieve some outcomes which neither can obtain independent of the others involvement. According to the Umbrella Final Agreement (the foundation agreement that these modern treaties are based on), co-management is the intended norm when it comes to natural resource development in Yukon, and the term relates to ideas like covenantal relationship (Newman 2011), and co-equal partnership (Papillon and Rodon 2017).

Co-management structures dominate in Yukon, and these institutions find their genesis in the Umbrella Final Agreement and First Nation-specific Final Agreements reached with eleven Yukon First Nations between 1993 and 2005. Where protest does occur over resource development, we argue it is because one party in the relationship has neglected their obligations; however, because of the constitutionally-protected nature of the treaty and related co-management governance institutions, such abrogation will not generally be tolerated by Canadian courts. An example of this phenomenon in practice is the legal fight over the Peel Land Use Plan, a fight resolved in the Supreme Court of Canada in late 2017. The Peel case, which started as a dispute between the Yukon government and the First Nations of Na-Cho Nyäk Dun and Tr'ondëk Hwëch'in over land use planning, evolved into a debate about ungenerous treaty interpretation that received international attention.

The chapter is organized as follows. We begin with a brief overview of recent Yukon history, including the long series of events that led to the creation of the Umbrella Final Agreement. We then explain the importance of the modern treaties that were negotiated following the Umbrella Final Agreement (UFA) and highlight how their content established co-management governance of natural resources as the intended norm. Three conflicts related to resource development then are covered, including those that resulted in the recent Supreme Court of Canada decision regarding the Peel Land Use Plan. Our concluding remarks focus on the lessons our observations can offer policy makers in other jurisdictions.

Settler Arrivals and the Call for Treaties in Yukon

Spurred by the negative impacts of the 1890s gold rush in the Dawson City region of Yukon on the traditional lifestyles of many First Nations, Chief Jim Boss of the Ta'an Kwäch'än Council sent a letter to the federal government in 1902 calling for protection of lands and game for Indians. This marked the first written expression of a long period of dissatisfaction among Yukon First Nations' citizens with the federal government. Events between 1902 and 1973 sustained this dissatisfaction, including forced relocations for the sake of administrative convenience, residential schools, the construction of the Alaska Highway and a pipeline from Norman Wells in Northwest Territories through Yukon, placer and hard rock mines across the territory, copper mining in the Whitehorse area, and the massive open-pit Faro Mine site.

In 1973, a delegation of Yukon Chiefs presented Prime Minister Pierre Elliott Trudeau with *Together Today for our Children Tomorrow*, a proposal intended "to find out what kind of Settlement we feel will be 'fair and just' to both our people and to our White Brothers" (CYI 1973, 7). This proposal spoke about collaboration and partnership, arguing that "if we are successful [in negotiations] then the date of our agreement will be a day for all to celebrate... If we are successful, the day will come when ALL Yukoners, will be proud of our Heritage and Culture, and will respect our Indian identity. Only then will we be equal Canadian brothers" (CYI 1973, 17). *Together Today* was critical of existing treaties in place elsewhere in Canada, while also taking a position that relationship-building was inherently valuable:

> When the treaties in the prairies were signed, they were a plan to help the Indian to adjust to the Whiteman's way of life. It was an attempt to change him from a hunter to a farmer... We all know it didn't work. But maybe it was an "honest attempt" by the Whitemen to help the Indian change (CYI 1973, 17).

The year 1973 also saw the passage of the federal Comprehensive Claims Policy, a policy that provided a very different procedural base for modern treaty-making compared to the Historic and Numbered Treaties (see Alcantara 2013). It sparked negotiations between Canada and Yukon First Nations that ultimately resulted in an Agreement-in-Principle (AiP) in the early 1980s. The AiP, however, was rejected at a First Nations gathering at Tagish in 1984 as offering too little on lands, resources, and self-government. In conversations with a former Chief of the Vuntut Gwitchin First Nation who was involved in negotiations on the AiP it was noted how difficult it was to walk away from an agreement worth more than $600 million to Yukon First Nations, but that the 1984 agreement was doomed to failure without recognition of self-government.

Following the 1984 rejection, and subsequent thinking of the unique First Nation-distinct approach, the UFA approach was developed. This framework document defined a collection of common interests while remaining flexible enough to allow for modifications based on the unique interests of each First Nation. In total, eleven of fourteen Yukon First Nations have concluded Final Agreements with the territorial and federal government. These are modern treaties that use the UFA as their foundation and include sections unique to the individual First Nation to which they apply.

By 1993, four Yukon First Nations had negotiated Final Agreements. Parliament enacted legislation in 1995 creating new, constitutionally protected treaties with Champagne & Aishihik First Nations, the First Nation of Na-Cho Nyäk Dun, Teslin Tlingit Council and the Vuntut Gwitchin First Nation. Seven more Final Agreements followed: Selkirk First Nation's and Little Salmon/Carmacks First Nation's were settled in 1997; Tr'ondëk Hwëch'in's was concluded in 1998; Ta'an Kwäch'än Council's was reached in 2002; Kluane First Nation's in 2003; and Kwanlin Dün First Nation's and Carcross/Tagish First Nation's in 2005.

In addition to the Final Agreements, which are the modern treaties protected by the Canadian Constitution, each First Nation negotiated and implemented Self-Government Agreements. These SGAs are not protected by the Canadian constitution but are complementary and supportive of the co-management aspects of the treaties. For instance, self-governing First Nations can pass legislation for their lands and people that reinforce the land rights provisions of the treaties. There are many parts of the SGAs that speak to the importance of co-ordination and the interrelationship between First Nation and public laws.

White River First Nation, Liard First Nation and Ross River Dena Council do not have signed modern treaties. Though negotiations are ongoing, it is unclear where these discussions will end up. (For a general history of land claims in Yukon and relationship to public government, see Cameron and White, 1995.)

The Importance of Modern Treaties

Why are these modern treaties so fundamental to partnership and co-management governance of Yukon? First, these treaties are a recognized component of Canada's constitutional framework. According to the Supreme Court of Canada, "through s. 35 of the *Constitution Act, 1982*, [the modern treaties] have assumed a vital place in our constitutional fabric. Negotiating modern treaties, and living by the mutual rights and responsibilities they set out, has the potential to forge a renewed relationship between the Crown and Indigenous peoples" (*First Nation of Nacho Nyak Dun v. Yukon*, 2017, para 1). Unlike the Historic and Numbered Treaties, where implementation was left to the parties to roll out through ongoing relationships, modern treaties provide clearer guidance on institutional structures, processes, and authority. Furthermore, as the Supreme Court of Canada explained in *First Nation of Nacho Nyak Dun v. Yukon* (2017, para. 7), "the Umbrella Final Agreement and the specific Final Agreements that implement its terms are the product of decades of negotiations 'between well-resourced and sophisticated parties' (*Little Salmon*, at para. 9)." In other words, their value is both in their stature as constitutional documents and in their detail, detail that works against incomplete implementation. Both modern treaties and related co-management have also been criticized at various points as a means of maintaining Crown control over Indigenous peoples and lands through the politics of recognition (Coulthard 2014; Charlie 2017) and forced adoption of Euro-Canadian processes (Nadasdy 2004; Irlbacher-Fox 2009; King 2013). Whether First Nations and Crown actors are in fact equally well resourced in modern treaty negotiations is also disputed (Alcantara 2008).

Values of partnership and co-management are ubiquitous throughout the text of the UFA and Final Agreements. These values influence the very fundamentals of land and resource governance in the territory by recognizing First Nation ownership of a portion of Yukon lands. Ownership of "settlement lands" is split into two classes, with Category A settlement lands including surface and subsurface ownership rights, and Category B settlement lands providing for only surface ownership. Between the eleven Yukon First Nations with signed modern treaties, there is roughly 41,595 square kilometres, or 8.5%, of the territory designated as settlement lands.

As noted in the Supreme Court ruling in the Peel Land Use Planning decision, "in exchange for comparatively smaller settlement areas, the First Nations acquired important rights in both settlement and non-settlement lands, particularly in their traditional territories" (*First Nation of Nacho Nyak Dun v. Yukon*, 2017, para. 46). Barry Stuart, Yukon chief land claims negotiator, is quoted verbatim in the Court's decision:

> It became abundantly clear that [the First Nations'] interests in resources were best served by creatively exploring options for shared responsibility in the management of water, wildlife, forestry, land, and culture. Effective and constitutionally protected First Nation management rights advanced their interests in resource use more effectively than simply acquiring vast tracts of land [as settlement lands]. (*First Nation of Nacho Nyak Dun v. Yukon*, 2017, para. 46)

The trade-off made by Yukon First Nations during treaty negotiations was sacrificing maximum land ownership for the guarantee of significant involvement in management over all resource activities in Yukon. Stuart notes this covers management of "water, wildlife, forestry, land and culture" (*First Nation of Nacho Nyak Dun v. Yukon*, 2017, para. 46). Though the signatories had to "cede, release and surrender" Indigenous title to much of their traditional territory (see Charlie 2017), they also set the foundation for a new concept of Canadian governance based on sharing of values and interests. In this context, ownership of the levers of governance no longer rests completely with a dominant Crown government, but in the institutions set up through the modern treaties. As the Supreme Court's Peel decision explains, "the language of s. 11.6.3.2 must be read in the broader context of the scheme and objectives of Chapter 11 of the Final Agreements, which establishes a comprehensive process for how the territorial and First Nation governments will collectively govern settlement and non-settlement lands, both of which include traditional territories" (*First Nation of Nacho Nyak Dun v. Yukon*, 2017, para.

42). In this instance, the focus is on Chapter 11 (Land Use Planning), but the message applies to the entire governance framework created by the UFA. Protest is often fuelled by a feeling of isolation and distance from the elite who control the forums of governance. Through the spaces of governance created by the UFA, this isolation is reduced; however, this reduction can only be sustained so long as decision-makers respect the process. Failing to do so may, in turn, spark further protests that force leadership to return to following the expectation created by the UFA related to co-management in Yukon.

The Components of Modern Treaties

Co-management is promoted by twelve chapters in the UFA. In our view, these chapters can be divided into four broad thematic categories: chapters addressing balance between protection and use (the "wise stewardship" chapters); those focusing primarily on conservation and protection; a third with attention to specific resource management; and a final category associated with the economy and governance. Some chapters touch on multiple themes, but this categorization is still a useful guide to understanding the UFA.

The first of three chapters under the "wise stewardship" theme, Chapter 11 (Land Use Planning) establishes a Land Use Planning Council with authority over all non-municipal lands in Yukon. This Council is comprised of one nominee from the Council of Yukon Indians (now the Council of Yukon First Nations) and two nominees from the Yukon government. Two objectives of the chapter highlight the co-management intent:

> 11.1.1.1 to encourage the development of a common Yukon land use planning process outside community boundaries; and

> 11.1.1.6 to ensure that social, cultural, economic and environment policies are applied to the management, protection and use of land, water and resources in an integrated and coordinated manner so as to ensure Sustainable Development.

Broad regional land use planning processes are provided for, as well as the authority to focus on specific areas through sub-regional and district land use plans. However, planning at the lesser levels must be in conformity with a regional land use plan, by nature a co-managed outcome. More will be said on this point below during our discussion of the Peel Land Use Plan.

Chapter 12 (Development Assessment) can also be counted in the "wise stewardship" theme and creates the Yukon Environmental and Socio-economic Assessment Board (YESAB). An independent body set up through federal legislation, YESAB is responsible for assessing every development project in the territory, whether on Crown, municipal, or a First Nation's Settlement Lands. These assessments must be conducted before any government can provide an authorization for a project to proceed. YESAB's enabling legislation guarantees First Nations representation on the board and its executive committee. This legislation—the Yukon Environmental and Socio-economic Assessment Act (YESAA)—also establishes requirements for First Nations and community consultation as part of the assessment processes including board member appointments.

Chapter 14 (Water Management) is the third "wise stewardship" chapter. Although the territorial Water Board pre-dates the UFA, it is still recognized as a key co-management body in Chapter 14 because of the economic, environmental, and cultural importance of water in the territory. Water rights of Yukon First Nations are described, and the Water Board is to have one-third of its members nominated by Yukon First Nations, reinforcing the principle of co-management (s. 14.4.1).

Under the conservation and protection theme are Chapter 10 (Special Management Areas), Chapter 13 (Heritage), and Chapter 16 (Fish and Wildlife). Special Management Areas are intended "to maintain important features of the Yukon's natural or cultural environment for the benefit of Yukon residents and all Canadians while respecting the rights of Yukon Indian People and Yukon First Nations" (UFA s. 10.1.1). There is considerable interaction among these three chapters, owing to the potential impacts a Special Management Area may have on heritage, fish, and wildlife.

Chapter 13 defines a common interest of Yukon residents "to promote public awareness, appreciation and understanding of all aspects of culture and heritage in Yukon and, in particular, to respect and foster the culture and heritage of Yukon Indian People" (s. 13.1.1.1). The Yukon Heritage Resources Board is established through this chapter and, similar to the Water Board and YESAB, encourages co-management by requiring an equal number of appointees from Yukon First Nations and the Yukon government. Chapter 13 also creates a Yukon Geographical Place Names Board with equal First Nation and public government representation.

Chapter 16 creates a complex institutional structure around fish and wildlife management. The intent is to recognize pan-territorial and regional involvement in resource management. In this case co-management is embedded in the Chapter's objective of "ensur[ing] equal participation of Yukon Indian People with other Yukon residents in Fish and Wildlife management processes and decisions" (s. 16.1.1.4). The territorial Fish and Wildlife Management Board includes protected representation for First Nations, as do the regionally focused Renewable Resource Councils (RRCs), of which there is the right set out in the treaties for each of the eleven First Nations with Final Agreements to establish an RRC.

Specific resource management chapters also exist within the UFA. Chapter 17 (Forest Resources) speaks to the importance of shared values and coordinated management of the resource. As with fish and wildlife, RRCs are empowered through this chapter to make recommendations on "the coordination of Forest Resources Management throughout Yukon and in the relevant Traditional Territory" (s. 17.4.1). Their recommendations must encourage the sustainability of forest resources and demonstrate a watershed-based approach to planning (s. 17.5.5).

Chapter 18 (Non-Renewable Resources) follows with detailed provisions regarding management of non-renewable resources, specifically mineral rights, quarries, and access rights on Crown and Settlement Land. Where the potential for conflict exists between a person holding a mineral right and a First Nation who acquires the land as part of Settlement, Chapter 8 authorizes the Yukon Surface Rights Board to address the dispute. In the spirit of co-management, Yukon First Nations nominate half of this board, and panels set up to hear disputes either favour the First Nation nominees or public government nominees depending on whether the dispute falls on First Nation or Crown-owned property. (Though the Yukon Surface Rights Board exists, it is famously underused.)

The final category of chapters of the UFA relates to the economy and governance. Again, these chapters encourage co-operation, and cover resource royalty-sharing in Chapter 23, and economic development in Chapter 22. Chapter 24 is particularly important because of its focus on self-government. Chapter 24 does not constitute an agreement in-and-of-itself, but instead creates the parameters for the negotiation of SGAs that are external to the UFA. This was the basis for subsequent SGAs that explicitly recognize that Yukon

First Nations can draw down powers to govern their own affairs through passing their own laws.

Self-Government & Overlapping Authorities in Yukon

Reading chapter 24 alongside a SGA provides a sense of the complex relationships among the powers of the First Nation, the contents of the Land Claims Agreement, and public government legislation. For instance, the SGAs make it clear that the Land Claims Agreement is superior to the SGA and associated First Nation legislation; laws passed by the First Nation cannot contravene the Land Claims Agreement. At the same time, the First Nation holds the jurisdiction to "enact laws [for the] management and administration of rights or benefits which are realized pursuant to the Final Agreement..." (see for instance Kwanlin Dün First Nation Self-government Agreement, ss. 13.1 and 13.1.1). Similarly, where a First Nation passes laws that relate to matters covered by its Final Agreement, those laws must be consistent with what is set out in the treaties. For example, when exercising its right to enact laws on Settlement Land relating to "gathering, hunting, trapping or fishing and the protection of fish, wildlife and habitat" or "control or prevention of pollution and protection of the environment" (Kwanlin Dün First Nation 2005, ss. 13.3.4 and 13.3.20) it can only do so in a manner that complements the processes already in place due to the relevant chapters (12 and 16) of the First Nation's Final Agreement.

Where there are matters that present legislative overlap between territorial and First Nation governments, the SGA clarifies that, except in defined areas such as taxation, the First Nation law renders the territorial law inoperative (this applies in all SGAs). Yet, the SGAs are also filled with provisions that encourage co-operation. Section 25 of the Kwalin Dün First Nation SGA, for instance, called "Compatible Land Use," frames the way in which consultation is to happen, in both directions, where a land use on either public land or Settlement Land may impact the neighbouring land. In a similar manner, Section 26 of the same agreement gives the First Nation the authority to "enter into agreements with another Yukon First Nation, a municipality, or Government, to provide for such matters as municipal or local government services, joint planning, zoning or other land use control" (Kwanlin Dün First Nation 2005, s. 26.2.1). Section 28 sets out that "The Parties wish to coordinate Yukon, Kwanlin Dün First Nation and municipal legislative regimes on Settlement Land and Non-Settlement Land within the Community

Boundaries for the City of Whitehorse and the Marsh Lake Local Advisory Area." Clearly, the architects of self-government saw the building of institutional and legal inter-relationships as advantageous to all parties.

This brief description of the UFA, the Land Claims Final Agreements, and the SGAs illustrates an intention to develop a co-managed decision-making regime. One final example not included in these agreements, but that is important in demonstrating the objective of co-management for the territory, is found in the 2001 Devolution Transfer Agreement. The DTA is a tri-party agreement (Canada, Yukon, and First Nations) transferring jurisdiction from Canada to Yukon for land and resources "Administration and Control," which in constitutional parlance is in effect ownership, in 2003. Because of the importance of Yukon's ability to control the legislative regime over Yukon Crown lands and resources post-devolution, agreement was reached that, where there are substantive changes contemplated by Yukon for any of Yukon's successor legislation over land and resources, a Successor Resource Legislation Working Group would be created to provide substantive consultation with First Nations over this work, including: "(a) priorities for development of successor legislation; (b) any opportunities identified for the development of a common or compatible regime in respect of particular successor legislation and First Nations' legislation" (Minister of Public Works and Government Services Canada 2001, Appendix B s. 4.0). At the time of writing, the Working Group has not been formed, which reflects the second conclusion of this essay, that progress to implement the spirit and intent of these visionary agreements depends on leadership of the day to ensure that the principles are respected and acted on.

Examples of Conflict in Yukon

The following are three examples of where, despite the constitutional relationship between First Nations and public government created through the UFA and treaty process, there have been conflicts over land use decisions: *Beckman vs. Little Salmon/Carmacks First Nation*, the five-year review of YESAA, and the case of the Peel Watershed. These examples highlight the importance of co-operative working relationships between leadership in both First Nations' and public governments. Without these leadership relationships, and a willingness to find shared interests, the words of the treaty will not come to life as intended. In many cases, disputes can lead to protracted and expensive journeys through the courts, and often end on the doorstep of the Supreme Court of Canada.

EXAMPLE #1: *BECKMAN V. LITTLE SALMON/CARMACKS FIRST NATION*

The courts were instrumental in establishing a concrete interpretation of the treaties negotiated based on the UFA. The first notable decision came from the Supreme Court in *Beckman v. Little Salmon/Carmacks First Nation* (2010). The conflict in this case was between the Yukon government (Beckman being its responsible authority) and Little Salmon/Carmacks First Nation. The issue was whether the Crown had properly consulted with the First Nation before authorizing a grant of agricultural land, a grant that had an impact on a trapper who was also a citizen of the First Nation. Ultimately, the Supreme Court decided that the government had fulfilled its consultation obligations, but in the decision made some important comments on the nature of the treaties and the relationship between the Crown and First Nations.

At the heart of the Court's decision was whether the Little Salmon/Carmacks First Nation Final Agreement precluded the duty of the Yukon government to consult the First Nation. The Yukon government argued that the treaty was the full expression of the relationship, and because there was no language in the treaty requiring consultation, the obligation did not exist. The Supreme Court rejected this argument, with Justice Binnie writing for the majority of the Court:

> While consultation may be shaped by agreement of the parties, the Crown cannot contract out of its duty of honourable dealing with Aboriginal people—it is a doctrine that applies independently of the intention of the parties as expressed or implied in the treaty itself. (*Beckman v. LS/CFN*, 2010, para. 5)

In other words, although the treaty holds great sway in determining procedures to give effect to the general intentions of the partners to the treaty, the treaty is still only one aspect of the ongoing relationship. Binnie also spoke to the relational nature of governance established by the treaties:

> The reconciliation of Aboriginal and non-Aboriginal Canadians in a mutually respectful long-term relationship is the grand purpose of s. 35 of the Constitution Act, 1982. The modern treaties, including those at issue here, attempt to further the objective

of reconciliation not only by addressing grievances over the land claims, but by creating the legal basis to foster a positive long-term relationship between Aboriginal and non-Aboriginal communities. Thoughtful administration of the treaty will help manage, even if it fails to eliminate, some of the misunderstanding and grievances that have characterized the past. Still, as the facts of this case show, the treaty will not accomplish its purpose if it is **interpreted by territorial officials in an ungenerous manner or as if it were an everyday commercial contract.** The treaty is as much about building relationships as it is about the settlement of ancient grievances. The future is more important than the past. A canoeist who hopes to make progress faces forwards, not backwards" (*Beckman v. LS/CFN,* para. 10, emphasis ours).

The treaty is not a simple contract intended to remedy past wrongs but is an expression of the will of the parties in framing the relationship of the future (Borrows and Coyle, 2017). Narrow or "ungenerous" interpretation of the treaty does not meet the test fulfilling the honour of the Crown. Personalities of those presently in leadership positions matter a great deal in treaty relationships and are fundamental to the success of treaty implementation.

Another key point from *Beckman* is that the Supreme Court is reinforcing a recurring theme that treaties are not about only one party but are about a relationship between the interests and rights of both Indigenous and non-Indigenous Canadians. Therefore, obligations and interests must be considered from both perspectives, and both must be considered in government decision-making. Binnie notes that "Underlying the present appeal is not only the need to respect the rights and reasonable expectations of Johnny Sam [trapper and LS/CFN citizen] and other members of his community, but the rights and expectations of other Yukon residents, including both Aboriginal people and Larry Paulsen [Yukon resident who applied for the offending land grant], to good government" (para. 34).

EXAMPLE #2: THE FIVE-YEAR REVIEW OF YESAA
The second example of dispute between the parties on interpretation of the treaties and their underlying intent to provide for co-management of Yukon land and resources, relates to the review of the Yukon Environmental and Socio-economic Assessment Act (YESAA), which was designed to occur

every five years. As noted earlier, the YESA process is a critical co-management institution set up through the UFA and treaties (Chapter 12) to ensure that there is thorough examination of potential environmental and socio-economic impacts of projects in Yukon. YESA is a cornerstone of the complex matrix of institutions based in the modern treaties that is intended to balance conservation and development interests within the context of a society where First Nations' and non-First Nations' rights must be upheld.

In 2015 and 2016 the federal and territorial governments attempted to push through amendments to YESAA without adequate consultation with the other treaty-holder, Yukon First Nations. Four particular amendments to the Act were not part of an all-party five-year review that was wrapped up in 2012, and it is to these four amendments that Yukon First Nations took exception both on substance and process. Briefly, the four objectionable changes related to: giving binding policy direction to the Government of Canada over the YESA Board; allowing the federal minister to delegate authority to a territorial minister; setting maximum timelines for assessments, and; dropping the requirement for an assessment on the renewal of projects.

Ultimately the four changes erode the intended independent nature of the assessment process, which is a fundamental principle captured in Chapter 12 (Development Assessment) of the UFA. Through one change, the federal minister would be authorized to issue binding policy directives to the YESA Board and with no requirement to consult with the other treaty partners. Finally, regarding the tightening of timelines, First Nations had long argued that there should be more time allotted given sheer volume of projects coming to them for review as part of the YESA process, and the limited resources available to First Nations to take on this review adequately.

On process, due to the fact that the Final Agreements under the UFA are treaties, any changes to them, or instruments used to implement them, require agreement from all parties. The four amendments were imposed by Canada on First Nations without appropriate consultation, which is required where fundamental change to the treaties' underlying principles is concerned.

Chapter 12 of the UFA outlines the values the signing parties agreed to. Among these values are particular objectives relating to the co-management aspects of the unique institution that is YESA. The objectives of Chapter 12 set out the importance of "the traditional economy of Yukon Indian People and their special relationship with the wilderness Environment" (s. 12.1.1.1) and goes on to emphasize that YESAB is to protect and promote "the well-being of

Yukon Indian People and of their communities and of other Yukon residents and the interests of other Canadians" (s. 12.1.1.3). Again, the theme of sharing among *all* residents—First Nations and non-First Nations—is clearly expressed. In effect, the YESA process was set up at arm's length from all governments (federal, territorial and First Nations), and framed to ensure that care and attention would be given to the comprehensive management of Yukon lands and resources. Over a decade passed between the signing of the UFA and the date when YESAB started its work as the overarching assessment body for all Yukon (November 28, 2005). A considerable amount of effort was expended by all parties to get the mechanics worked out to implement the process.

The parties reached agreement on a wide range of adjustments to the Act, but despite this progress, there remained three matters where Yukon First Nations' positions were not resolved. No agreement was reached on adequacy of funding, a subsequent mandated review of the YESA process was not accepted by Canada, and no agreement was reached to require engagement between a Decision Body (set up in the Act as federal departments and agencies, the territorial government, or a First Nation if a project is on Settlement Land) and a First Nation whose Treaty Rights might be affected by a project in advance of issuance of a Decision Document (a critical stage in the overall regulatory process that can set conditions on environmental and socio-economic matters before a project can commence). Despite these unresolved differences, the review was concluded.

Changes to YESAA entered the Parliamentary system through the Senate in June 2014 as Bill S-6, "An Act to amend the Yukon Environmental and Socio-economic Assessment Act and the Nunavut Waters and Nunavut Surface Rights Tribunal Act." At the Senate Energy, Environment and Natural Resources Committee hearings, both First Nation and non-First Nation Yukoners expressed strong displeasure that unilateral action had been taken by governments without the approval of the third treaty partner. Note that this was not just First Nations protest, but an expression from a broad range of Yukoners that unilateral action by government to affect the underlying co-management rights captured in the institutions created through the modern treaty is unacceptable. This protest was of First Nations and non-First Nations citizens unified against a Crown government, not a disaffected Indigenous population resisting against the settler population. In short, the resistance to Bill S-6 was a demonstration of shared acceptance of the treaty relationship responsibilities that one party had spurned. More and more, as we will see in the examination of the Peel Land Use Planning process, this is the form of protest most recently found in the Yukon context.

First Nations' leaders (including Council of Yukon First Nations Grand Chief Ruth Massie, Little Salmon/Carmacks First Nation Chief Eric Fairclough and Champagne and Aishihik First Nations Councillor Mary Jane Jim) who appeared before the Senate Committee reinforced a number of key points regarding the treaty relationship. To Yukon First Nations, the YESA process is considered a cornerstone of the treaties. It is a reflection of the principle of shared management between public and Indigenous governments for all environmental, social, and economic assessment matters in Yukon. As noted earlier, a good portion of land in traditional territories throughout Yukon were given up in the treaty negotiations in favour of a trust relationship through co-management of all lands. This agreement saw First Nations retaining Indigenous title to only ~9% of Yukon in exchange for this co-management framework over the full territory. The unilateral amendments dictated by Canada were viewed by leadership as fundamentally undermining the principles of the treaties.

An interesting aside to this story is that Yukon First Nations were not given individual standing before the Senate Committee. This amalgamation happened despite their protest that this ignored the fact that the eleven Yukon First Nations have independent treaty relationships with Canada. This was seen as either a demonstration of the ignorance of Ottawa as to the nature of the treaties, or worse, a blatant disregard for the fundamental nature of the distinct treaty relationship.

Despite overtures by Yukon First Nations to recommence discussions on the amendments that did not benefit from consultation, Canada ignored the offer. Bill S-6 with the offending provisions received Royal Assent June 18, 2015. In October of that year, the Teslin Tlingit Council, Little Salmon/Carmacks First Nation, and Champagne and Aishihik First Nations filed suit against the federal government in the Yukon Supreme Court, calling for the repeal of those amendments that had not been the subject of adequate consultation. Subsequently, and following the 2015 election which saw a change in government in Ottawa, the repeal of the four concerning provisions of YESAA was brought forth through Bill C-17, "An Act to amend the Yukon Environmental and Socio-economic Assessment Act and to make a consequential amendment to another Act."

Underscoring the point that leadership can make or break the treaty relationship, the change in government in Ottawa in October 2015 changed much regarding the fate of the amended Act. The new government and its minister of Indigenous and Northern Affairs committed to reversing the offending provisions and to a dialogue with Yukon First Nations on how to finalize the changes agreed to during the five-year review. In 2016 this turnaround was echoed in Yukon when a new majority Liberal government took power with an anchor platform commitment to resolve long-standing disputes between First Nations and the Yukon government, and an agenda to engage with First Nations so as to implement the spirit and intent of the treaties. Needless to say, the new territorial government strongly supported Canada's work to repeal the offending provisions of Bill S-6. Bill C-17, repealing the four offending amendments of Bill S-6, received Royal Assent December 14, 2017.

EXAMPLE #3: THE PEEL WATERSHED LAND USE PLAN

Our third example of conflict in Yukon involved the Peel Land Use Plan and the related Supreme Court of Canada case (*First Nation of Nacho Nyak Dun v. Yukon*, 2017 SCC 58). The appellants included the First Nation of Na-Cho Nyäk Dun, Tr'ondëk Hwëch'in, the Yukon Chapter of the Canadian Parks and Wilderness Society, the Yukon Conservation Society, Gill Cracknell, Karen Baltgailis, and Vuntut Gwitchin First Nation. Interveners included the Attorney General of Canada, Gwich'in Tribal Council, and the Council of Yukon First Nations, while the Yukon government served as the respondent.

Thomas Berger, legal counsel for the appellants, noted that engagement on the Peel Land Use Plan was substantial. There were 10,000 submissions to the Commission on the recommended regional land use plan, including 2,000 from Yukoners and 8,000 from outside the territory. The planning process set out in the UFA was designed to find resolution and balance among competing and (potentially) conflicting values. In an area more than twice the size of Belgium, one containing significant iron and coal deposits, environmental and cultural values were pitted against mineral interests. In the absence of a planning process perceived as legitimate by all stakeholders, the Peel region would become the centre of considerable public protest.

Much of the discussion focused on whether the courts were being asked, in the words of the Supreme Court's Chief Justice Beverley McLachlin, to interject through a "micromanaging Judicial kind of supervision" in the business of the parties to the treaties. Specifically, given the Yukon government's failure to follow the process outlined in Chapter 11 of the UFA, at what stage of the process should the Court instruct the parties to go back to so that the process could be properly followed? At the Supreme Court of Yukon, Justice Veale directed the parties to go back to the point where the Peel Land Use Planning Commission had finalized its draft Plan. The reasons for decision are complicated, and not relevant to the main points raised here surrounding public protest. Suffice it to say, returning to the point in the process identified by Veale as appropriate would prevent the government from rewriting the plan, which was what they had in fact done, and in doing so effectively ignoring Chapter 11 altogether. Given the significant loss by the Yukon government at the trial level, Justice Veale's decision was appealed to the Yukon Court of Appeal, where Justice Bauman ruled to send the parties back to an even earlier stage in the Chapter 11 process. In reality, this would have meant a complete retread of the planning process. This became the subject considered by the Supreme Court of Canada.

There are a number of points in the Peel decision that are relevant to the future of co-management. First, it is critical that all parties respect the details of the treaties. In the case of Peel, "[Yukon] did not respect the land use planning process in the Final Agreements and its conduct was not becoming of the honour of the Crown" (*First Nation of Nacho Nyak Dun v. Yukon*, 2017, para. 7). The time leading up to the Supreme Court of Canada case saw the premier of Yukon framing co-management institutions, in this case the Land Use Planning Commission, as unaccountable and a threat to democracy in the territory (CBC 2016). Such statements serve to delegitimize co-management institutions in the public view (Clark and Joe-Strack 2017). Here we see the magnitude of influence and consequence that the behaviour of leaders of the day can have on a treaty relationship and the realization of co-management promised therein. Reflecting on this strained relationship, Tr'ondëk Hwëch'in Chief Roberta Joseph said at a press conference immediately following the release of the Peel decision: "We've been on a long, twisting journey to hold the Yukon government accountable for promises made during the land claims process," (Blewett 2017).

Second, the Supreme Court clarified the boundaries of judicial authority when it comes to interpreting the treaties: "It was not open to the Court of Appeal to return the parties to an earlier stage of the planning process... The Court of Appeal improperly inserted itself into the heart of the ongoing treaty relationship between Yukon and the First Nations" (*First Nation of Nacho*

Nyak Dun v. Yukon, 2017, para.7). The decision of the Supreme Court notes, "Yukon must bear the consequences of its failure to diligently advance its interests and exercise its right [provided in the treaty] to propose access and development modifications to the Recommended Plan. It cannot use these proceedings to obtain another opportunity to exercise a right it chose not to exercise at the appropriate time" (para. 61). In other words, it is critical to respect the procedures described in the treaty, and not engage in outcome-shopping.

Third, Justice Karakatsanis noted in the Supreme Court decision that "in a judicial review concerning the implementation of modern treaties, a court should simply assess whether the challenged decision is legal, rather than closely supervise the conduct of the parties at each stage of the treaty relationship" (para. 4). This is another boundary on judicial authority, one that is reiterated at paragraph 33 while also recognizing that modern treaties "in this case... set out in precise terms a co-operative governance model."

It is of little value to describe here the motives that may have driven the Yukon government to ignore clearly set out provisions of the modern treaty, which resulted in a protracted conflict leading ultimately to the Supreme Court of Canada for resolution. There are many theories on this question, and no clarification from the political leadership of the territorial government of the day as to why they chose the course they did. The fact is that, for whatever reason, the Yukon government as one of the parties ignored the clearly defined requirements set out in the modern treaty. This resulted in substantial conflict and protest, not between Indigenous and non-Indigenous Yukoners, but between a strong representative group of both Indigenous and non-Indigenous parties (from a wide cross-section of Yukon, Canada and indeed the world) who protested the actions of the territorial government and what appeared to be a blatant disregard for the provisions of the treaty.

Conclusion

The Yukon's constitutionally protected co-management governance model provides numerous avenues for Yukon residents to influence decision-making. It is an institutional arrangement that has worked against conflict in the form of protest between First Nations people and non-First Nation governing structures by bringing the two together through management institutions. Where conflict does occur, it has been sparked in our examples by one party in the relationship neglecting their clearly defined obligations. Through the treaty mechanisms—YESAB, Water Board, Land Use Planning Council,

Renewable Resource Councils and Heritage Resources Board to name the key ones that affect resource management in the territory—citizens have many avenues to bring their perspectives to the governance elite. Only where governments ignore the co-management processes and relationships set up through the treaty partnership does protest result, and that in today's treaty context is usually First Nation and non-First Nation citizens rallying to oppose directions taken or decisions made by Crown governments.

Yukon's recent history since the 1960s has seen very little protest where Indigenous citizenry, alienated from the decision-making elite, has found itself at odds with a predominantly non-Indigenous governing populace. We suggest this is because of the development of a co-management approach to governance in Yukon that occurred through the negotiation of treaties, the subsequent operation of co-management institutions, and the decisions of courts that have given definition to the interpretation of the treaties. We also suggest that, regardless of what is written down, fully realizing these co-management intentions depends greatly on the leadership of the day. Yukon's experience can offer lessons on building relationships between multiple First Nations governments and public governments through shared co-management bodies that may be valuable elsewhere in Canada.

First, Yukon's experience suggests that a precondition of positive relationships is the creation of stable and accepted institutional spaces that govern the processes of decision-making. The form, function, and leadership of these spaces ought to be negotiated between equal partners, rather than dictated by one to the other. Ultimately all citizens, Indigenous and non-Indigenous, should be able to see themselves in the makeup of the institutional bodies. If Indigenous and public governments are both owners of the co-management institutions, they will both be more inclined to view the decisions of these bodies as legitimate, and as the proper forum for debate over critical land and resources decision options. This point is critical so that groups within society who have a rightful place in the decision-making process (in this instance, the Indigenous population) are not alienated from that process.

Second, Canadian governments must be willing to accept, within mandates to negotiate new treaty and self-government arrangements with Indigenous Nations, the incorporation of the Indigenous Nations' values, particularly so where co-management institutions are concerned. These values must have a direct influence over the process of governance, particularly in regard to engagement and consultation with the Nations over resource development proposals. Although not discussed in detail in this chapter, it is this values foundation in the UFA and modern treaties that is so critical to Yukon First Nations, thus driving several First Nations to press the issues of Bill S-6 and the Peel Watershed Land Use Plan through the Canadian courts system to preserve the values that are fundamentally important to their success. These changes—relative to the status quo of existing institutions of governance—will increase public legitimacy of decisions made by these institutions. It ought to be stressed that this legitimacy will only be granted by both Indigenous and non-Indigenous governments and publics where these new decision-making institutions are guided by leadership appointed from each community.

Third, the creation of mutually beneficial institutional partnerships can be a lengthy process, fraught with missteps and stalled negotiations, as demonstrated in the ongoing negotiations processes starting in the early 1970s for three of the fourteen Yukon First Nations. There are concrete benefits to remaining committed, specifically in terms creating mutually legitimate decision-making bodies. Relationship-damaging conflict that can lead to protest can be avoided by proactively developing institutions that are legitimate to all parties. In the case of First Nations, this requires sustained negotiation that gradually builds agreement on practical issues like ownership of land, self-government, and the devolution of authority over service delivery. Ink drying on new treaties and SGAs is not the end point in development of a co-management relationship, but the starting point.

Co-management is the intent of the modern treaties in Yukon and the institutions designed to realize those treaties. Implementation of these institutions has been ongoing for the last two decades. Yukon's experience in constructing this approach to the governance of lands and resources presents a model of relationship-building between First Nations and Canadian governments that ought to inform decision-makers across Canada. (Indeed we are seeing progress in British Columbia where the province has set up tables to discuss appropriate forms of regional co-management). It is a demonstration of the possibility of finding a way forward that not only respects the autonomy of First Nations, but creates a formal, systematic role for First Nations' governments as real partners in governing in this region of Canada. Ultimately what Yukon has experienced over this same period is not the protest of Indigenous people alienated from the decision-making instruments of public government, but coalitions of Indigenous and non-Indigenous

Yukoners with the shared interests and aims to bring to account public government that either does not understand or rejects its treaty obligations and the co-management governance framework resulting from modern treaties.

References

Alcantara, C. 2013. *Negotiating the Deal: Comprehensive Land Claims in Canada.* University of Toronto Press: Toronto.

Alcantara, C., K. Cameron, & S. Kennedy. 2012. "Assessing Devolution in the Canadian North: A Case Study of the Yukon Territory," *Arctic* 65, no. 3: 328–38.

Armitage, D., F. Berkes, A. Dale, E. Kocho-Schellenberg, & E. Patton. 2011. "Co-management and the Co-production of Knowledge: Learning to Adapt in Canada's Arctic." *Global Environmental Change* 21, no. 3: 995–1004.

Beckman v. Little Salmon/Carmacks First Nation, 2010 SCC 53, [2010] 3 SCR 103.

Berkes, F., P. George, & R. J. Preston. 1991. "Co-management: The Evolution in Theory and Practice of the Joint Administration of Living Resources. *Alternatives* 18: 12–18.

Blewett, Taylor, 2017. "'This is a great day for the Peel watershed'" Whitehorse Star, December 1, 2017, https://www.whitehorsestar.com/News/this-is-a-great-day-for-the-peel-watershed.

Borrows, J. and Coyle M, eds. 2017. *The Right Relationship: Reimagining the Implementation of Historical Treaties.* Toronto: University of Toronto Press.

Cameron, K & G. White. 1995. *Northern Governments in Transition.* Montréal: The Institute for Research on Public Policy.

Campbell, A. & K. Cameron. 2016. "Constitutional Development and Natural Resources in the North.: In *Governing the North American Arctic: Sovereignty, Security and Institutions*, ed. D. A. Berry, N. Bowles & H. Jones (London: Palgrave Macmillan), 180–99.

Canadian Broadcasting Corporation (CBC). 2016. "Peel Watershed: Pasloski Explains Reasons for appeal." *CBC News*, January 13, 2016. https://www.cbc.ca/news/canada/north/peel-watershed-darrell-pasloski-explains-reasons-for-appeal-1.2899452.

Charlie, L. 2017. "Modern Treaty Politics in the Yukon." *Briarpatch Magazine*, March 1, 2017, 1–8. https://briarpatchmagazine.com/articles/view/modern-treaty-politics-in-yukon

Clark, D. & J. Joe-Strack. 2017. Keeping the "Co" in the Co-management of Northern Resources. *Northern Public Affairs*, April 2017, 71–74.

Coulthard, G. 2014. *Red Skin White Masks: Rejecting the Colonial Politics of Recognition.* Minneapolis: University of Minnesota Press.

Council of Yukon First Nations. 1993. Umbrella Final Agreement. Whitehorse, YT. https://cyfn.ca/agreements/umbrella-final-agreement/

First Nation of Nacho Nyak Dun v. Yukon (Government of), 2014 YKSC 69.

First Nation of Nacho Nyak Dun v. Yukon, 2015 YKCA 12.

First Nation of Nacho Nyak Dun v. Yukon, 2017 SCC 58, [2017] 2 SCR 576.

Irlbacher-Fox, S. 2009. *Finding Dahshaa: Self-government, Social Suffering and Aboriginal Policy in Canada*. Vancouver: UBC Press.

King, Hayden. 2013. "Co-managing the future?" *Northern Public Affairs*, Special issue 2013: 27–31. https://web.archive.org/web/20160529102427/http://www.northernpublicaffairs.ca/index/special-issue-2013-free-digital-download/.

Kwanlin Dün First Nation. 2005. Kwanlin Dün First Nation Self-government Agreement. Ottawa: Minister of Indian Affairs and Northern Development.

Minister of Public Works and Government Services Canada. 2001. Yukon Northern Affairs Program Devolution Transfer Agreement. Ottawa: Minister of Public Works and Government Services Canada.

Nadasdy, P. 2004. *Hunters and Bureaucrats: Power, Knowledge and Aboriginal-State Relations in the Southwest Yukon*. Vancouver: UBC Press.

Natcher, D., S. Davis, And C. G. Hickey. 2005. "Co-management: Managing Relationships, not Resources." *Human Organization* 64: 240–50.

Newman, D. 2011. "Contractual and Covenantal Conceptions of Modern Treaty Interpretation." *The Supreme Court Law Review: Osgoode's Annual Constitutional Cases Conference* 54, no. 17: 475–91.

Papillon, M. & T. Rodon. 2017. "Indigenous Consent and Natural Resource Extraction Foundations for a Made-in-Canada Approach." *IRRP Insight* 16, July 2017. https://irpp.org/wp-content/uploads/2017/07/insight-no16.pdf

Stuart, B. 1992. "Land Claims Agreements as a Mechanism for Resolving Resource Use Conflicts." In *Growing Demands on a Shrinking Heritage: Managing Resource-use Conflicts.*, ed. J. O. Ross, and Monique Saunders (Calgary, AB: Canadian Institute of Resources Law), 129–54.

Yukon Indian People. 1973. *Together Today for Our Children Tomorrow*. Whitehorse, YT. https://cyfn.ca/wp-content/uploads/2013/10/together_today_for_our_children_tomorrow.pdf

Inuit Engagement in Resource Development Approval Process: The Cases of Voisey's Bay and Mary River

Thierry Rodon, Aude Therrien, and Karen Bouchard[1]

In this chapter, we look at the engagement of Inuit communities in two min-ing projects, namely Voisey's Bay and Mary River, both located in regions where Inuit have signed land claim settlements. Voisey's Bay is a nickel mine in Nunatsiavut that submitted a development proposal for evaluation in 1994, while negotiations were underway on the Labrador Inuit land claim that was settled in 1997, and began operating in 2005, as the Nunatsiavut government, negotiated through the Labrador Inuit Land Claim Agreement (LILCA), was being created. The signing of this land claim is intimately linked to the Voisey's Bay mining project development, as it was used as a leverage to accelerate negotiations (O'Faircheallaigh 2015). The entire con-sultation process took place before the signing of the LILCA, which meant that an ad hoc engagement process had to be negotiated before the mining project's approval. By contrast, Mary River is an iron mine located on Baffin Island in Nunavut, a Canadian territory created in 1999 through the Nunavut Land Claim Agreement (NLCA) that was signed in 1993. In this particular case, since the mining project was proposed in 2008 and approved in 2012, Inuit engagement was framed by the NLCA.

The engagement of Indigenous Peoples in the resource development ap-proval process throughout Canada has dramatically changed over the past thirty years. Indigenous resistance and litigation in these two case studies have paved the way to several landmark decisions by the Supreme Court of

Canada that formally recognize Aboriginal Rights and redefine the government's role in resource development.

Aboriginal Rights in Canada stem from the long-standing occupation, possession, and use of the traditional lands by Indigenous societies prior to European contact. While some historical treaties were signed in the nineteenth and early twentieth centuries, most of Canada's lands remained unceded Indigenous territories.[2] This includes the North (Yukon, Northwest Territories, and Nunavut), significant portions of BC, large segments of the Maritimes and the entire province of Québec. In order to address this situation, a land claims process was developed in the 1970s by the federal government through negotiated agreements with First Nations (Scholtz 2006). This conversely enabled the institutionalization of Indigenous participation in resource development by way of an impact assessment (IA) process co-managed with Indigenous representatives and that has gone as far as obliging proponents to sign Impact and Benefit Agreements (IBAs) with Indigenous organizations in the most recent agreements.

In this context, one could firstly question the ability of these engagement processes (IAs and IBAs) to provide the leverage required for Indigenous organizations and communities to control development on their lands and to increase their engagement in these approval processes; and secondly, ask whether land claim agreements improve the engagement of Indigenous Peoples in the approval of resource development projects (Papillon and Rodon 2019). These questions appear crucial when it concerns the control and self-governance that Indigenous Peoples are striving to regain over their traditional lands. Furthermore, with the passing of Bill C-15, the United Nations Declaration on the Rights of Indigenous Peoples Act (the UNDRIP Act or the Act), into law on 21 June 2021, the principle of free, prior, and informed consent (FPIC) is now a legal norm for Indigenous Peoples' engagement in resource development.

In order to answer these questions, we will first provide some background context, then present a concise description of Indigenous rights in Canada and of the consultation and participation mechanisms that currently shape Indigenous engagement in resource development projects. Following that, we will analyze Inuit engagement in the approval processes of two mineral development projects in Inuit Nunangat: the Mary River project in Nunavut and the Voisey's Bay project in Nunatsiavut.

These case studies show that while the IA and IBA processes allow proponents to fulfill their duty to consult and to secure the consent of Indigenous organizations, they do not guarantee that the expectations and aspirations of community members will be met. Furthermore, the engagement process of land claim agreements doesn't necessarily lead to an effective and meaningful engagement (Rodon 2017).

An Emerging International Norm: Free, Prior, and Informed Consent (FPIC)

Free, prior, and informed consent is increasingly being considered as a new norm for Indigenous engagement in development projects worldwide. In 2007, the United Nations adopted the Declaration on the Rights of Indigenous Peoples (UNDRIP), a comprehensive international framework on the rights of Indigenous Peoples. While providing a clear definition of the minimum standards for the dignity and well-being of Indigenous Peoples worldwide, the goals and standards it sets forth are not, however, binding. The initial resistance of Canada and other British common-law settler societies (Australia, New Zealand, and the United States) to signing this document has proven its significance. One of this framework's most contentious elements is the concept of free, prior, and informed consent applied to contexts of resource development on Indigenous territory. In 2010, Canada endorsed UNDRIP while expressing concerns about FPIC when used as a veto. Finally, on May 10, 2016, the federal minister of Indigenous Affairs, Carolyn Bennett, announced at the UN Permanent Forum on Indigenous Issues that "Canada [was] a full supporter of the Declaration without qualification" and that the federal government intended "nothing less than to adopt and implement the declaration in accordance with the Canadian Constitution" (Bennett 2016). The Royal Assent of the UNDRIP Act in 2021 marks a historic milestone in Canada's implementation of UNDRIP, especially given Section 5 of the UNDRIP Act, which requires the federal government "to take all measures necessary to ensure that Canada's federal laws are consistent with the Declaration, and to do so in consultation and cooperation with Indigenous peoples" (Duncanson et al. 2021).

Two interpretations of this concept currently prevail. The first is a more process-oriented vision that simply requires that governments and proponents make an effort to obtain the consent of Indigenous communities. The second, more substantive in nature, considers that FPIC requires that both a deliberative process amongst the community and a negotiation process with the proponent take place (Papillon and Rodon 2019). As such, FPIC must entail discussions conducted freely and with all relevant information about the project and its impacts before any form of consent is given. Negotiations must necessarily occur between community representatives and the proponents after the deliberative process has taken place with community members (Papillon and Rodon 2017b). A project's outcomes would also necessitate negotiations with the members of the concerned communities and see their interests reconciled with those of the proponent (Papillon and Rodon 2017a). Communities must also be able to refuse projects throughout the FPIC process.

Aboriginal Rights and Indigenous Consultation in Canada

In Canada, a series of landmark decisions by the Supreme Court, such as *Haida* (2004), *Taku River* (2004) and *Mikisew Cree* (2005), established the Crown's duty to consult and sometimes accommodate Indigenous Peoples when proposed activities are believed to potentially have adverse impacts on their rights and related interests (AANDC 2011).

The strength of a nation's Aboriginal Rights and the potential negative impacts of the proposed activity on these rights influence the Crown's duty to consult. If the impacts of proposed projects are limited and the Aboriginal Rights of the concerned communities are weak (for example, not recognized by the federal government or any treaty), the Crown may only have an obligation to notify the Indigenous communities on proposed development activities. In cases where government activities are predicted to cause major negative impacts on Aboriginal Rights, substantial consultations and accommodations are needed. Consultation activities are held at stages deemed fitting by the concerned government department or agency charged with enacting the Crown's duty to consult, in accordance with their operational realities as well as the societal interests at stake (AANDC 2011). If the negative impacts and Aboriginal Rights of the concerned Nation are both strong, it might be necessary to obtain the consent of the concerned Indigenous community.[3]

While the Crown is ultimately responsible for consultation processes, the Crown's duty to consult can be, and very often is, delegated to the company or government in charge of a project's planning and implementation (the proponent). The proponent may consider this delegation of power as a means of reducing the legal uncertainties surrounding their project. In order to fulfill their obligations to consult Indigenous Peoples, the Crown and proponents use two mechanisms: IBAs and IAs.

Indigenous Participation in the Context of Land Claim Agreements

The Supreme Court of Canada's decision in *Calder et al. v. Attorney-General of British Columbia* (1973), which asserted that the Nisga'a Tribal Council had never relinquished their lands to the Crown, led to the recognition of the existence of Aboriginal titles as a concept in Canadian common law. This ruling led to the Comprehensive Land Claims Policy and the implementation of land claims agreements, also known as modern treaties, by the federal government. This policy enables the provincial and federal governments, as well as Indigenous groups, to negotiate unsettled land claims agreements.[4] The purpose of these agreements is to settle Indigenous land rights and titles through financial compensations, the definition of surface and subsurface rights, and by establishing the rights of Indigenous communities to participate in the management of resources on their lands (Rodon 2017). The right to participate in resource management is usually implemented through co-management boards that oversee land management and the impact review process. Land claim agreements have more recently made the signing of IBAs between proponents and the Indigenous land claim organizations mandatory, thus requiring a form of consensual agreement on the terms and conditions of resource development.[5] This inclusion does not, however, correspond to substantive free prior and informed consent since community participation in IBA negotiations are not mandatory.

Impact Assessment Processes

In Canada, the consultations required for major resource development projects occur, for the most part, during impact assessments (IA)—processes in which proponents play a key role. The legislative and regulatory framework supporting IA processes is quite complex. The federal government adopted its first environmental impact assessment legislation in 1973. Provinces have since established their own distinctive impact assessment processes for projects that fall under their jurisdiction. Land claims agreements with Indigenous Peoples have also led to the creation of specific processes in the concerned treaty area. The IA process therefore varies according to a project's location. Project proponents are usually required to gather relevant information and to produce reports on their project's foreseen environmental impacts as well as the actions that can be done to reduce these effects (mitigation measures). Proponents must also hold public consultations with Indigenous communities and all other interested parties. Participants are invited to express their concerns during these hearings.

While IAs represent an important participatory exercise that allow Indigenous communities, representatives, and local communities to voice their concerns and to discuss and confront project proponents, their participation remains superficial and passive since they ultimately have little ability to shape the decision-making process (O'Faircheallaigh 2007; Papillon and Rodon 2017a). Hence, consultations merely provide an opportunity for local communities to comment as well as to better understand a project's implications and to identify suitable mitigation and accommodation measures. The hearing process is also based "on liberal democratic cultural values" that do not typically "invite or incite disagreement, debate, or activism" (Scobie and Rodgers 2013). It is therefore not surprising that the conclusions of IA processes are increasingly challenged in court by Indigenous communities who deny their legitimacy as consultation processes (Papillon and Rodon 2017a).[6]

Impact and Benefit Agreements

Other mechanisms used to secure the consent of Indigenous communities are impact and benefit agreements (IBAs). In Canada, IBAs are private contractual agreements that have increasingly become a standard practice for the mining industry. These are seen to provide a form of consent that has been considered to constitute a community's expression of agreement to a proposed project, as determined by the terms and conditions negotiated in the agreement. As such, IBAs somewhat act as a testimony of the concerned communities' acquiescence and thus protect proponents from litigation. IBAs have been defined as a mandatory process in the most recent modern land claim agreements, as with the NLCA and the LILCA. The signing of IBAs were mandatory for the authorization and implementation of the projects in these two cases.

IBAs are private and usually confidential agreements negotiated between project proponents and Indigenous organizations. These agreements include, amongst other things, monitoring and mitigation measures, employment and training benefits, and financial compensation for the communities in exchange for their support in the project's implementation and operation. As such, IBAs constitute legally binding agreements that ensure that the community won't enter into litigation (Papillon and Rodon 2017b).

However, since IBAs are fundamentally private agreements, they are negotiated between representatives of the concerned Indigenous organizations and the proponents, and do not necessarily allow community deliberations. The absence of public deliberations is often interpreted as a means of exclusion, triggering feelings of frustration among community members that stem from a perceived lack of interest in local concerns and preoccupations (Papillon and Rodon 2017a). IBAs may additionally be signed before the end of the IA process, which restricts the community's access to important information regarding a project's potential or predicted impacts and the ability of affected communities to voice their preoccupations to their representative and to oppose the project (Papillon and Rodon 2017b).

The Voisey's Bay Project

The Voisey's Bay mine is an open pit mine operated by Vale Inco, which extracts nickel, copper, and cobalt in Nunatsiavut. Located in an area of northern Labrador without terrestrial links to other communities, the mining site employs approximately 450 people through the fly-in/fly-out model. The mine is located 35 km from the Inuit community of Nain and 80 km from the community of Davis Inlet. The Labrador Inuit live in five communities north of Voisey's Bay, and the Labrador Innus live in two communities south of the Voisey's Bay mine. The Indigenous population was, between 1996 and 2000, approximately 30% of the Labrador population (Laforce 2012). While the Labrador Innu and Inuit nations were both similarly engaged in the mine's approval process, our analysis will essentially focus on the engagement process of the Labrador Inuit communities.

The Voisey's Bay project was first proposed in 1994 when Inuit were fighting for their formal recognition as an Indigenous Nation. This formal recognition would be achieved through the signing of the Labrador Inuit Land Claims Agreement in 2005. The mine's IA process was not, therefore, established by a land claim agreement. The process was rather determined by a memorandum of understanding signed in 1997 between the governments of Newfoundland and Labrador, the federal government, the Labrador Inuit Association, and the Innu Nation. This provided an opportunity for the signatories to fully participate in the IA process of the Voisey's Bay project. The IA's assessment panel was required to include a representative for each of the four involved parties. The memorandum of understanding also demanded the signature of an IBA, and the conclusion of land claims agreements with the Innu and Inuit. These conditions represented key elements for the approval of the proposed project (Laforce 2012).

The Impact Assessment

The initial project proponents began discussing the extractive project's development with Inuit and Innu Nations between 1994 and 1996. Interviews conducted by Kenny (2015) reveal that negotiations were difficult at first since the proponents did not seriously consider their two Indigenous counterparts or their land claim. Relations improved once Innu people organized protests at the mine site in Voisey's Bay. In response to their opposition, the mining company hired more experienced negotiators. However, negotiations stopped in 1996 when Vale Inco purchased the Voisey's Bay deposits from the previous owners. By then, both the Labrador Inuit Association (LIA) and the Innu Nation were engaged in land claims negotiations with the provincial government for lands that included the Voisey's Bay area (Heritage Newfoundland and Labrador 2011). Negotiations between the LIA and the Innu Nation with the proponent for the IBA as well as with the provincial government for the environmental assessment process restarted a year later, in 1997 (Archibald and Crnkovich 1999; Kenny 2015).

When Vale Inco acquired the project in 1996, Inuit lacked the necessary information to fully take part in the decision-making process since they had only been given a three-page document presenting a descriptive summary of the proposed project (Kenny 2015). They additionally feared a narrow definition of the project footprints by Vale Inco, a definition that would exclude or marginalize Inuit knowledge (Kenny 2015). The LIA therefore prepared and submitted their own report, titled *Seeing the Land Is Seeing Ourselves* (Williamson 1996) which was completed at the same time as the standard environmental assessment process. Their document became a reference throughout the planning processes (Kenny 2015). The Innu Nation and the LIA additionally organized information campaigns and undertook successful litigation and civil disobedience activities to increase pressure on the proponent and provincial government to reach an agreement on the terms of the environmental assessment process (Kenny 2015). The impact assessment of the Voisey's Bay mine began after the signature of a memorandum of understanding in 1997 and the formation of a joint review panel where the Innu Nation and the Labrador Inuit Association representatives sit alongside the federal and provincial governments. The parties agreed to participate in a joint environmental impact assessment (Gibson 2002). Since the Innu Nation and the LIA had no land claim agreements, both parties made it clear that the conclusion of such agreement would be a key element of the environmental assessment and would be necessary before the Voisey's Bay mine could begin operation (Laforce 2012).

Following the submission of Vale Inco's Environmental Impact Statement in December 1997, the joint review panel, established earlier with the signature of the memorandum of understanding, held public and technical hearings throughout the year 1998 in the ten communities of Labrador and in St. John's (Archibald and Crnkovich 1999; Gibson 2006; Laforce 2012). The Innu and Inuit parties also engaged in "protests, site occupations and court actions to ensure that their voices were heard, and their concerns addressed" (Gibson 2006). From the beginning of August 1997, the Innu and Inuit, who had been arguing with the proponent and the government that the construction of roads and the airstrip would undermine the integrity of the environmental assessment process, initiated an on-site protest and began legal action on that matter.[7] They later won the case, obliging Vale Inco to stop its work on the project's infrastructure (Gibson 2006).

The joint review panel concluded its work in March 1999. Their report stated that the proponents had, amongst other things, to sign IBAs with the Innu Nation and LIA in order for the project to proceed (Gibson 2006). The completion of the land claims negotiations with the provincial government was also declared mandatory to the project's continuation (Gibson 2006).

The IBAs

In parallel to the IA process, the LIA organized consultations, workshops, and research to establish its members' priorities for the IBA (O'Faircheallaigh 2015). One year after the signature of the agreement-in-principles concerning Inuit land claims in 2001, an IBA was approved by referendum by 82% of the Labrador Inuit population and signed in 2002 (Laforce 2012). Two rounds of information sessions had previously been conducted in all of the five Inuit communities of Nunatsiavut (Kenny 2015). The Labrador Inuit Land Claims Agreement was signed in January 2005, and the mine started its operations in 2005.

Summary of the Voisey's Bay Project Case

As explained above, Inuit communities of Labrador played an integral role in both the definition of the IA process and the IBA. Inuit organizations initially engaged in a conflictual relationship with the proponent during the impact assessment process since they did not believe that they were taken seriously by the company's representatives. The community members and representatives of both nations were highly mobilized throughout the IA process and IBA negotiations (through protests, information campaigns, workshops, and civil disobedience movements, etc.). Community members were not only invited to attend public hearings but were summoned to partake in protests and civil disobedience. By doing so, they came to play a more active role in the decision-making process. The IBA was also signed three years after the conclusion of the impact assessment process. While it remains confidential to this day, the IBA was shared with all the Labrador Inuit communities and adopted by a referendum. The population was therefore fully informed about the content of the IBA and participated in its approval. The communities additionally took part in the deliberation processes of the IA and IBA. Inuit communities were thus able to give their consent to the project. The considerable involvement of community members throughout the process also limited the tensions between the regional and local organizations by allowing the latter to play an important part in the decision-making process. The absence of land claim agreements did not undermine Inuit engagement during the process. On the contrary, Inuit organizations used the land claim negotiations as leverage in their negotiations during the IA and IBA processes and to help community mobilization.

The Mary River Project

The Mary River mine, owned by Baffinland Iron Mines Corporation (BIMC), is located between Pond Inlet and Igloolik on Baffin Island, Nunavut. The mine is located on Inuit-owned land, where Inuit own surface and subsurface rights that are managed by the Qikiqtani Inuit Association (QIA). The approbation process of the Mary River mining project began in 2008, and the first approval of the project was given by the Government of Canada in December 2012.

As opposed to Voisey's Bay, the Mary River project was developed fifteen years after the signing of the Nunavut Land Claim Agreement (NLCA). The NLCA establishes Inuit ownership of approximately eighteen percent of the land in Nunavut and mineral rights to two percent of these lands, a cash settlement, and the creation and administration of the territory of Nunavut by an elected government. The Agreement also provides for the creation of three designated Inuit organizations, one being the QIA. The QIA is a not-for-profit organization representing the thirteen Inuit communities of the Qikiqtani region and has the mandate to protect and promote Inuit rights and values, as well as lands of cultural significance to Inuit. The NLCA further put into place three co-management institutions mandated to oversee resource development projects, including the Nunavut Planning Commission (NPC), which is "responsible for the development, implementation and monitoring of land use plans that guide and direct resource use and development in the Nunavut Settlement Area"; and the Nunavut Impact Review Board (NIRB), which is charged with assessing the potential biophysical and socio-economic impacts of proposed developments in Nunavut.[8] Inuit organizations appoint half of the members of the NIRB and the NPC to ensure representation of Inuit interests in decision-making. The NLCA stipulates that Inuit Impact and Benefit Agreements (IIBAs) are mandatory for any major development project, such as mining. IIBAs are negotiated with the designated Inuit regional organizations that are in charge of managing Inuit land—in this case, the QIA.

Impact Assessment

The IA process for the Mary River mine started in 2008 and 2009 with the publication of the NIRB's feasibility study (Saywell 2008; Rogers 2009). It was followed by two rounds of technical reviews and public hearings in 2011 (NIRB 2012). While this was happening, several concerns were raised by community members, the Government of Nunavut, and the QIA regarding the lack of baseline information and communication (George 2011a; Williams 2015). The mine submitted its final environmental impact statement in February 2012, and the final hearings were scheduled in July 2012 in Iqaluit, Igloolik, and Pond Inlet. These were broadcasted on IsumaTV in an attempt to enforce a more deliberative engagement model for the Inuit community (George 2012a,

2012b; Scobie and Rodgers 2013). Forty-one community members from eight communities[9] in Nunavut participated in the final hearings (NIRB 2012).

During the hearings, one of the main discussion topics was possible alternative transportation modalities of the iron ore from the mining site, located in Mary River to the Milne Inlet port, located near the Pond Inlet community, and destined for the European market. During the hearings, the Government of Nunavut criticized the important impact a railway would have on the North Baffin caribou herd and insisted that BIMC develop a more detailed mitigation plan (Dawson 2012). Makivik Corporation, the legal representative of Nunavik's Inuit, also voiced their concerns about the year-round shipping route (Murphy 2012). The QIA, for their part, supported the project, saying it was the right choice for the Inuit, but stressed the lack of baseline information[10] (CBC News 2012a; Williams 2015). The mayors of Igloolik and Hall Beach, who originally objected to the port location, changed their minds, stating that they would not oppose the project as long as they received adequate compensation (CBC News 2012a). In 2011, the mayors of the two communities sent letters to the NIRB explaining their position. While "grave reservations over the Steensby site" were continuously held by the community of Igloolik, Paul Quassa (at the time the mayor of Igloolik) insisted that the benefits also had to be considered (CBC News 2011). From January 2012 onwards, the new mayor of Igloolik, Nicholas Arnatsiaq, also supported the project. Many Igloolimiut were, however, more skeptical during the final hearings (CBC News 2012b). While supporting the project, the Pond Inlet community expressed important concerns about the new proposals put forward by the mine. Amongst other things, the hamlet of Pond Inlet insisted that the project had to guarantee that it would not impact the access to country food and ensure the protection of their land (NIRB 2014).

Moreover, during these hearings, community members raised important concerns about the consultation process and whether Inuit organizations, such as the QIA, the Government of Nunavut, and the mayors of Igloolik and Hall Beach acted in their interests (Williams 2015). Some expressed concern about the lack of possibilities for community members to fully participate in the hearings and local representatives felt excluded from the decision-making process and considered that their institutions were not working in their interest (Williams 2015). IsumaTV, a website for Inuit media and art, played an important role with respect to this matter. Feeling that the IA process was more about the delivery of information rather than a platform conducive to deliberation, IsumaTV recorded and collected Inuit testimonies about the project. They also created a blog, recorded a series of community events and individual interviews, and broadcast call-in radio shows on the event. Their active role during the hearing led the NIRB to include the news media as one of the tools the company would, thereafter, be required to use to inform Inuit communities of their project's development (Scobie and Rogers 2013). Aside from this element, as Williams (2015) noted, the numerous public interventions "failed to have a meaningful impact on the information that was included in the final assessment." The project was finally approved by the Government of Canada in December 2012. Over the course of the same month, the company obtained a project certificate from the NIRB.

Modifications to the Proposal and Phase Two Project

In January 2013, a month after the project's final approval, the proponent requested permission from the NIRB to execute a phased approach and to amend their project certificate. The company planned on slowing down the mine's construction and delay the project's implementation because of a decrease in steel prices (Bell 2013). Rather than sending iron ore by train to a deepwater port in Steensby Inlet, the company would convey the extracted minerals by truck on an all-weather road to a port in Milne Inlet (The Canadian Press 2013). Because of the importance of these changes, in February 2013, the NIRB decided, with the agreement of the federal government, to reconsider Mary River's project certificate (CBC News 2013; George 2013). The NIRB and the federal approved the amended Mary River project in spring 2014.

In October 2014, however, BIMC submitted additional amendments for a Phase Two project: the company aimed to triple the amount of ore shipped through Milne Inlet, from 4.2 million tones to about 12 million tones, for ten months every year (from June until March), which required icebreaking in Eclipse Sound near Pond Inlet and into Baffin Bay (Bell 2014; CBC News 2014). This proposal further entailed an additional 150 voyages per year, floating fuel storage, ice management vessels, and a significant increase of haul truck traffic along the tote road between Milne Inlet and Mary River (Nunatsiaq News 2015).

In an unprecedented opposition, the NPC unanimously rejected BIMC's amended proposals for the Mary River project in April 2015, explaining that their submission did not conform to the land use plan, since icebreaking activities "would prevent or prohibit wildlife harvesting and traditional activities" (CBC News 2015a; Gregoire 2015a). In April 2015, Charlie Inuarak, the mayor of Pond Inlet, also insisted on the significant impact of icebreaking on wildlife harvesting and traditional activities that these changes could entail, echoing concerns shared by several community members (CBC News 2015b). The QIA and Nunavut Tunngavik Inc. (NTI) both supported the community's position (Bell 2015; CBC News 2015c).

The company, however, challenged the NPC's refusal, and asked the federal government for an exemption from the land use plan (Bell 2015). In a letter sent to the minister of AANDC, the Government of Nunavut supported the mine's request and asserted that they supported a decision that would allow the mine to bypass the land use plan (Gregoire 2015b). The Government of Nunavut's position was also endorsed by the mayor and council of Pond Inlet, who changed sides in July 2015, four months after he had said he supported the NPC's decision (CBC News 2015d). They felt that the best way to address the impacts of the new proposal was through public hearings with the NIRB (CBC News 2015e). In July 2015, AANDC granted the exemption to the mine. This was a controversial decision that was seen as bypassing the NLCA impact process. However, given the significance of the proposed changes, BIMC was required to resubmit its proposal for Phase Two to the NIRB and delay the already planned public consultations.

In 2016, the company made more changes, asking for the construction of a railway from the Mary River site to the Milne Inlet port as a means of replacing the road it had previously requested (Rohner 2016; Skura 2016). Community representatives expressed concern about the project's multiple changes. In the words of Abraham Qammaniq, Hall Beach's community director, "Where do we draw the line? They're not thinking of the land. They're not thinking of the people" (Skura 2016).

Final hearings took place in November 2019. However, the hearings were adjourned only five days after it started at the request of NTI that complained of a lack of time to review the documents and inadequate consultation from BIMC. The motion was supported by all interveners, including the QIA president: "[T]here's just too many outstanding questions that haven't been resolved. From my perspective, if you're going to make a decision for your future, you've got to ensure you have all the information available to make that sound decision. It just wasn't quite there" (Tranter and Anselmi 2019). This happened a few days after it was revealed that the company was promoting to private investors that it planned shipping up to 18 million tonnes of iron ore every year rather than 12 million tonnes as indicated in the proposal under review (Tranter 2019). This news furthered the distrust toward BIMC.

Because of the COVID-19 pandemic and given the significant opposition and the limit of technical meetings held via teleconference, the hearings were put on hold on April 24, 2020 (Deuling 2020). The NIRB stated that the review process would only resume once travel restrictions were lifted and when Nunavummiut would be allowed to return to work and have public gatherings (Deuling 2020).

Despite significant Inuit opposition to BIMC's expansion project, especially within the five communities of North Baffin, the NIRB resumed public hearings on the expansion of the Mary River iron mine from 26 January to 6 February 2021 in Pond Inlet, with restricted in-person access, online streaming, and television broadcasting (Bell 2021). Frustrated with this process, as we will see in the next section, six Inuit hunters from Pond Inlet and Arctic Bay went to block the Mary River airstrip.

The hearings continued throughout the spring across impacted communities until April 25 (Murray 2021). BIMC subsequently made changes to its proposal in response to Inuit concerns, and hearings resumed during the fall of 2021. This was the fourth attempt at completing the hearing regarding the proposed Phase Two expansion. Once the hearings are completed, BIMC is expected to submit final statements within one month, and the NIRB would have to prepare its final submission for the minister of northern affairs (Venn 2021b). At the date of writing, the review process was still underway.

Negotiating Inuit and Impact Benefit Agreements

In parallel to the Impact Assessment process, BIMC was also renegotiating its IIBA with the QIA (George 2011b). Unlike the IBAs for the Voisey's Bay mine, where there were no land claim agreements signed between the government and the Innu and Inuit Nations, and thus no obligation for IBAs, the IIBA for the Mary River project was required under Article 26 of the NLCA. During the negotiation of the IIBA, the QIA did not disclose any elements of the agreement's content. No information sessions and referendums were held. The QIA and BIMC reached an agreement on the terms and conditions of the IIBA in September 2013, only a few months after the project was granted the necessary approval to move forward (Nunatsiaq News 2013a). A plain-language guide was released and available for the public consultation of local communities after the IIBA was signed (Nunatsiaq News 2013b). In December 2013, the QIA released a public version of the IIBA without the detail on the financial arrangements and in May 2016, the full IIBA was made public. The QIA did so in an effort to be more transparent and open (Nunatsiaq News 2013c). The full disclosure of the IIBA occurred one month before a conflict resolution mechanism, and arbitration procedures were launched between the QIA and BIMC to settle a dispute over royalty payments and employment levels. This led both parties into arbitration in April 2017 (Nunatsiaq News 2017). The Arbitration Panel made a unanimous ruling in favour of the QIA and determined that BIMC owed the QIA approximately $7.3 million (Nunatsiaq News 2017).

The tensions between the Inuit organization and the local Inuit communities did not, however, lessen after the disclosure of the IIBA. Following the beginning of the arbitration procedures initiated by the QIA, six Nunavut communities, namely Hall Beach, Igloolik, Pond Inlet, Clyde River, Arctic Bay and Resolute Bay, submitted a petition to the NTI in March 2017, requesting their separation from the QIA in order for them to form their own Inuit organization.[11] The secession, which was initiated by Pond Inlet, the most affected community, is primarily due to the disagreements about the use of the royalty payments received from BIMC, currently saved in a legacy fund established by the QIA (Van Dusen 2017). This separation request was rejected by NTI.

As the company submitted amendments to the project in 2016, the QIA demanded a renegotiation of the IIBA. This time however, consultations and community visits were conducted by the QIA prior to the renegotiation of the IIBA. The new IIBA signed in 2019, called the Inuit Certainty Agreement, contains a range of provisions intended to support Inuit interests "in terms of financial transfers (advance and royalty payments), employment, contracting/subcontracting, and training opportunities, as well as social and environmental initiatives" (Loxley 2019, 3). The amended IIBA increases Inuit training and employment at the mine. It also changes the formula for royalty payments, an element that was at the heart of a previous dispute between BIMC and the QIA (Brown 2020). Finally, the new IIBA allowed an Inuit oversight of the project by putting into place an Inuit-led environmental monitoring and financial commitment to build daycares in the affected communities. The QIA's president considered that the new agreement "put Inuit in the driver's seat" (Tranter 2020). Those changes in the IIBA reflect, according to the

QIA, the comments received following public consultations in 2018 (Brown 2020). However, signing the Inuit Certainty Agreement was seen as providing a form of consent prior to the completion of the NIRB process and the final approval by the federal authority.

This led to further tension with the Northern communities and on February 4, 2021, seven Inuit men from Pond Inlet and Arctic Bay, who called themselves the Nuluujaat Land Guardians, drove their skidoos to the Mary River mine and blocked the landing strip, cutting the mine's resupply channels and preventing the miners from exiting the site. Specifically, the protestors feared that their concerns regarding the expansion's negative impact on the caribou population and other wildlife in the area, including narwhal, on which Inuit depend for subsistence, were not being considered by their representatives or the mining company (Beers 2021). In order to stop the protest, the mining company's lawyers were able to obtain a court injunction. However, the blockade ended on February 11 after the mayor of Pond Inlet's mediation (Beers 2021). Negotiations with an elected official, based on constructive dialogues and a proposal responding to the protestors' demands, were more fruitful than the court injunction.

This public expression of discontent toward the extractive operations in Mary River illustrates the frustration engendered by such development projects within communities adjacent to the mine site. It further demonstrates how Inuit express their grievance when official processes and communication channels appear ineffective, but also how they engage in activism in the hopes of enacting meaningful political change. It is worth noting that the Nuluujaat Land Guardians subsequently met with federal Department of Northern Affairs and its minister, Dan Vandal, in May 2021 to "discuss the strengths and values of their communities," as well as "land-based economic options for current and future generations of north Baffin residents ... who do not wish to be involved in mining" (Venn 2021a). This conversation, which happened outside official processes, shows how such a protest catalyzed changes that transgress the event's conclusion.

Finally, in a surprising reversal brought by the increasing pressure on the QIA from Inuit communities impacted by the Mary River project, the QIA announced in March 2021 that it was withdrawing its support of BIMC's Phase Two expansion proposal (QIA 2021). Without the QIA's support, this expansion is unlikely to occur.

Analysis of the Mary River Case

In the Mary River case, the NLCA obliged all concerned parties to negotiate an IBA and set the conditions for the impact assessment. No protests were required for these negotiations to take place. The concerns of local Inuit communities were channelled through established co-management institutions as well as through Inuit organizations created by the NLCA, and their concerns were heard during public hearings. Furthermore, because of the NLCA, the mine had to follow an established process and thus could not minimize the role that the local and regional organizations had to play.

However, the concerns of local community members and the positions of their local and regional representatives often appeared divergent. While important criticisms were raised by community members on the impact of the railway and year-round shipping on wildlife, their concerns and objections often appeared minimized. The hamlets of Pond Inlet, Igloolik and Hall Beach were all, initially, very critical of the Mary River project. However, they changed their position over the course of the environmental assessment process by deciding to support the project so long as they received adequate compensation from the mining company. While the mayors of Pond Inlet, Igloolik, and Hall Beach still outlined the potential negative impacts of the transportation of iron ore, the positive economic impacts justified the project's implementation. For that reason, some community members attending the public hearings expressed their concern toward the way local and regional organizations represented their opinion (Williams 2015). Furthermore, the numerous changes made by the mining company after receiving approval from the NIRB divided Inuit organizations and communities over the process itself. Finally, the secretive nature of the negotiations that led to the first IIBA (the local communities were not informed of the agreement's content before its signature), could possibly explain in part the skepticism and criticisms voiced during the public hearings. The second IIBA was also negotiated behind closed doors, but at least community consultations were held before the negotiation process started. This didn't prevent criticism from some Inuit communities who felt that the IIBA was signed before the IA process was conducted or complete, which led to the blockade of the Mary River airstrip by Inuit hunters who felt their concerns were not addressed. Therefore, both the IA and the IBA processes have not been able to provide a real community engagement, and this is reflected in the multiples episodes of dissension. In the end, the QIA had to change position because of the pressure from local communities.

Conclusion

These two cases show important variations in the form and extent of community engagement. In both cases, there was a good level of engagement throughout the IA processes, although only in the Nunatsiavut case was there a real community engagement process during the development of the IBA. This engagement included both a deliberative process and a referendum. In the case of Nunavut, information regarding the IBA was only shared with Inuit beneficiaries after the signing of the agreement. The negotiation of the second IBA provided for more engagement, although that didn't prevent dissension among Inuit organizations. In addition, there was no deliberative process on any of the agreements.

In the case of Voisey's Bay, even without a land claim agreement framework, the Inuit negotiators, as well as the Labrador Inuit population, demonstrated a strong engagement both during the IA and IBA processes. This could be explained by the fact that, right from the beginning, negotiations had to take place to define the IA process and that the IBA process was linked to the land claim negotiation. Thus, considerable mobilizations occurred during the different negotiation phases to ensure that Innu and Inuit from Labrador took part in the IA process and that their rights were respected. Since the Labrador Inuit were very involved throughout the process and because the land claim agreements and IBAs were negotiated simultaneously, it appeared sensible to vote for their approval by referendum, especially considering that the IBA was a precondition to the signing of the land claims agreement.

For the Labrador Inuit negotiators, strong opposition from community members could have jeopardized the signing of the Labrador Inuit Land Claims Agreement. This consequently led to a process akin to FPIC, since it involved forms of consultations and deliberations amongst all Labrador Inuit.

In the Mary River case, the engagement processes were established by the NLCA, but as shown above, both the IA and the IIBA were considered unsatisfactory by a number of Nunavummiut. In the case of the IA process, several people felt that they had not been heard or considered, although, through the pressure of the civil society, the IA was made more accessible to community members. As noted by Scobie and Rodgers (2013), IA processes can often "channel and control community residents' engagement" instead of encouraging it. Negotiations that occurred as part of the IIBA processes were limited to a small group of experts and negotiators. While the QIA, as the designated Inuit organization representing Inuit communities of the region, was mandated to negotiate the IBA, community members were not directly involved, and there was no community consultation nor deliberation. This engendered tensions that subsequently forced the QIA to release the non-financial clauses. With the arrival of a new the QIA president, the financial clauses of the Inuit organization's IBA were finally released. It was, however, too late for community members to influence the decision-making process since the IBA had already been signed.

The Mary River mine had a considerable impact on the Nunavummiut. Firstly, BIMC's incapacity to deliver the financial compensation (royalties) and reach the employment targets promised in the IIBA led to an arbitration process, which was resolved in favour of the QIA but introduced doubts on the company's capacity to meet its commitments. Secondly, the decisions of the federal government to bypass the NPC has shown that the impact assessment process can be easily overruled by the federal government. Finally, tensions arose between the five northern communities and the QIA over the use of the royalties of the Mary River project. This led the communities of North Baffin to formally request their separation from the QIA in order to create their own organizations as permitted by the NLCA. This "secessionist" movement was finally stopped by the refusal of NTI to consider their request and by the efforts of the new the QIA president to re-engage the northern communities' leadership. It could partly be attributed to what could be considered a lack of transparency and deliberation in the negotiation of the IIBA. The negotiation of the second IIBA provided more consultation beforehand, but negotiations were still conducted by a small team and were not approved by the impacted communities or their residents. Finally, the fact that the IIBA was signed before the IA was conducted also created tensions, since it looked like the QIA had consented to the project while the impacted communities had not yet had the chance to participate in the IA process and thus fully ascertain the project's potential repercussions. Finally, the QIA decided to withdraw its support to the second phase of the project, putting an end to this project and to the dissension. Dissensions can be very damaging for small communities and should be considered as a negative externality of the IA and IIBA processes.

As we have seen, the FPIC principles that stem from UNDRIP are emerging as a new norm for Indigenous engagement in resource development. In the case of Voisey's Bay, all the engagement processes were conducted before UNDRIP was adopted, although, in the case of the IBA, a deliberative process was established. In the case of Nunavut, the NLCA only implemented a consultation process through the IA and a negotiation process with the IIBA. As demonstrated, this could have led to the dissent of some Nunavummiut who felt that their concerns were not addressed or even considered. The ambiguity inherent to such consultation and authorization processes appears to call for the implementation of a real FPIC process. These cases further highlight the need to clarify the objectives of consultation and the definition of FPIC.

NOTES

1   The authors wish to acknowledge the important contribution of Luc Brisebois and Bethany Scott from QIA, who helped us in the revision of this article as well as Rosalie Côté-Tremblay for her assistance in the research. However, the views and opinions expressed in this article are the authors' own and do not necessarily reflect the official policy or position of their respective employers.

2   In the Canadian context, unceded lands or territories refer to Indigenous lands that have not been acquired by treaty or by an act of war.

3   See *Delgamuukw v. British Columbia*, 1997.

4   In 2016, there were 29 comprehensive land claim agreements and self-government agreements signed in Canada and 74 unsettled land claims (AANDC, 2016).

5   For example, this is the case with the Nunavut Land Claim Agreement (1993), with the Labrador Inuit Land Claims Agreement (2004), with the Sahtu (1993) and the Gwich'in (1992) comprehensive land claims agreements and with the Tłı̨chǫ Agreement (2003).

6   Between 2010 and 2014, Canadian appeal tribunals (federal, provincial, and territorial) heard 35% more cases on the duty to consult than between 2005 and 2009 (Papillon and Rodon 2017a).

7   *Labrador Inuit Association v. Newfoundland (Minister of Environment and Labour)*, (1997) 157 Nfld. & P.E.I.R. 164 (NFTD).

8   The third is the Nunavut Water Board (NWB).

9   Out of the thirteen communities in the Qikiqtani region.

10 QIA criticized, amongst other things, a lack references and a lack of evidence concerning the project's impact on caribou (Williams 2015).

11 NTI has the signatory of the NLCA is responsible to statute on the demand to create a new designated Inuit Organization. At this time, there is one Designated Inuit organization (DIO) for each Nunavut regions, Kitikmeot, Kivalliq and Qikiqtaluk.

References

Aboriginal Affairs and Northern Development Canada (AANDC). 2011. *Aboriginal Consultation and Accommodation—Updated Guidelines for Federal Officials to Fulfill the Duty to Consult.* Ottawa: Government of Canada. https://www.rcaanc-cirnac.gc.ca/eng/1100100014664/1609421824729.

Archibald, Linda, and Mary Crnkovich. 1999. *If Gender Mattered: A Case Study of Inuit Women, Land Claims and the Voisey's Bay Nickel Project.* Ottawa: Status of Women Canada.

Beers, Randi. 2021. "Mary River Mine Protesters Announce the End to Blockade." *Nunatsiaq News,* February 11, 2021. https://nunatsiaq.com/stories/article/mary-river-mine-protesters-announce-end-to-blockade/

Bell, Jim. 2013. "Baffinland Slashes Scope of Nunavut's Mary River Project." *Nunatsiaq News,* January 10, 2013. https://nunatsiaq.com/stories/article/65674baffinland_slashes_scope_of_nunavuts_mary_river_project/

———. 2014. "Nunavut Iron Producer Proposes Big Changes for Mary River Baffinland seeks expansion of Milne Inlet, winter shipping, ramped up iron ore volumes." *Nunatsiaq News,* November 5, 2014. http://www.nunatsiaqonline.ca/stories/article/65674nunavut_iron_producer_proposes_big_changes_for_mary_river/ .

———. 2015. "Inuit Org wants Valcourt to Reject Baffinland Request for Land Use Exemption." *Nunatsiaq News,* May 22, 2015. https://nunatsiaq.com/stories/article/65674inuit_org_wants_valcourt_to_reject_baffinland_request_for_land_use_exe/#:~:text=The%20Qikiqtani%20Inuit%20Association%20has,Baffin%20Regional%20Land%20Use%20Plan .

———. 2021. "Despite Inuit Opposition, Mary River Mine Hearing to go Ahead Next Week." *Nunatsiaq News,* January 22, 2021. https://nunatsiaq.com/stories/article/despite-inuit-opposition-mary-river-mine-hearing-to-go-ahead-next-week/

Bennett, Carolyn. 2016. "Speech Delivered at the United Nations Permanent Forum on Indigenous Issues, New York, May 10." May 10, 2016. https://www.canada.ca/en/indigenous-northern-affairs/news/2016/05/speech-delivered-at-the-united-nations-permanent-forum-on-indigenous-issues-new-york-may-10-.html.

Brown, Beth. 2020. "New Inuit Benefit Agreement Worth $1B over Life of Mary River." *CBC News,* July 07, 2020. https://www.cbc.ca/news/canada/north/baffinland-signs-environmental-agreement-qikiqtani-inuit-association-1.5639858?fbclid=IwAR3eFAMRfRqGwMBSFTlQiGB0bP0Bp-TdQ7jWwVgeV39qsw447eMXH4DmH4k

Calder et al. v. Attorney-General of British Columbia, [1973] S.C.R. 313.

CBC News. 2011. "Baffin Mayors Soften Stance on Iron Mine Port." *CBC News,* November 9, 2011. http://www.cbc.ca/news/canada/north/baffin-mayors-soften-stance-on-iron-mine-port-1.1049887.

———. 2012a. "Nunavut Braces for Massive Mary River Mine." *CBC News,* September 13, 2012. http://www.cbc.ca/news/canada/north/nunavut-braces-for-massive-mary-river-mine-1.1179502.

———. 2012b. "Final Baffinland Hearings Move to Igloolik." *CBC News*, July 24, 2012. http://www.cbc.ca/news/canada/north/final-baffinland-hearings-move-to-igloolik-1.1194777.

———. 2013. "Baffinland Headed Back to Nunavut Regulators." *CBC News*, April 4, 2013. http://www.cbc.ca/news/canada/north/baffinland-headed-back-to-nunavut-regulators-1.1348367.

———. 2014. "Baffinland Pitches Year-round Shipping from Milne Inlet." *CBC News*, October 3, 2014. http://www.cbc.ca/news/canada/north/baffinland-pitches-year-round-shipping-from-milne-inlet-1.2822346.

———. 2015a. "Oceans North Canada Applauds Decision on Baffinland Shipping." *CBC News*, April 14, 2015. http://www.cbc.ca/news/canada/north/oceans-north-canada-applauds-decision-on-baffinland-shipping-1.3031588.

———. 2015b. "Pond Inlet Mayor Says Residents Share Fears about Baffinland Shipping." *CBC News*, April 10, 2015. http://www.cbc.ca/news/canada/north/pond-inlet-mayor-says-residents-share-fears-about-baffinland-shipping-1.3027724.

———. 2015c. "QIA, NTI team up against Baffinland's request for NPC exemption." *CBC News North*, June 9, 2015. http://www.cbc.ca/news/canada/north/qia-nti-team-up-against-baffinland-s-request-for-npc-exemption-1.3105701.

———. 2015d. "Baffinland Iron Mines Granted Land Use Plan Exemption by Federal Minister." *CBC News*, July 14, 2015. http://www.cbc.ca/news/canada/north/baffinland-iron-mines-granted-land-use-plan-exemption-by-federal-minister-1.3151834.

———. 2015e. "Pond Inlet Council Sides with Baffinland, Premier in Regulatory Dispute." *CBC News*, July 2, 2015.

Dawson, Samantha. 2012. "Mary River Railway Could do Big Damage to Caribou." *Nunatsiaq News*, July 19, 2012. http://www.nunatsiaqonline.ca/stories/article/65674mary_river_railway_could_do_big_damage_to_caribou_gn/.

Delgamuukw v. British Columbia, [1997] 3 S.C.R. 1010.

Deuling, Meagan. 2020. "Baffinland Expansion Meetings Cancelled Again." *Nunatsiaq News*, April 27, 2020. https://nunatsiaq.com/stories/article/baffinland-expansion-meetings-continue-to-be-canceled/

Duncanson, S., M. O'Neill Sanger, K. Twa, and C. Brinker. 2021. Federal UNDRIP Bill Becomes Law. *Oster*. Accessed 10 May 2023. https://www.osler.com/en/resources/regulations/2021/federal-undrip-bill-becomes-law.

George, Jane. 2011a. "Draft EIS for Nunavut's Mary River Mine Sparks Stinging Technical Review." *Nunatsiaq News*, October 7, 2011. https://nunatsiaq.com/stories/article/65674draft_eis_for_nunavuts_mary_river_mine_sparks_criticism/.

———. 2011b. "Baffinland Gets its Marching Orders from NIRB." *Nunatsiaq News*, December 15, 2011. https://nunatsiaq.com/stories/article/65674baffinland_gets_its_marching_orders_from_nirb/.

———. 2012a. "Iqaluit Technical Review Puts Spotlight on Nunavut's Mary River Iron Mine Project." *Nunatsiaq News*, May 2, 2012. https://stage.nunatsiaq.com/stories/article/65674iqaluit_technical_review_puts_spotlight_on_nunavuts_mary_river_project/.

———. 2012b. "Baffinland Gives NIRB Final EIS for Mary River: Nunavut Impact Review Board Now Reviewing Huge Environmental document." *Nunatsiaq News*, February 20, 2012. https://stage.nunatsiaq.com/stories/article/65674iqaluit_technical_review_puts_spotlight_on_nunavuts_mary_river_project/.

———. 2013. "Prepare for Another Review, Nunavut Board tells Baffinland." *Nunatsiaq News*, February 12, 2013. https://nunatsiaq.com/stories/article/65674pepare_for_another_review_nunavut_board_tells_baffinland/.

Gibson, Robert. 2002. "From Wreck Cove to Voisey's Bay: The Evolution of Federal Environmental Assessment in Canada." *Impact Assessment and Project Appraisal* 20, no. 3: 151–59.

———. 2006. "Sustainability Assessment and Conflict Resolution: Reaching Agreement to Proceed with the Voisey's Bay Nickel Mine." *Journal of Cleaner Production* 14, no. 3: 334–48.

Gregoire, Lisa. 2015a. "Nunavut Regulatory Org Says No to Baffinland." *Nunatsiaq News*, April 9, 2015. https://nunatsiaq.com/stories/article/65674nunavut_regulatory_org_says_no_to_baffinland/.

———. 2015b. "Nunavut Premier's Leaked Letter to Ottawa Disappoints Board Chair." *Nunatsiaq News*, June 1, 2015. https://nunatsiaq.com/stories/article/65674nunavut_premiers_private_letter_to_ottawa_disappoints_board_chair/.

Haida Nation v. British Columbia (Minister of Forests), [2004] 3 S.C.R. 511.

Heritage Newfoundland and Labrador. 2011. "The Voisey's Bay Mine." Heritage Newfoundland and Labrador. July 12, 2018. http://www.heritage.nf.ca/articles/economy/voiseys-bay.php.

Kenny, Caitlin. 2015. "Navigating Complex Planning Processes: The Experiences of Two Aboriginal Governments with Large Mineral Development Proposals in their Traditional Territories." Master thesis, University of Guelph.

Laforce, Myriam. 2012. "Régulation du projet minier de Voisey's Bay au Labrador vers un rééquilibrage des pouvoirs dans certains contextes politiques et institutionnels?" In *Pouvoir et régulation dans le secteur minier: leçons à partir de l'expérience canadienne*, ed. Bonnie K. Campbell, Myriam Laforce and Bruno Sarrasin (Québec: Presses de l'Université du Québec), 157–90.

Loxley, John. 2019. *Assessment of the Mary River Project: Impacts and Benefits*. Ocean North. https://oceansnorth.org/wp-content/uploads/2019/02/Assessment-of-the-Mary-River-Project-Impacts-and-Benefits-final-draft.pdf

Mikisew Cree Nation v. Canada (Minister of Canadian Heritage), [2005] 3 S.C.R. 388.

Murphy, David. 2012. "Makivik Demands Changes to Baffinland's Mary River Shipping Route." *Nunatsiaq Online*, July 20, 2012. https://stage.nunatsiaq.com/stories/

article/65674makivik_demands_changes_to_baffinlands_mary_river_shipping_route/.

Murray, Nick. 2021. "Wildlife concerns still lingering as public hearings into Baffinland's expansion resume." *CBC News North*, April 13, 2021. https://www.cbc.ca/news/canada/north/narwhal-wildlife-concerns-baffinland-mary-river-mine-iron-ore-expansion-nunavut-1.5985301

Nunatsiaq News. 2013a. "QIA, Baffinland Strike Deal on Inuit Benefits, Commercial Lease for Nunavut Iron Project." *Nunatsiaq News*, September 6, 2013. https://nunatsiaq.com/stories/article/65674qia-baffinland_reach_agreement_on_inuit_benefits_commercial_lease_for_/.

———. 2013c. "QIA releases public version of Mary River IIBA." *Nunatsiaq News,* December 9, 2013. http://www.nunatsiaqonline.ca/stories/article/65674mary_river_iiba_made_public/. https://stage.nunatsiaq.com/stories/article/65674mary_river_iiba_made_public/.

———. 2015. "Valcourt Exempts Nunavut Iron Mine Expansion from Land Use Plan." *Nunatsiaq News,* July 14, 2015. https://nunatsiaq.com/stories/article/65674breaking_valcourt_exempts_nunavut_iron_mine_expansion_from_npc/.

———. 2016. "Nunavut Review Board Sends Mary River Scheme Back to the NPC." *Nunatsiaq News*, December 20, 2016. https://nunatsiaq.com/stories/article/65674nunavut_review_board_sends_mary_river_scheme_back_to_the_npc/.

———. 2017. "Arbitration Hearing on QIA-Baffinland Royalties Dispute Starts April 18." *Nunatsiaq News*, April 18, 2017. https://nunatsiaq.com/stories/article/65674arbitration_hearing_on_qia-baffinland_financial_dispute_starts_april_1/.

Nunavut Impact Review Board (NIRB). 2012. *Final Hearing Report: Mary River Project.* Cambridge Bay: NIRB.

———. 2014. *Public Hearing Report: Mary River Project: Early Revenue Phase Proposal.* Cambridge Bay: NIRB.

O'Faircheallaigh, Ciaran. 2007. "Environmental Agreements, EIA Follow-up and Aboriginal Participation in Environmental Management: The Canadian Experience." *Environmental Impact Assessment Review* 27, no. 4: 319–42.

———. 2015. *Negotiations in the Indigenous World: Aboriginal Peoples and the Extractive Industry in Australia and Canada.* London: Routledge.

Papillon, Martin, and Thierry Rodon. 2017a. "Proponent-Indigenous Agreements and the Implementation of the Right to Free, Prior and Informed Consent in Canada." *Environmental Impact Assessment Review* 62: 216–24.

———. 2017b. "Indigenous Consent and Natural Resource Extraction: Foundations for a Made-in-Canada Approach." *IRPP Insight* 16: 1–26.

———. 2019. "From Consultation to Consent: The Politics of Indigenous Participatory Rights in Canada." In *The Prior Consultation of Indigenous Peoples in Latin America: Inside the Implementation Gap*, ed. C. Wright & A. Tomaselli (London: Routledge), 261–75.

QIA (Qikiqtani Inuit Association). 2021. "QIA Board Resolves to not Support the Mary River Phase Two Proposal. Qikiqtani Inuit Association." March 5, 2021. Accessed May 10, 2023. https://www.qia.ca/qia-board-resolves-to-not-support-the-mary-river-phase-two-proposal/

Rodon, Thierry. 2017. "Institutional Development and Resource Development: The Case of Canada's Indigenous Peoples." *Canadian Journal of Development Studies* 40, no. 2: 1–18.

Rogers, Sarah. 2009. "Some Nunavik Residents Worried about Mary River." *Nunatsiaq News*, September 22, 2009. http://nunatsiaq.com/stories/article/918_Some_Nunavik_residents_worried_about_Mary_River/ .

Rohner, Thomas. 2016. "Baffinland Pitches Mary River—Milne Inlet Railway for Nunavut Iron Mine." *Nunatsiaq News*, February 19, 2016. https://nunatsiaq.com/stories/article/65674baffinland_milne_inlet-mary_river_railway_for_nunavut_iron_mine/

Saywell, Trish. 2008. "Robust Economics for Baffinland's Mary River Project." *The Northern Miner*, February 25–March 2, 2008. http://www.canadianminingjournal.com/features/robust-economics-for-baffinland-s-mary-river-project/.

Scholtz, Christa. 2006. *Negotiating Claims: The Emergence of Indigenous Land Claim Negotiation Policies in Australia, Canada, New Zealand, and the United States.* New York: Routledge.

Scobie, Willow, and Kathleen Rodgers. 2013. "Contestations of resource extraction projects via digital media in two Nunavut communities." Études/Inuit/Studies 37, no. 2: 83–101.

Skura, Elyse. 2016. "Baffinland Proposes Changing Mary River Project's Shipping Road to a Railway." *CBC News North*, February 18, 2016. http://www.cbc.ca/news/canada/north/baffinland-new-change-railway-shipping-1.3453469.

Taku River Tlingit First Nation v. British Columbia (Project Assessment Director), [2004] 3 S.C.R. 550, 2004 SCC 74.

The Canadian Press. 2013. "Iron Miner Seeks Delay on Railway and Port for Baffin Island Project amid Financing Squeeze." *The Financial Post*, January 11, 2013. http://business.financialpost.com/news/mining/iron-miner-delays-railway-and-port-for-baffin-island-project-amid-financing-squeeze.

Tranter, Emma. 2019. "Nunavut Board Rejects Oceans North Motion to Suspend Iron Mine Assessment." *Nunatsiaq News,* November 3, 2019. https://nunatsiaq.com/stories/article/nunavut-board-rejects-oceans-north-motion-to-suspend-iron-mine-assessment/

———. 2020. "Qikiqtani Inuit Association and Baffinland Sign New Multimillion-dollar Benefit Agreement." *Nunatsiaq News*, August 14, 2021. https://nunatsiaq.com/

stories/article/qikiqtani-inuit-association-and-baffinland-sign-new-multimillion-dollar-benefit-agreement/

Tranter, Emma & Elaine Anselmi. 2019. "Baffinland Hearing Abruptly Ends, with Sessions Cancelled in Pond Inlet. *Nunatsiaq News*, Nov. 7, 2019. https://nunatsiaq.com/stories/article/baffinland-hearing-abruptly-ends-with-sessions-cancelled-in-pond-inlet/

Van Dusen, John. 2017. "High Arctic Communities Consider Splitting from QIA." *CBC News*, February 6, 2017. http://www.cbc.ca/news/canada/north/qia-split-proposed-1.3969477.

Venn David. 2021a. "Northern Affairs Minister Meets with Mary River Mine Protesters." *Nunatsiaq News*, June 8, 2021. https://nunatsiaq.com/stories/article/northern-affairs-minister-meets-with-mary-river-mine-protesters/.

Venn, David. 2021b. "NIRB Hearing on Baffinland Expansion to Resume Monday." *Nunatsiaq News*, October 31, 2021. https://nunatsiaq.com/stories/article/nirb-hearing-on-baffinland-expansion-to-resume-monday/

Williams, Andrew. 2015. "Governmentality and Mining: Analyzing the Environmental Impact Assessment for the Mary River Mine." Master thesis, Carleton University.

Williamson, T. 1996. Seeing the Land Is Seeing Ourselves: Labrador Inuit Association Issues Scoping Report. Prepared for the Labrador Inuit Association. Nain, Labrador.

"It's Time to Make Things Right": Protests and Partnerships in the Implementation of Livelihood Rights in Mi'kma'ki

L. Jane McMillan, Janice Marie Maloney, and Twila Gaudet

This chapter shares a history of the Mi'kmaq Rights Initiative and the rise of the Kwilmu'kw Maw-klusuaqn Negotiation Office (KMKNO).[1] Our narrative examines the strategies employed by the Mi'kmaq of Nova Scotia to rebuild Indigenous nationhood, access their livelihood rights, and gain control over the management, distribution, and implementation of their treaty-protected resources. Generating and sustaining a nationhood collectivity against the capitalist imperative of economic individualism is a challenge for many First Nations. KMKNO works to counter colonially induced poverty, and to overcome settler ignorance of Treaty Rights, while fighting against divisive and contradictory policies imposed federally and provincially that undermine nation-to-nation relations. They seek remedies to complex problems of economic and political insecurity by fostering unity through effective communications, inclusivity, and the rigorous maintenance and protection of Indigenous and Treaty Rights. It is very difficult work managing the expectations, interests, and needs of the unique communities that comprise the Mi'kmaw nation in Nova Scotia. Through trial and error, grit, and determination, promising pathways to Indigenous prosperity, livelihood autonomy and freedom are emerging in Mi'kma'ki.

This chapter first grounds the consultation and negotiation processes in Mi'kma'ki, the territory of the Mi'kmaq Nation, within the pre-Confederation Peace and Friendship Treaties. The consequences of colonialism and the failure of the signatories, and generations of settlers, to honour those treaties and Indigenous Rights, set the stage for Mi'kmaw resistance. Secondly, as presented here, the Mi'kmaq took a calculated risk and chose treaty litigation as a path to protect their rights. After successfully affirming their Treaty Rights through the courts in the *Simon, Marshall,* and other decisions, the Mi'kmaq of Nova Scotia took significant steps to unify as a nation and to build the scaffolding to construct mechanisms for protecting and managing their rights. Thirdly, we describe those steps in the story of the Made-in-Nova Scotia Process and detail the principles underpinning the governance activities of KMKNO. Highlighted are the general tensions the Mi'kmaq face internally and externally as they navigate the diverse needs of their membership and confront the challenges of the uneven, competitive, inadequate, and often unpredictable approaches to consultation and negotiation taken by federal, provincial, and corporate proponents in the context of implementing their livelihood rights in the context of the *Marshall* decision.

Peace and Friendship Treaties: The Precursors for Contemporary Consultation and Negotiation

The Mi'kmaq peoples known as L'nu have lived in Mi'kma'ki, the Atlantic region, since time immemorial. Their creation stories identify sacred connections to their territories, and when shared teach peoples their clan histories, value systems, modes of governance, and about their relationships with each other (Augustine 2016). Over time they developed highly sophisticated governance and legal principles that protected the environment, respected their ancestors, and fostered generations of prosperity. Honouring family relations (*msit no'kmaq*—all my relations) is vital to Mi'kmaq daily life and is captured in the concepts that guide their individual and collective interactions with each other and the universe. The Mi'kmaq believe that the spirits of their ancestors reside in the land, sea, and sky, and they take seriously the responsibility to honour and protect the legacies of their ancestors for future generations. Over the course of at least 14,000 years, well before the arrival of European explorers and settlers, the Mi'kmaq peoples developed vast trading networks, sophisticated national political and legal structures, and a rich social and cultural history (Hoffman 1955; Paul 2006).

Due to their geographic location, the Mi'kmaq Nation has endured one of the longest periods of colonial encounter. As such, they have a lot of experience in engaging and negotiating with newcomers in their territories. The first sustained interactions between the Mi'kmaq and Europeans occurred following the arrival of French missionaries and settlers in the early 1600s (Henderson 1997). Early relations between the French and the Mi'kmaq were generally amicable, and the two groups co-operated and co-existed. The French attempted to assimilate the Mi'kmaq through a process that included the conversion of Mi'kmaq peoples to Catholicism to strengthen social and cultural ties between them and the original inhabitants. The French and Mi'kmaq formed partnerships based on reciprocity and mutual recognition, and the benefits each group could provide for the other (McMillan 2011). The French settlers were particularly dependent on the Mi'kmaq for survival in the harsh environment. The relationship began to shift with the arrival of more French settlers and the rise of the fur trade, which disrupted the existing balance of power between the nations. The relationship was altered further by the arrival of European conflicts to the shores of Mi'kma'ki.[2]

As the British moved into the territory of Mi'kma'ki, they did not follow the more amicable French example, instead developing hostile relations. The British colonialists largely ignored the Mi'kmaq peoples, except in instances where their activities interfered with commercial and settlement plans (McMillan 2011). British colonial authorities were concerned about the potential threat posed by the Mi'kmaq, who were experts in defending their territories on land and sea. Worried that they might continue to take up arms against the British, or that they would re-join forces with the French in their effort to regain control of Acadia, the British sought ways to ensure that the Mi'kmaq would remain peaceful and co-operative with the new British authorities. Treaties were one way of doing this; scalping proclamations, starvation, germ warfare, and terrorism were others (Upton 1979; Whitehead 1991; Prins 1996).

Recognizing the Mi'kmaq as a powerful military threat to their plans for occupation and settlement, the British entered into Peace and Friendship treaty negotiations. The first treaty was signed in 1725–26 (Wicken 2002). The intent of the treaty, from the British perspective, was to regulate the activities of the Mi'kmaq in order to enable the peaceful colonization and settlement of Mi'kma'ki. For the Mi'kmaq, the intent was to protect their sacred relations with their territories and resources in perpetuity (Wicken 2002; Wildsmith 1992; McMillan 2018). The Mi'kmaq practised treaty diplomacy, *kisa'mue-mkewy*,[3] amongst their citizens and allies, and had processes of community engagement through *mawiomi* (formal gatherings) that included storytelling, ceremonies and rituals, by which they came to a collective understanding of their treaty obligations reflecting their world views (Young, T. 2018). The 1725–26 Treaty laid out protections for the inherent customary rights of the Mi'kmaq, including hunting, fishing, and planting. It was renewed several times between 1749 and 1778, including in 1749 and in 1752, when seven new articles were added. Following the British capture of Louisbourg and the loss of French "control" of Cape Breton, the British again signed several treaties with the Mi'kmaq in an attempt to quell resistance and ensure stability (McMillan 2011; Wicken 2012). The Treaties of 1760 and 1761 established agreements between the parties in regard to the harvest and sale of natural resources, among other things.[4]

At no time did the Mi'kmaq ever abandon their sovereignty or cede any of their lands to the French or the British.[5]

As an orally oriented culture, the Mi'kmaq relied on storytelling to translate knowledge generationally. The ability to recite genealogies and to demonstrate connectedness to places and to each other was central to social interactions and vital to the maintenance of treaty relations. Though the treaties of peace and friendship and the Royal Proclamation guaranteed protection of Mi'kmaq customary land use rights, and defined protocols that assured the exchange of gifts and annual renewal ceremonies, these promises were soon ignored by the British as a result of the influx of settlers and the unfettered colonial appetite for wealth accumulation. Waves of new colonists, hungry for the resources to fuel their capitalist aspirations, began to occupy Mi'kma'ki and soon forced the Mi'kmaq from their traditionally bountiful territories into the most marginal areas (Prins 1996; Paul 2006; Wicken 2012). The failure of the British to maintain their treaty relationships became apparent as the Mi'kmaq were forcefully excluded from the resource economy and treacherously dominated by discriminatory legislation, such as fishing and hunting regulations that protected settler interests over Indigenous Rights. They were violently pushed away from their traditional livelihoods, thus interrupting their long-held sacred connections to territory and jeopardizing prosperity.

Colonization is a process, not an event (Wolfe 1999). Mi'kmaq peoples were further marginalized by settler society with the passage of the British North America Act of 1867, which gave jurisdiction over Indigenous peoples to the newly created federal government. The official policy of the Canadian state became dedicated to the elimination of Indigenous peoples. The Indian Act, 1876, the most discriminatory legislation in Canadian history, was one of many paternalistic tools used to pursue the goals of cultural genocide and to advance the agenda of assimilation through suffocating state control over every minute detail of Indigenous peoples' lives.[6]

It is worth remembering that the Mi'kmaq have not been passive victims in this history. Many people actively protested colonial aggressions through various tactics, such as guerrilla warfare, continuing with ceremonies through clandestine meetings, and embedding the traditional political body of the Grand Council within the Catholic Church. These efforts ensured that the culture, language, and indomitable spirits of the Mi'kmaq Nation are alive and well today. In 2022, legislation in Nova Scotia recognized Mi'kmaw as Nova Scotia's first language. There are numerous notable examples of ways in which the Mi'kmaq specifically, and Indigenous peoples more generally, have resisted colonization, and assert and protect their rights through the courts. These legal battles are instrumental in the establishment and institutionalization of Mi'kmaq consultation and negotiation processes.

Treaty Litigation: Forging the Pathway to Making Things Right

Even with settlers' denial of their treaty obligations that were set out in the covenant chain of Peace and Friendship Treaties made between 1725 and 1778, and despite the imposition of discriminatory laws and racist policies entrenched in British law that criminalized Mi'kmaq livelihoods, and systemically alienated them from their territories and resources, the Mi'kmaq persisted as a nation. They passed their treaty knowledge on from generation to generation around kitchen tables and in formal annual gatherings at St. Anne's Mission in Potlotek. For centuries, the Mi'kmaq made many petitions to the British Crown to negotiate better treatment and respect for their Treaty Rights. When this failed, they turned to the courts.

Consistent with colonial attitudes and systemic discrimination, the courts did not at first recognize the Treaty Rights of the Mi'kmaq Nation. The Canadian justice system was particularly hostile to Indigenous Peoples; provisions in the Indian Act prohibited them from hiring lawyers for decades or from gathering in defence of their rights. Treaties signed before Confederation were thought to be extinguished. For example, Grand Chief Gabriel Sylliboy, the head person of the Mi'kmaq Nation, argued in 1928 that he had a 1752 treaty that protected his right to hunt and sell furs in a case that went to the Nova Scotia Court of Appeal. The Court of Appeal unequivocally rejected Sylliboy's claim of a treaty right to hunt. The Grand Chief was convicted, and the court further stated that Sylliboy had no Treaty Rights (Wicken 2012; Young, J. 2015). Despite this loss, the Mi'kmaq continued to keep the treaties alive in their national consciousness and livelihood strategies (Battiste, M. 2016; McMillan 2018). As a result of Mi'kmaq advocacy, Grand Chief Gabriel Sylliboy was pardoned by the Nova Scotia department of justice in 2017, as a gesture of reconciliation (Nova Scotia 2017).

Tracing the complex history of Indigenous Rights litigation is beyond the scope of this chapter, but it must be noted that a series of cases across the country built the arguments to establish a clear duty of the Crown to consult with Indigenous Peoples and to prioritize Indigenous and Treaty Rights in decision-making processes involving resource development.[7] The germinal case *Calder v. Attorney-General of British Columbia* (1973) recognized Aboriginal Rights based on original occupancy. Afterward, the Nova Scotia Court of Appeal held that the Mi'kmaq had the right to hunt on reserve lands free of provincial game laws and that they held usufruct rights in reserve lands in *Isaac v. The Queen* (1975).

In 1982, partially as a result of the previous decade of political activism and tribal council mobilization, as Indigenous peoples adamantly rejected the 1969 White Paper policy of the Pierre Trudeau government, the rights of Indigenous peoples were formally recognized in the newly repatriated Canadian Constitution.[8] Section 35.1 of the Constitution Act, 1982 recognized and affirmed the existing Aboriginal and Treaty Rights of the Aboriginal Peoples of Canada. The exact meaning of section 35.1 was left ambiguous, particularly with regard to the questions of the meaning of "existing" rights and the exact definition of how these rights can be proven. In light of this uncertainty, many conflicts over resources turned to the courts for clarification, thus leading to a new era of Indigenous Rights litigation. Rather than acting honourably, the state has made every effort to limit Indigenous Rights.

Two important cases dealing with Mi'kmaq Rights came about in the period after 1982, most notably *Simon v. The Queen* (1985), in which the Supreme Court of Canada held that the treaty of 1752 was an existing treaty and it guaranteed certain hunting rights, and *R. v. Denny, Paul and Sylliboy* (1990), which found that the Mi'kmaq have an Aboriginal Right to fish for food.

Arguably the most significant case for Mi'kmaq Rights was *R. v. Marshall* in 1999 (Wildsmith 2001; McMillan 2018). Donald Marshall was a Mi'kmaw man from Nova Scotia who first gained notoriety for being wrongfully convicted of murder when he was seventeen years old. Marshall spent eleven years in prison until he could prove his innocence and was acquitted in 1983. Infamously one of the first wrongful convictions to come to the public's attention, it was a story so horrifying in its revelations of blatant and systemic racism, that it shook the foundations of the Canadian legal system and exposed the widespread discrimination against Indigenous peoples before the law (McMillan 2018). Donald Marshall's wrongful conviction resulted in a Royal Commission of Inquiry to find out what went wrong in his prosecution and presented eighty-two recommendations to address systemic faults in the administration of justice (Hickman 1989, 1).

In trying to recover from the trauma of his wrongful conviction, Donald Marshall turned to his culture and traditions for healing, and he went fishing for eels. Jane McMillan was his fishing partner and spouse at the time and she learned that the significance of Mi'kmaq relationships with marine life were incorporated in every facet of their life for thousands of years, from cosmological belief systems to political and family organization. The premises of Mi'kmaq traditional fisheries were both spiritual and practical, focusing mainly on the well-being and survival of families and community members. The early Mi'kmaq fished, hunted, and collected. Their subsistence activities were governed by the concept of *netukulimk*, which guided harvesting practices aimed at responsible harvesting and co-existence (Prosper et al. 2011). In fishing and selling eels, Marshall was carrying out livelihood activities as had his ancestors before him (McMillan 2012).

Subsistence customs reflected the holistic interconnectedness of Mi'kmaq laws embedded in their tribal consciousness governing their behaviour, particularly in relation to establishing means for survival and food security, such as sharing, providing, and honouring procurement skills. *Netukulimk* denoted the proper customary practice of seeking bounty provided by *Kisu'lk* (Creator) for the self-support and well-being of the individual, family, and the nation, and thus was intimately tied to Traditional Rights. One's place to hunt and fish, taken in its broadest sense, is the tract on which one practices *netukulimk* (McMillan and Prosper 2016). Oral histories, creation stories, myths, petroglyphs, and archival records reveal ritual practices, ceremonies and spiritual concepts relating to resource use, including extraction protocols, taboos, and prohibitions, as indicators of customary stewardship and are primary sources of Mi'kmaw laws (Denys 1908; Hoffman 1955; Paul 2006; Borrows 2010; McMillan 2021). The Mi'kmaq prospered in their fisheries for thousands of years (McMillan and Prosper 2016). In fishing and selling eels, Donald Marshall was carrying out what he believed to be his Treaty Right to earn a livelihood unmolested. However, the joyous relief Donald Marshall experienced exercising his Treaty Rights as an eel fisher was short-lived when Donald, Jane, and Peter Martin were charged with illegal fishing (McMillan 2019).[9]

This incident became the focus of a treaty test case that considerably altered Indigenous and settler resource relations in the Atlantic provinces of Canada. In carrying out an inherent right and treaty-protected practice, Donald Marshall Jr., was charged with three counts under the Maritime Provinces Fishery Regulations: fishing eels without a licence, fishing eels in a closed zone with prohibited gear and selling eels without the authority of a licence (McMillan 2012).[10]

When the Supreme Court of Canada handed down the verdict in *R. v. Marshall* on September 17, 1999, the decision confirmed something the Mi'kmaq people had known for generations—that the rights enshrined in the Peace and Friendship Treaties of 1760–61 had not been extinguished by colonization, and that these rights should help to define the relationship between the Mi'kmaq people and the Canadian state (Coates 2000). The court did not elaborate on how the rights of the Mi'kmaq people should be implemented, instead leaving this open-ended and to be resolved outside of the judiciary through consultation and negotiation.

Fears that Indigenous people would take to the waters and harvest everything at once were heightened when the Department of Fisheries and Oceans (DFO), following its own interpretation of the Supreme Court decision, showed excessive force in restricting Mi'kmaq access to the waters. Video footage of hulking government vessels battering small Mi'kmaw dories to force the occupants overboard into the open ocean and other violent confrontations played out on the nightly news.

The *Marshall* decision sparked increased surveillance and monitoring for all fishers. Racism and competition strained Indigenous and settler relations, pre-empting any potential for co-operation and collaboration in fishery access and co-management. Given the fragile state of the fishery, acrimony had increased not only between settler and Indigenous peoples but also within these groups as well. Despite the opinion of the Supreme Court, Mi'kmaw claims to self-governance in their territories, control over resource management, and equitable access were in practice denied. Media accounts propelled racist animosity towards Indigenous harvesters by perpetuating negative stereotypes and exaggerating instances of overfishing and the use of illegal gear.

In response to unreasonable limits to their livelihoods, the Mi'kmaq began to re-conceptualize and re-implement a holistic approach to the exercise of their Treaty Rights. In doing this, Mi'kmaq and their leadership returned to the concept of *netukulimk* as the values and moral principles reference base upon which to operate Mi'kmaq resource stewardship and governance.[11]

The court's ruling led to a great deal of confusion and conflict, as was seen in communities such as Burnt Church, where tensions erupted into violent clashes between Mi'kmaq and non-Indigenous fishers (Isaac 2001; King 2014). In part because of these hostilities and due to the strength of the outrage of commercial fisheries associations toward the *Marshall* decision, the court took the unprecedented step of issuing a clarification of their original ruling, known as *Marshall (No. 2)* (1999). This rare elucidation of the Court's ruling included the recommendation that further definition of the Treaty Rights of the Mi'kmaq people should be addressed through a process of "consultation and negotiation ... rather than by litigation" (*R. v. Marshall (No. 2)*, 1999, para. 22). Negotiation, when fair and honourable, is preferable to litigation, as it is more closely aligned with Mi'kmaq cultural approaches to justice, which emphasize dialogue, consensus building, compromise, and mutual respect rather than adversarial conflict (McMillan 2016). However, Mi'kmaq are well versed in fighting for their rights, every step of the way, even at the negotiation tables.

From Litigation to Consultation and Negotiation: The Made-in-Nova Scotia Process

In Canada, Indigenous Rights are in part defined and delimited through litigation and negotiation. The implementation and exercising of Indigenous Treaty Rights are highly contentious processes, often confounded by jurisdictional contests between federal and provincial governments over fiduciary responsibilities, and by pervasive systemic discrimination that devalues Indigenous knowledge and favours assimilation or elimination over recognition (Borrows and Coyle 2017). The legitimacy of Canadian claims of sovereignty over Indigenous Peoples and their lands and resources are being challenged through Indigenous peoples' reinvigoration of identity politics, the successful pursuit of Treaty Rights and constitutional litigation, the unqualified adoption of the *United Nations Declaration on the Rights of Indigenous Peoples* (United Nations 2007), and the national movement of reconciliation (Asch, Borrows, and Tully 2018; Borrows et al. 2019).

In response to the negative legacy of colonization, Indigenous communities across Canada are demanding not only participation in, but control over the decision-making and institution building processes that will positively influence the quality of their lives and reflect their constitutionally and treaty-protected rights. Key legal successes and constitutional recognition are linked with Indigenous Peoples' productive mobilization of the spirit and capacity for positive and empowering transformations. But litigation is risky; it is expensive, and slow, and dispositions are often narrowly interpreted by governments in application, even when the Supreme Court of Canada affirms broad application of Indigenous Rights. It is often the case that agents and institutions of the Crown view decisions affirming Treaty Rights as losses (McMillan 2018). This consciousness facilitates a persistently adversarial environment when it comes to consulting and negotiating Indigenous Rights with federal, provincial, and corporate entities.

The Mi'kmaq have successfully litigated for recognition of their Treaty Rights. As a nation, they decided to not participate in the federal claims commission program, but instead established a unique course of action for consultation and negotiation. The Chiefs created an office to diligently manifest Treaty Rights in Nova Scotia to benefit the members of the Mi'kmaq Nation. The negotiation office maintains that they work for the Assembly of Chiefs, that the Chiefs provide them their mandate and the Chiefs make the decisions. They hold firm that they DO NOT negotiate Treaty Rights and they ARE NOT negotiating a modern treaty.

The *Marshall* decision instigated a redistribution of access to natural resources, allowing for increased opportunities for economic development and autonomy. The potential to remedy patterns of dependency and subjugation for Mi'kmaq communities and other Indigenous peoples across the country in favour of sustainable community advancement through the affirmation of Treaty and Aboriginal Rights, and through the substantiation of traditional knowledge, marks an unprecedented turn in colonial relations (McMillan 2016).

The Mi'kmaq leveraged the *Marshall* decision and their livelihood Treaty Rights to demand reliable, productive, and respectful consultation and negotiation relationships with proponents. The Mi'kmaq are interested in self-governance and in developing co-management agreements to establish predictability in access to and sustainability of resources. A key priority is the incorporation of Mi'kmaq resource harvesting governance principles such as *netukulimk*. In 1999, the Supreme Court recognized the 1760–1761 Treaties in *R. v Marshall* as a right to livelihood. This case was significantly transformative for the Mi'kmaq Nation. It substantiated the Made-in-Nova Scotia Process, first organized in 1997 when the Mi'kmaq Chiefs of Nova Scotia, the Government of Nova Scotia, and the Government of Canada signed the Tripartite Memorandum of Understanding (MOU), which was an agreement between the three parties to begin discussions regarding issues and "matters of mutual concern." The Tripartite Forum approach was based on one of the eighty-two recommendations of the Royal Commission on the Donald Marshall Jr. Prosecution (Hickman 1989).

Negotiated by senior Mi'kmaq advisors Viola Robinson, former commissioner of the Royal Commission on Aboriginal Peoples, and law professor Joe B. Marshall, as well as the legal team Bruce Wildsmith and Eric Zscheile, who dedicated their professional lives to advocating for Mi'kmaq Rights, the MOU was signed as a result of pressures to address outstanding rights-related issues, particularly *with* regard to natural resource development. The Mi'kmaq position was, and firmly remains, that they would not be bound by the federal government's comprehensive land claims policy.[12] The MOU was not intended to act as a formal process by which the parties could negotiate specific rights or title claims—it simply represented a commitment by the parties to begin discussions. Following this political commitment to work together to address outstanding issues, representatives from the three parties met to explore options with a view to the creation of a formal negotiation and consultation process. The Mi'kmaq began to build capacity for negotiation within.

After the *Marshall* fishing case, the federal government, through the DFO, responded by entering into separate agreements with eleven of thirteen bands in Nova Scotia, each of the bands in New Brunswick and Prince Edward Island, and three in Quebec, to control their entrance to the fisheries and regulate access to the resource. The Mi'kmaq of Nova Scotia found this tactic divisive and decided to reassert their nationhood in negotiations with federal and provincial governments to regain control over the decision-making processes and to protect the full implementation of their Treaty Rights.

During the great fishery hostilities of 2000–2001, the parties agreed to a joint statement asserting willingness to work together to resolve outstanding issues. Grand Council, Chiefs and tribal councils held exploratory talks to determine the substance of their Treaty Rights. In 2002, through band council resolutions, the Chiefs of the thirteen Mi'kmaw communities agreed to sign an umbrella agreement to confirm the willingness of the Mi'kmaq and the federal and provincial governments to work together to enter into discussions to define, recognize, and implement Mi'kmaw rights. The parties developed terms of reference for consultation, appointed negotiators, and held deliberations on the Made-in-Nova Scotia Process framework agreement. The agreement set out three distinct goals: the continuation of the Tripartite Forum; the commencement of negotiations with a view to the creation of a Framework Agreement on treaty and Aboriginal Rights negotiations; and the initiation of negotiations for the development of a Terms of Reference for a consultation process (Umbrella Agreement 2002).

In 2004, the Made-in-Nova Scotia Process was retitled Kwilmuk Mawklusuaqn (Kwilmu'kw Maw-klusuaqn, "We Are Seeking Consensus"; KMKNO), or the Mi'kmaq Rights Initiative, formalized in a framework agreement in 2007. The agreement outlined negotiation procedures for Treaty Rights as applied to fish, wildlife, forestry, and land. It took a long time to reach a memorandum of understanding, but the process was based on respectful relations and has since led to significantly productive dialogues on governance and on social, cultural, and economic issues.

Kwilmu'kw Maw-klusuaqn Negotiation Office—the Pillars

With the establishment of the KMKNO, the Mi'kmaq were able to invest more time into research and community engagement for input on decision-making. Participatory decision-making was a power long denied by assimilative federal policies, systemic discrimination, and diluted by proponent ignorance of both the duty to consult and of Indigenous Rights generally. Throughout the negotiation process, it was made very clear to the public that the new accord will not be used as an attempt to re-negotiate the Mi'kmaq treaties, nor would it constitute a process leading to their extinguishment, such as in the federal comprehensive claims policy. Throughout the history of KMKNO, maintaining this fact in the consciousness of the nation has been difficult and periodically there are public outcries that KMKNO is "selling out Mi'kmaq treaty rights."[13] Forging collective governance for exercising Indigenous Rights is controversial work that challenges colonial consciousness and pressures governments and private businesses to do things differently to come to agreements that honour the Peace and Friendship Treaties. Nation-to-nation consensus is complex, political, and often unobtainable in the current reconciliation framework where the federal rules and regulations appear as unbendable and sustain colonial structures that oppress and dispossess (Manuel 2017).

Despite the challenges, negotiations for the Framework Agreement continued after the pilot project. An Agreement was officially signed in 2007, and set out the process by which negotiations would take place, as well as the subject matter that could be discussed.[14] The envisioned goal of this process, as noted in the Framework Agreement, was the eventual creation of a "Mi'kmaq of Nova Scotia Accord" that sets out "the manner in which the Mi'kmaq will exercise constitutionally protected rights respecting land, resources and governance" (Made-in-Nova Scotia Framework Agreement 2007). The goal was to empower communities to take control of their own affairs and to create opportunities for equitable participation in Canadian economy.

Chiefs Terry Paul and the late Lawrence Paul, at the time co-chairs of the Assembly of Nova Scotia Chiefs, stated the significance of the agreement: "We will finally be able to achieve what our ancestors set out to do for our people, to protect a way of life that would allow us to provide for ourselves and our families. It is time to make things right. And this negotiation process will help us achieve that" (Kwilmu'kw Maw-klusuaqn n.d.). The province saw the agreement as a landmark in relations between the Nova Scotia government and the Mi'kmaq. It was a significant moment in a spirit of good will and co-operation to build on common learning and a shared interest in fostering a strong Nova Scotia, culturally and economically.

On Treaty Day 2008, the Assembly of Nova Scotia Mi'kmaq Chiefs signed the Mi'kmaq of Nova Scotia Nationhood Proclamation, signalling their commitment, through the Kwilmu'kw Maw-klusuaqn Mission Office (KMKNO), to develop a cohesive system of governance.[15] The chiefs recognized the need to heighten transparency and accountability if they were going to be effectively and equitably responsive in decision-making regarding Treaty Rights implementation. This proclamation, in combination with the framework agreement, guides the Mi'kmaq Rights Initiative negotiations with the Crown and proponents.

In 2010, the Agreement on Consultation was signed to address the direction provided by the Supreme Court of Canada's *Haida* (2004), *Taku River* (2004) and *Mikisew Cree* (2005) decisions. The rulings framed the federal and provincial Crowns' legal duty to consult and where appropriate accommodate, particularly when Crown conduct may adversely impact established or potential Aboriginal and Treaty Rights.

The mission of the KMKNO is to address the historic and current imbalances in the relationship between Mi'kmaq and non-Mi'kmaq people in Nova Scotia and secure the basis for an improved quality of Mi'kmaq life. KMKNO undertakes the necessary research, develops consensus positions on identified issues, and creates public and community awareness in a manner that supports the ability of the Assembly to fully guide the negotiations, the implementation, and exercise of constitutionally protected Mi'kmaq Rights. It is committed to moving forward at a pace determined by the Mi'kmaq themselves, and to balancing individual First Nations autonomy with the collective Mi'kmaq identity, governance, and decision-making required to re-institute Mi'kmaq ways of operating. Five pillars directing the work of the KMKNO are:

1. To achieve recognitions, acceptance, implementation and protection of treaty, title, and other rights of the Mi'kmaq in Nova Scotia;

2. To develop systems of Mi'kmaq governance and resource management;

3. To revive, promote and protect a healthy Mi'kmaq identity;

4. To obtain the basis for a shared economy and social development; and

5. To negotiate toward these goals with community involvement and support.

KMKNO Consultation Processes

The Terms of Reference (ToR) for the Mi'kmaq-Nova Scotia-Canada consultation agreement were signed in 2010 to set the process for consultation between the Crown (represented by either Canada or Nova Scotia) and the Mi'kmaq of Nova Scotia. The Mi'kmaq can participate in the consultation process through committees that are established by the Assembly of Nova Scotia Mi'kmaq Chiefs. These committees are appointed by and report to the Assembly of Chiefs, and the Assembly has control over the composition and tenure of the committees. The ToR do not restrict consultation activity solely to the committees appointed by the Assembly; individual bands can conduct their own consultation if they so choose, and bands have the option to remove themselves from consultations if they see fit (KMKNO Terms of Reference, 2010). The options are clearly laid out in the ToR and are designed to protect a community's unique needs and importantly to provide opportunity for communities to decide how to proceed. As per the ToR, the parties jointly review the terms every three years. For communities who have opted out of a particular consultation, the review process enables them to return to the tables.

According to the consultation Terms of Reference, which are unique to Nova Scotia and the first of its kind for Indigenous nations in Canada, a proponent—as per the Supreme Court of Canada in *Haida* (2004), *Taku* (2004) and *Mikisew Cree* (2005), has no legal duty to consult with the Mi'kmaq except where resource-based projects have potential impacts to the environment. If there are potential impacts, the province must engage in consultation, particularly when regulatory permits and licences are issued, and they may delegate certain procedural aspects of consultation to proponents. Proponents may include private industry, consulting firms, government departments and municipalities. When the federal or provincial government is going to make a decision that could potentially impact Mi'kmaq Rights and title, they are required to formally notify the Assembly by writing a letter to the Chiefs and councils and to the KMKNO.

Once the letters are received by the Assembly, individual communities can decide whether to take the lead on a particular file on the behalf of the Assembly, or they can proceed with consultation on their own, or they can have consultations run through the KMKNO office with the Lead Chiefs of the relevant portfolio overseeing the discussions. First Nation communities frequently defer to the KMKNO for their technical support expertise. Once

KMKNO receives the letter, they co-ordinate the consultation on behalf of the Assembly, unless a community indicates otherwise. Consultation can occur at any stage of a project, from the planning stages to on-site monitoring. Discussions can focus on the protection of resources, cultural and archaeological concerns, Mi'kmaq use and occupancy, historical connections to territory, and the impacts of project construction and operations. While improvements in uptake are occurring, there are still situations where the governments have not adequately triggered a consultation process due to "failure to consistently follow the terms of reference, consultation funding, communications, time gaps, and legislated timeframes" (Indigenous and Northern Affairs Canada 2015).

The duty to consult exists to protect the collective rights of Indigenous peoples. At consultation, the concerns of the Mi'kmaq are brought forward to the Crown. It is not a veto process, nor is it a way to get approval from the Mi'kmaq. It is a forum for addressing Mi'kmaq concerns before the Crown makes a final decision on a project. Without a formal process, the concerns of the Mi'kmaq would not necessarily be heard or addressed. The KMKNO has framed participation in consultation as a responsibility of Mi'kmaq to respond to protect their rights. Advisory groups are created to decide what should be examined, issues to be addressed, and to identify next steps. Advisory groups consist of Elders, researchers, scientists, resource users, conservationists, and people who represent the best interests of the Mi'kmaq. The information they review and collect is brought to the Assembly throughout the consultation process for the input and guidance of the leadership. The Assembly provides instruction by passing resolutions. The dialogue continues between the Assembly, the advisory groups, and the government. Not all consultations result in agreement, but without the dialogue the Mi'kmaq Nation would not have the ability to drive change. The dialogue relies largely on the honour of the Crown. If the Assembly is not satisfied with the accommodations made by the Crown, then the Mi'kmaq can go to court for infringements of Aboriginal and Treaty Rights and title. With the passing of the United Nations Declaration on the Rights of Indigenous Peoples Act in 2021, the duty to respect and recognize the human rights of Indigenous peoples raises the standards and imperative of implementing Treaty Rights, self-governance, and federal and provincial accountability in consultations and negotiations.

By participating in consultation, KMKNO is not giving up any rights claims. They position themselves as protecting time immemorial rights and it is a collective duty to ensure that Mi'kmaq lands and resources will be enjoyed for many years to come. Their slogan is "It is time to make things right." Information about consultations is disseminated through newsletters, press releases, community notices, and articles in the *Mi'kmaq Maliseet Nations News* and through their website, Facebook, YouTube, and X accounts.

The KMKNO consultation team provides feedback on legislation, regulations, and policy. They advocate for and recommend specific items. Potential changes to any government legislation or policy must consider the following:

- Recognize that the Mi'kmaq of Nova Scotia have rights;

- Support and promote responsible resource management, consistent with recognition and affirmation of existing Treaty and Aboriginal Rights;

- Recognize the Mi'kmaq assert co-ownership of natural resources;

- Recognize the Terms of Reference for a Mi'kmaq-Nova Scotia-Canada Consultation Process and that the Province needs to take its duty to consult seriously;

- Recognize there is a unique relationship with the Mi'kmaq of Nova Scotia;

- Be socially responsible;

- Be reflective of the needs of the Mi'kmaq;

- Recognize there is an exception that benefits agreements are developed with the Mi'kmaq prior to project approvals; and

- Identify MEKS as tools used in consultation.

Legislation and regulations currently or recently under review by the consultation team include the following: Children and Family Services Act, Mineral Resources Act, Marine Renewable Energy Act, Environmental Goals and Sustainable Prosperity Act, and Aquaculture regulations and the Fisheries Act. These are transformative areas of inquiry, with outcomes that directly affect the livelihoods of Mi'kmaq families and communities.

The Office of L'nu Affairs in Nova Scotia produced proponent engagement guidelines which emphasize communications, decision-making, and lasting outcomes that should benefit the Mi'kmaq Nation. It is a work in progress with the principles of engagement centred around:

1. Mutual respect—taking into account different interests, perspectives, cultures, understandings and concerns;

2. Early engagement—before final decisions are made— clear and reasonable timelines should be established and communicated, appropriate and proportionate in respect of the decision being made;

3. Openness and Transparency—open lines of communication, provision of timely, accurate, clear and objective information. The Mi'kmaq need to be informed of how their concerns have been considered, and where appropriate, addressed in the planning and decision-making process;

4. Adequate time to review / respond—appropriate and proportionate in respect of the decision being made for the Mi'kmaq to review the information, hold internal discussions, and respond. (Office of Aboriginal Affairs 2012)

KMKNO has a variety of departments mandated to conduct research related to negotiations and consultations to protect Treaty Rights. The Chiefs of the Assembly are responsible for particular portfolios to help co-ordinate and organize the vastly diverse and complex matters that come through the KMKNO's Consultation Department. The evolving portfolios are currently: Archaeology, Benefits, Child Family, Energy, Fisheries, Governance, Social, Cultural Tourism, Nova Scotia Power, Forestry, Wildlife, and Lands. The Lead Chiefs receive all authorities and instructions from the Assembly. Their role is to meet and gather information relevant to their portfolios and present it to the Assembly. In addition to the Chiefs, the Grand Chief and the Grand Captain of the Mi'kmaq Grand Council—the traditional governing body of the Mi'kmaq Nation—are ex officio members of the Assembly.

The Governance portfolio, for example, has the challenging job of determining membership and citizenship. The central discussions are focused on the contentious issues of eligibility to practice Indigenous Rights and who is entitled to receive benefits. The Assembly of Mi'kmaq Chiefs have relied on federally issued Indian Status cards. Since the 1980s, the Native Council of Nova Scotia, representing non-status and off-reserve Indigenous peoples, has issued to their members Aboriginal and Treaty Rights Access cards (ATRA) to access harvesting rights. Enforcement officers once recognized both cards. The Assembly of Mi'kmaq Chiefs asked the province to enter into formal consultation to ensure that the Mi'kmaq maintain control over identifying their membership and verifying who has access to Mi'kmaq harvesting rights (Googoo, R. 2017). In 2022, the Supreme Court of Nova Scotia certified a class-action lawsuit filed by the Native Council of Nova Scotia because the ATRA passport holders lost access to hunting moose in the Cape Breton Highlands. The Newfoundland agreement of recognition of the Qalipu members who now reside in Nova Scotia and the emergence of "Eastern Métis" groups add layers of complexity and increase contestation over the questions of membership and benefits. KMKNO is in the process of creating a system whereby Mi'kmaq determine their own membership using the traditional concepts of *wejikesin* and *ekinawatiken*—translated as "we must go back to our communities and seek their feedback and approval at the outset" (Battiste, J. 2014).

A key priority for the Mi'kmaq Rights Initiative is access to and management of resources. In 2009, KMKNO conducted extensive community negotiations to establish moose hunting guidelines for the nation and are continuing to examine how Mi'kmaq can create a fair and open process for exercising their authority to hunt. The Mi'kmaq continue to work with the federal and provincial Departments of Natural Resources and Environment and Climate Change to institutionalize their Adaptive Moose Management Plan, which includes collaborating to address harvest levels, instituting Mi'kmaq-controlled Harvester Identification and a Mi'kmaq-directed reporting mechanism to monitor harvest levels and locations. This community engagement process is the hallmark of effective, meaningful, and generative Indigenous Rights consultation and implementation in the Atlantic. The cultural significance of the moose hunt cannot be underestimated in its knowledge translation capacities and for its food security redistribution activities when tonnes of meat are shared with community members and organizations who help those struggling on social income assistance (CBC News 2016). Non-Indigenous hunters, however, continue to protest any priority rights of the Mi'kmaq to hunt moose.

KMKNO's Perspective—Protests and Partnership in Nation Rebuilding

The KMKNO works for the Assembly of Chiefs, and the Chiefs are elected by their constituents. The concerns of the constituents drive the mandates of the Chiefs, which in turn influence the priorities of the negotiation and consultation processes. It is ideally a community-driven process. The Assembly generated the five pillars, and these remain the guideposts for implementing Mi'kmaq treaties and Indigenous Rights and title. Harvesting rights (moose and fisheries) were selected as priority areas because despite the constitutional and Supreme Court of Canada affirmations of these rights, there are still conflicts on the ground that need to be resolved to ensure Mi'kmaq are able to access resources and exercise their rights to their full potential without getting charged with violations of hunting and fishing regulations, or trespassing. As the Mi'kmaq work through regulatory control issues, livelihood rights become prioritized.

In order to maintain the community-driven nature of the KMKNO processes, the organization is challenged to sustain engagement on both the mundane and controversial issues it deals with on a day-to-day basis. There are hundreds of ongoing consultations that require meaningful ratification by the membership. The staff of KMKNO understand and take to heart their responsibilities in what is a nation rebuilding process. It is an all-consuming responsibility according to the executive director:

> We always talk with our staff and ourselves, you never leave the work, for us you never leave it at your desk. For us you go home and most of us live in community or our families, we are community members, you always hear about Treaty Rights. You open your window and you look out and you see the traps in the water. You know everything is just right there, you are always in it. You never leave work per se and you never leave your community.[16]

For the director of consultation, the role of Treaty and Indigenous Rights protection is embedded in her lineage, and it is her familial duty to carry out her commitment to the nation.

> I approach it as a personal responsibility. We are in a unique process and I think we have a personal responsibility, not only

a professional responsibility to share the information, to ask the questions of our communities' members, and to take the information they give us back to the tables. It's at the gas station, it's at birthday parties, you don't get away from it, but it is part of our responsibility as a Mi'kmaw person and I think that comes with the dedication and responsibility and that is why you see our negotiators and our team being there for so long. It is that personal investment.[17]

The work is very challenging, with so much at stake on a day-to-day basis. The team takes the responsibility of representation seriously and are increasingly skilled at balancing diverse interests. During the most contentious scrimmages, they are tenacious in their willingness to fight for justice and have the very important role of translating those interests to non-Indigenous audiences, who are often poorly versed in Mi'kmaq knowledge systems, treaty relationships, and Indigenous Rights. Finding the right balance between economic development and protecting the environment are daily efforts for the consultation and negotiation teams:

We are at the table and we have to find a good balance. We need be able to talk to people, even though I say we are tired of fighting, we need to be able to say to people here is what is going on in the areas, here is where we are at. Sometimes I feel that we are a shield for that warrior anger.[18]

A further challenge is keeping nationhood front and centre while respecting the decision of an individual band to pursue its own consultation process. The push and pull factors of collective consultation can get disrupted when federal and provincial policies divide a community, on cost/benefit measures of economic remunerations and the inherent connectedness to the land and its resources that require Mi'kmaw specific stewardship as embodied in the principles of *netukulimk*. Protest can be both productive and destructive for KMKNO. It is a factor beyond their direct control, but if read carefully it can provide valuable insights on the concerns of the community, which can then be translated for the Assembly to determine how best to act in the interests of their members.

Maintaining the collective while respecting community autonomy is a substantial challenge in the evolution of KMKNO. Nationhood gets put to the test when individual bands decide that it is in their best interest to step out of the process. In 2013, the Sipekne'katik band removed itself from KMKNO activities and announced its intention to develop their own consultation process, in order to seek greater input from individual band members. This was a strategy to respond to specific community concerns. Sipekne'katik left the Assembly of Nova Scotia Mi'kmaq Chiefs following disagreements over the Alton Natural Gas Storage Project (Googoo, M. 2016). Sipekne'katik was followed by Millbrook First Nation in May 2016, when the band announced they would be leaving both KMKNO and the Assembly of Chiefs. Sipekne'katik had a changeover in Chief and council during the 2016 election and has since rejoined with the Assembly and the KMKNO on selected files. The Millbrook band withdrew, arguing that the KMKNO process was unclear and was shielded from the scrutiny of the majority of the Mi'kmaq people. The band also expressed their concerns that the negotiation office had expanded beyond its original mandate of treaty implementation. This concern was shared by Mi'kmaw scholar Dr. Sherry Pictou who worried that the KMKNO process is being co-opted by the comprehensive land claims process and will become a victim of the domestication of UNDRIP. This is a process which subsumes UNDRIP's authority into Canadian sovereignty under s. 35 of the Constitution and thus undermines the spirit and intent of Mi'kmaq Treaty Rights and the potential of the declaration to end dispossession and lead to full implementation of Indigenous Rights (Pictou 2018; Manuel 2017). However, the passage of Bill C-15 has potential to ameliorate these concerns and Dr. Pictou is now a District Chief, making significant contributions to the protection of Mi'kmaw livelihood rights and *netukulimk* fishery plans, thus ensuring KMKNO and the Assembly resist co-optation and reject assimilation.

Differing conceptions of how rights should be discussed and implemented has led to both protest and partnerships between the thirteen Mi'kmaq communities in Nova Scotia. A dramatic example of the challenges of effective communication was seen in 2013 in the context of Idle No More, when two Mi'kmaq activists undertook a hunger strike to protest the Made-in-Nova Scotia Process (Howe 2013). The opponents of the process argued that there had been insufficient consultation between government and Indigenous leaders, as well as a lack of consultation between Mi'kmaq leaders and their communities (McMillan, Young, and Peters 2013). After eleven days, the Assembly of Chiefs agreed to halt negotiations until their communities could be better educated regarding the ongoing discussions, thus ending the hunger strike (Howe 2013). Days after the hunger strike ended, Mi'kmaq community members in Cape Breton raised concerns about the KMKNO process, specifically regarding the clarity and accountability of the negotiation process. Several people argued that the process was insufficient as the Mi'kmaq Chiefs dominated it and did not include satisfactory consultation with Mi'kmaq community members (Howe 2013):

> My husband, at one point when we were going through Idle No More, we were attacked a lot and we are so passionate about what we do and it is so important that we are there to do our best to protect (the rights) and we cannot do it alone. There is a role for everyone. When you look at the community groups and the warriors, on some of those consultation files I would love for them to get mad and go and do that (protest) because we need the teeth behind it and we need someone at the table. There is a role for everybody. But when we were being attacked every day, someone told me "you go tell them you are the desk warriors, you are the warriors that fight for this every single day, not just the flash items that come up, it is not for oh I don't like this project, it is for the consistency, that continual push. We fight every day."[19]

The issues of unambiguous accountability are at the root of successful nation rebuilding and productive conflicts have arisen in the recent years of the KMKNO. As expressed by the hunger-striking activists, community members, and individual First Nation communities, the process has been marked by a perceived lack of clarity and confusion regarding the exact goals and actions of the KMKNO. The protestors who undertook the hunger strike pointed out that many of the issues are due to the structure of the band and council system, which is drawn from colonial Indian Act policies and legislation reflecting Western concepts of representative democracy rather than traditional Mi'kmaq conceptions of consensus-based decision-making (Howe 2013). As with most other issues interfering with reclaiming nationhood, the tensions within the KMKNO may be traced back to the impacts of colonialism, treaty denial, and the disruption of Mi'kmaq systems of governance and dissolution of decision-making powers. As Janice Maloney and Twila Gaudet note in the interview, "They know they are stronger together."

Livelihood Fisheries—It's Time to Make Things Right

The Fisheries portfolio and working group is set up under the primary negotiation table known as the Main Table, and has membership from the federal Department of Fisheries and Oceans, Indigenous and Northern Affairs Canada, Nova Scotia's Department of Fisheries and Aquaculture, and the Office of L'nu Affairs.[20] The technicians supporting the KMKNO are currently working on a detailed mandate to negotiate fisheries matters with the goals of supporting moderate livelihood as per the *Marshall* decision and to establish Mi'kmaq laws and authorities, pursuant to Mi'kmaq harvest and management plans. The robust portfolio is focused on rights-based fisheries implementation; sustainable harvesting; fisheries economic development; food, social and ceremonial fisheries; communal commercial fisheries; and aquaculture. These discussions are complex and challenging, particularly as the Crown's position continues to be adversarial rather than conciliatory, and the DFO did not attend the tables to engage with Mi'kmaw led and determined livelihood rights management plans.

Although the *Marshall* decision recognized Mi'kmaw and Indigenous Rights, the plethora of policies, rules, and regulations imposed on Indigenous fishers in order to "include" them in the commercial fishery effectively marginalized their livelihood rights. For instance, officials with the DFO doggedly refused to recognize autonomous community-based management plans such as those put forward by the Listuguj, Esgenoopetitj, Sipekne'katik, Potlotek and Pictou Landing Mi'kmaw communities that resisted being constrained by what they saw as stop-gap measures and narrow interpretations of their rights. Instead, these communities wanted autonomy over resource management and harvesting decisions, and they wanted control over access, procurement, and the distributions of benefits. This autonomy included jurisdiction over livelihood, commercial, as well as food, social and ceremony fisheries. The solution to centuries of broken treaty promises, they argued, was an integrated, sustainable fisheries management program informed by Indigenous ecological knowledge and governed by Indigenous legal principles.

The Supreme Court of Canada said there was a major difference between the Mi'kmaq livelihood fishery and the normal commercial fishery. In the regular commercial fishery, commercial fishers must comply with whatever regulations and licence conditions Canada in its wisdom sees fit to impose. But, while a Mi'kmaq livelihood fishery is subject to regulation by Canada, any such regulation of limitation on the exercise of the right *must be justified* by Canada, as the judge noted in their *R. v Marshall* decision: "In a series of important decisions commencing with *R. v. Sparrow*, [1990] 1 S.C.R. 1075, which arose in the context of the west coast fishery, this Court affirmed that s. 35 aboriginal and Treaty Rights *are* subject to regulation, provided such regulation is shown by the Crown to be justified on conservation or other grounds of public importance" (para. 6). In a livelihood fishery, limitations or restrictions on such matters as seasons and methods of harvest proposed by Canada, *have to be the subject of consultation* by the Mi'kmaw, and have to be justifiable.

The Supreme Court recognized Mi'kmaw and Wolastoqiyik (Maliseet) livelihood rights were to be exercised by authority of the local community. While catch limits can be identified to reflect moderate livelihood, the government cannot unilaterally impose seasonal limits. However, government practice, as noted above, has been one of exclusion. The regulatory framework of the DFO was not decolonized or meaningfully reorganized to honour and uphold Mi'kmaw livelihood rights, despite their mandate letters emphasizing reconciliation and nation-to-nation relationships.

This approach facilitates a persistently adversarial environment when it comes to consulting and negotiating how to secure the implementation of Indigenous Rights with federal, provincial, and corporate entities. As a result, the Crown, through the Ministry of Fisheries and Oceans, stubbornly do not come to the table to discuss restructuring the fishery to protect and prioritize livelihood. They employ a business-as-usual approach, only offering financial packages that pigeonhole livelihood rights into the confines of the commercial regulatory framework. A short-sighted, treaty-ignorant approach that is "unlawful because it failed to recognize or accommodate the treaty right to fish" (Metallic and MacIntosh 2020). This failure in proactive leadership impedes decolonization of the fishery and obstructs reconciliation. What should be a great moment in treaty relations has been muted by resentment, confusion, and reluctance to change. Adversarial spaces are not conducive to conciliatory actions. Instead, injustices are perpetuated, the balance of power remains askew, and livelihood rights get used as a pawn in a broader political strategy of divide and conquer. Mi'kmaw leadership is tired of this lack of respect and the injudicious treatment of their livelihood rights.

On September 17, 2009, the tenth anniversary of the fishing decision, Mi'kmaw leadership gathered in Halifax. It was the first anniversary without

Donald Marshall Junior, who had died on August 6 of that year. The Mi'kmaq nation were mourning, not only the loss of Junior, but also the failure of the Government of Canada to honour the Supreme Court decision and implement the rights set out in the 1760–61 Treaties. Chief Terry Paul's address admonished the governments' failure to recognize Mi'kmaw livelihood rights and demanded change.

In the 2015 mandate letters to his ministers, Prime Minister Trudeau stated that, "No relationship is more important to me and to Canada than the one with Indigenous Peoples. It is time for a renewed, nation-to-nation relationship with Indigenous Peoples, based on recognition of rights, respect, co-operation, and partnership" (Trudeau 2015). In his 2019 mandate letter to Minister Jordan, the third person in three years to hold the position of minister of Fisheries, Ocean, and the Canadian Coast Guard, he wrote:

> There remains no more important relationship to me and to Canada than the one with Indigenous Peoples. We made significant progress in our last mandate on supporting self-determination, improving service delivery and advancing reconciliation. I am directing every single Minister to determine what they can do in their specific portfolio to accelerate and build on the progress we have made with First Nations, Inuit and Métis Peoples. (Trudeau 2019)

In 2019, at the twentieth anniversary of the fishing decision hosted by KMKNO, the DFO, in a symbolic gesture, returned Donald Marshall Junior's eel nets they had confiscated in 1993. People were not in a celebratory mood at the gathering in Membertou, and the leadership and fishers expressed great frustration at having no protection in exercising their livelihood rights. Mi'kmaw harvesters reported that their gear was regularly vandalized, their boats burned, their traps cut; threats and intimidation were the order of the day and the DFO and RCMP could or would not do anything overtly to stop it. And in the weeks following September 17, 2020, the twenty-first anniversary of the Marshall decision, we witnessed with horror the attacks on Mi'kmaw livelihood harvesters escalate and reveal an astonishing level of racism when Sipekne'katik, Potlotek, and Pictou Landing exercised their legal livelihood fisheries. The extent of racialized violence was so dangerous that the Assembly of Nova Scotia Mi'kmaw Chiefs declared a State of Emergency on September

18, 2020 to protect Mi'kmaw harvesters, their families, and supporters. The Assembly co-ordinated assistance across organizations to protect the safety and security of Mi'kmaw affected by political unrest. But the violence continued to escalate as commercial fishing operations accused Mi'kmaw livelihood harvesters of threatening the conservation of the lobster stocks. During an emergency debate in the House of Commons during October 2020, Prime Minister Trudeau said "there is no place for racism in our country. The appalling violence in Nova Scotia must stop now. It's unacceptable, it is shameful, and it is criminal. Above all there is a right to live and fish in peace without being subject to threats and racism" (Zimonjic 2020).

Assimilation is not an option. Mi'kmaw leadership has consistently held firm that, as Indigenous peoples of Mi'kma'ki, they have treaty and constitutionally protected rights to exercise governance over all of their fisheries including food, social and ceremonial, communal commercial, and livelihood, and that they want self-government agreements to uphold, protect and honour those rights. The livelihood fishery is a legal fishery, it is not a symbolic fishery, it is a substantive fishery where the exercise of Mi'kmaw jurisdiction must be prioritized in order to meet the terms and obligations of the treaties. As stated in their submissions to the Royal Commission on Aboriginal Peoples, in terms of jurisdiction, "we have the freedom to manage and regulate our harvest, with levels based on need and on conservation. After we have taken what we need, other governments can manage what's left over on behalf of their citizens, but subject to our consent and our ability to establish that non-Indian use does not threaten the resources" (Royal Commission on Aboriginal Peoples 1992, 131).

After the racist attacks on Mi'kmaw fishers, the government made some efforts to calm the tensions between Indigenous and non-Indigenous communities. The DFO accelerated their efforts to compel First Nations, community by community, to enter into Rights Reconciliation Agreements, a version of the Marshall Response Initiative that was directed at engaging communities in the commercial fishery and participating in regulatory schemes that were at the complete discretion of DFO's minister. The agreements created divisions and orders that were counter to nationhood, to consensus seeking self-government, and are not an implementation of the treaty-protected right to livelihood. Lacking transparency, this method was not advancing the communal nature of Indigenous Rights; instead, it fostered uncertainty and generated disunity in the nation. Tensions over rights implementation were further flared as outspoken fishers' organizations threatened legal action amid false and alarmist claims that purported Mi'kmaw control over their treaty fisheries would undoubtedly jeopardize conservation and ruin the livelihoods of all in Atlantic Canada. The DFO were not engaging in the KMKNO in an honourable manner, "they were stuck in the mindset of their ministerial authority and licensing regime."[21]

Mi'kmaw parliamentarians were compelled to work toward an outcome to advance the collective interests of their communities and were keen to engage all sides "in a true spirit of reconciliation and cooperation to find a fair and durable solution."[22] The parliamentarians, after collaboratively engaging with Mi'kmaq and non-Mi'kmaq stakeholders, sought counsel with the Grand Council and cabinet ministers, and then proposed "a fresh approach to implementing the Marshall decision" based on a partnership between First Nations and the Crown, to generate an Atlantic First Nations Fisheries Authority. Working on behalf of all Mi'kmaq and Wolastoqiyik (Maliseet) Chiefs, and the Regional Chiefs of the Assembly of First Nations Paul Prosper, Roger Augustine, and Ghislain Picard, Senators Daniel Christmas (Nova Scotia) and Brian Francis (PEI) and Member of Parliament Jaime Battiste presented the Atlantic First Nations Fisheries Authority Plan to Ministers Jordan, Bennett (Crown-Indigenous Relations) and Miller (Indigenous Services) on 30 September 2020.

Drawing on the strengths of the educational sectorial self-government agreement of Mi'kmaw Kina'matnewey, an Atlantic First Nations Fisheries Authority was envisioned as a joint approach focused on economic growth of the Indigenous fisheries and bringing transparency to harvesting for commercial, moderate livelihood and food, social and ceremonial purposes. This structure offered a respectful path, a true nation-to-nation partnership approach. The Atlantic First Nations Fishing Authority would be governed by Mi'kmaw laws and the principles of sustainability and responsible harvesting embraced within *netukulimk* livelihood plans and *kisa'muemkewey,* the treaty diplomacy, which requires the honour of the Crown to engage with the nation as a whole. Such an authority would bring certainty to the Atlantic fishery, create a space for constructive dialogue, transparent resource management, even allyship. Significantly, it would substantiate treaty implementation and decolonize the fishery to the benefit of all, Indigenous and non-Indigenous alike. Nothing changed. The Crown, through its DFO agents, lacked vision.

On October 23, 2020, the federal government appointed Allister Surette as the Federal Special Representative with the mandate of acting as a neutral third party in an attempt rebuild relationships between non-Indigenous and Indigenous fishers. Unfortunately, Mr. Surette's Interim Report dated 6 January 2021 indicated that 81% of the individuals interviewed were non-Indigenous. The exclusion of Indigenous voices continues. From a Mi'kmaw perspective, no Federal Representative could act as a neutral third party, and the ministers of Crown-Indigenous Relations, Indigenous Services, and Fisheries and Oceans were not inclined to engage Mi'kmaq and Wolastoqiyik leadership in the proposed Atlantic First Nations Fishing Authority. They chose to stay on their colonial course.

On March 3, 2021, Minister Jordan issued a statement on a "new path for First Nations to fish in pursuit of a moderate livelihood" (Fisheries and Oceans Canada 2021). In the statement, she said, "we have never stopped working with First Nations to reach agreements and implement their right to a moderate livelihood." The Mi'kmaw disagree. Minister Jordan did engage with industry and appointed a Federal Special Representative to "mend broken relationships" but she *did not consult* with the Mi'kmaq, and arbitrarily imposed another licensing regime contrary to the Supreme Court ruling and constitutional protections (Metallic and MacIntosh 2020). People across Mi'kma'ki were outraged.

In response, Senator Dan Christmas issued a statement on March 4, noting that the government's "new path" was headed completely in the wrong direction, and that it falsely asserted that moderate livelihood is a threat to conservation, thus creating an unjustified and provocative infringement of section 35 constitutionally protected Aboriginal and Treaty Rights. Senator Christmas's statement expressed the profound frustration of Mi'kmaw and Wolastoqiyik leadership at the continued top-down, colonial methods to disempower and dispossess Mi'kmaw of their rights (Christmas 2021). Minister Jordan's myopic approach completely ignored the learned advice of PEI Senator Brian Francis, Senator Dan Christmas, and Cape Breton MP Jaime Battiste, as well as of the traditional and elected leaders of the Mi'kmaq and Maliseet nations.

Instead, Minister Jordan pursued an agenda that "dismisses the pursuit of a nation-to-nation, treaty relationship; it abrogates and derogates the constitutionally protected right of self-governance; it completely disrespects the Mi'kmaw traditional law of *netukulimk*—and it totally abandons the duty to consult, as there was absolutely no consultation with the Assembly of Nova Scotia Mi'kmaw Chiefs on this policy statement" (Christmas 2021).

Surette's final report was submitted to minister of Fisheries and Oceans and the Canadian Coast Guard, Bernadette Jordan, and minister of Crown-Indigenous Relations Carolyn Bennett on March 31, 2021. In the report, Surette states:

> I am grateful to the over 100 individuals that did meet with me, and some on multiple occasions.
>
> I had hoped to have more discussions with representatives from Indigenous communities. I have reached out to all Indigenous communities in the Maritimes and the Gaspé region and am very grateful to those that I had the opportunity to meet with and discuss the issue at hand.
>
> Regarding my numerous attempts to engage with certain Indigenous communities, for future reference, I would like to note barriers of why they declined to meet with me. In summary, the following were given as reasons to not meet with me: Fisheries is a matter of constitutionally affirmed Aboriginal and treaty rights, hence, Indigenous communities are engaged in formal agreements that govern their relationship with the Crown as well as in formal consultation processes. These First Nations that declined the invitation (which included the majority of Nova Scotia, amongst others) also indicated that they would want, at the least, a co-chair or a second person selected by them when agreeing to participate in a process that deals with issues of concern to them (Surette 2021).

By April 2021, the High Commissioner of the United Nations Human Rights Office was alerted by the Chair of the Committee on the Elimination of Racial Discrimination that the Committee had considered information it received under its early warning and urgent action procedure, related to allegations of acts of racist violence against Mi'kmaw peoples in Nova Scotia. The evidence of serious human rights violations experienced by Mi'kmaw livelihood fishers and their families was gathered and submitted by a team of Mi'kmaw lawyers on behalf of Sipekne'katik Mi'kmaw fishers with the support of the Chief Mike Sack and Council. The Committee on the Elimination of Racial

Discrimination (2021) called on Canada to investigate the racists acts of violence, investigate the alleged lack of response by Canada to protect Mi'kmaw from violence, prevent further acts of violence and to "respect, protect and guarantee the rights of Mi'kmaw peoples in relation to their fishing activities and territories, as well as their rights to be consulted, to food and cultural rights, including the measures taken to repeal federal and provincial laws, as well as policies and regulations that unduly limit such rights."

The report of the Standing Committee on Fisheries and Oceans, *Implementation of the Mi'kmaw and Maliseet Treaty Right to Fish in Pursuit of a Moderate Livelihood*, presented to the House of Commons May 13, 2021, made forty recommendations that largely aligned with the proposed Atlantic First Nations Fishing Authority. For example,

> Recommendation 1, that the Government of Canada recognize the Mi'kmaw and Maliseet right to a moderate livelihood fishery as a foundation of the Government of Canada's nation-to-nation relationship with the Mi'kmaq and Maliseet nations;

> Recommendation 8, that the federal government recognize the Mi'kmaw and Maliseet treaty right to harvest, sell fish, and co-manage moderate livelihood fisheries as the foundation of the Government of Canada's nation-to-nation relationship with Mi'kmaq and Maliseet nations;

> and

> Recommendation 11, that the Government of Canada acknowledge that Mi'kmaq and Maliseet have the rights to manage and develop resources for their economies with the guidance of their traditional governance institutions, Elders, and leaders, determining manner of ownership, access, manner and pace of economic development derived from the access and use of the resources within their traditional ancestral homeland territories, and within the Constitution and laws of Canada. (McDonald 2021).

These recommendations reflect what Mi'kmaw leaders have been insisting upon since the signing of the Peace and Friendship Treaties in the 1700s.

Mi'kmaw and Wolastoqiyik leaders continue to develop the proposed Atlantic First Nations Fisheries Authority. Seeking additional tools to protect Indigenous Treaty and Constitutional Rights, two Mi'kmaw Senators, the Honourable Dan Christmas (Nova Scotia) and the Honourable Brian Francis (PEI), with the support of Mi'kmaw member of Parliament Jaime Battiste, led the difficult, but successful, final debate to pass Bill C-15. The bill received Royal Assent and became law on national Indigenous Peoples' Day, June 21, 2021. The enactment provides that the Government of Canada must take all measures necessary to ensure that the laws of Canada are consistent with the *United Nations Declaration on the Rights of Indigenous Peoples* (United Nations 2007) and that the Canadian government must prepare and implement an action plan to achieve the objectives of the Declaration.

In September 2021, Minister Jordan lost her seat in the South Shore-St. Margarets riding under heated criticism of her handling of the dispute involving Indigenous fishing rights and her inability to appease the interests of non-Indigenous commercial fishers who vote in that riding.[23]

In December 2021, the prime minister's mandate letters directed that "every Minister [is] to implement the United Nations Declaration on the Rights of Indigenous Peoples) and to work in partnership with Indigenous Peoples to advance their rights" (Trudeau 2021). DFO Minister Murray, who resides in British Columbia, was directed to "work with Indigenous partners to better integrate traditional knowledge into planning and policy decisions" and to "advance consistent, sustainable and collaborative fisheries arrangements with Indigenous and non-Indigenous fish harvesters" (Trudeau 2021). The legal, social, technical capacities of the Mi'kmaw nations and KMKNO to take on the governance of an Atlantic First Nations Fishing Authority continue to expand.

Mobilizing Mi'kmaq Authority

The priorities of Mi'kmaw leadership remain the well-being, security, and sustainability of the rights of the nation, as they have for centuries. Honouring the Peace and Friendship Treaties are at the heart of Indigenous and settler relations. Their position is a steady, enduring patience that is gathering strength as Mi'kmaw resist the government's efforts to assimilate livelihood rights into a bureaucratic regulatory framework. With unwavering courage and steadfast belief in their rights to livelihood, Mi'kmaq leadership through KMKNO resist attempts to buy out, minimize or bury the Mi'kmaw Peace and Friendship Treaties.

At the forefront to cultural resurgence are the Lʼnu Saqmaw or Grand Chief of the Grand Council, Norman Sylliboy, Kji Keptin Antle Denny, and the Putus, along with their Council of Keptins, are the leaders and diplomats governing the seven districts that comprise Mi'kma'ki. The Grand Council is instrumental in *kisa'muemkewey*, treaty diplomacy, and in keeping the spirit and intent of treaties alive and in action. Lʼnu Saqmaw rejects any government interference with the exercise of Mi'kmaw livelihood rights; any plans issued by the DFO that attempt to regulate the fishery, such as the Rights Reconciliation Agreements, are directly in contravention of Mi'kmaw rights to self-determination and self-governance. Tired of the "divide and conquer" approach of the federal government, Grand Chief Sylliboy is working with the Grand Council and KMKNO to unify the nation, encouraging each community to build strong livelihood plans that are self-determined, community-led, and reflect the principles of *netukulimk* to collectively benefit all Mi'kmaw citizens. Lʼnu Saqmaw (Grand Chief) Norman Sylliboy expressed his view that the starting point for discussions should be seeking an understanding from where we come from by "honouring our ancestors"—*ta'n wetapeksi'k* in Mi'kmaq. To seek such an understanding, one must first carefully listen to the background and experiences of others (McMillan and Wien 2022).

A central responsibility of Lʼnu Saqamaw is to sustain treaty relations and the integrity of the Peace and Friendship Treaties through education. He encourages people to not sell their Treaty Rights and to refuse to sign any agreements that undermine Mi'kmaw rights to livelihood. Lʼnu Saqamaw Sylliboy is working with Keptins from across Mi'kma'ki to reignite customary protocols in the seven districts. Above all else, Lʼnu Saqmaw is clear that the government cannot put a price tag on Mi'kmaw treaty and constitutionally protected livelihood rights and is demanding transparency and inclusion in all discussions pertaining to the management of the resources. In a meeting with Mi'kmaw fishers Lʼnu Saqmaw Sylliboy stated:

> When the chiefs were discussing the agreements—it was a problem, you cannot put a price tag on our treaties. I told them don't use money, don't put a dollar on our rights. You cannot quantify, when you use dollar signs you cannot guarantee the future.[24]

At the direction of Mi'kmaw Chiefs and with the blessings of the Grand Council, KMKNO is working with the Unamaki Institute of Natural Resources, the Mi'kmaw Conservation Group, the Atlantic Policy Congress of First Nations Chiefs Secretariat, and other community-based experts to assist in the development of consensus-based standards for resource governance and management through the implementation of *netukulimk* livelihood fishery plans. At the heart of *netukulimk* plans are the principles of sustainability, the protection of Treaty Rights, and the safety and security of responsible harvesters. These are fisheries for the future, *Elmkinek'eway*—an organizing principle for the Atlantic First Nations Fisheries Authority.

In the absence of nation-to-nation recognition of self-government for fisheries, or the establishment of an Atlantic First Nations Fisheries Authority, individual communities such as Potlotek and Pictou Landing have advanced *netukulimk* livelihood plans with KMKNO to secure their economic well-being, protect and honour the resources, and hold harvesters accountable. Other communities have decided to co-ordinate their efforts by forming regional collectives. For example, the Kespukwitk Netukulimk Livelihood Fisheries Management Plan, a collaborative fishery management plan for Acadia, Bear River, and Annapolis Valley First Nations to exercise their Treaty Rights, was established in November 2021 with the support of District Chief Dr. Sherry Pictou and other Chiefs of the Assembly. Harvesters designated under the plan are currently authorized to fish up to 3,500 *jakej* (lobster) traps, up to 70 per harvester during established seasons in the waters of the traditional Kespukwitk District, which is one of the seven districts of Mi'kma'ki traditionally governed by the Grand Council.

The resurgence of *netukulimk* as the sacred foundation for treaty implementation is characteristic of Mi'kmaw ingenuity and emblematic of Mi'kmaw leadership. *Netukulimk* livelihood plans exemplify the Mi'kmaw philosophy to use the natural bounty provided by Creator for the self-support and physical, social, cultural, spiritual well-being. Mi'kmaq leadership are actively advocating for and building the legitimacy of *netukulimk* livelihood plans, both within their communities, that have long been suffocated by oppressive colonial policies of assimilation, and within the communities that have failed to recognize and honour Mi'kmaw inherent and Treaty Rights. It is an empowering and holistic approach to living well within the world and with each other, while simultaneously bringing forward enforceable harvesting practices and standards of sustainability.

Conclusion

The 2008 Nationhood Proclamation stated that the Mi'kmaq would seek to create new governance structures that better represent their interests and enhance the quality of life for Mi'kmaq people in Nova Scotia. There is presently a gap between the current, colonial-dominated governance structures that perpetuate conflicts within and between communities, and the future governance systems envisioned to improve the lives of Mi'kmaq people collectively through positive treaty relations, state fulfillment of its fiduciary obligations, and more responsible and reconciliatory recognition of Mi'kmaq Rights by federal and provincial ministries and corporations wishing to utilize Indigenous lands and resources. As negotiations continue regarding the reform and re-creation of governance structures, negotiators and community representatives will have to do what they can to counteract the negative pressures of the current system. In practical terms, this means putting more effort into community engagement and consultation. In order for meaningful alternative governance structures to be established, the people sitting at the negotiating table must do all they can to ensure the diverse opinions and values of the Mi'kmaq people are evenly represented in their decisions. By openly addressing issues of accountability and transparency, expanding opportunities for community feedback, the results of negotiations and consultation will continue to gain legitimacy and efficacy in rights implementation.

In July 2022, after hearing from Executive Director of KMKNO Janice Maloney and others, the Standing Senate Committee on Fisheries and Oceans released its report *Peace on the Water: Advancing the Full Implementation of Mi'kmaq, Wolastoqiyik and Peskotomuhkati Rights-Based Fisheries* (Manning 2022). It puts forward ten recommendations including a three-step plan to move forward with the full implementation of the rights-based fisheries:

1. To immediately review, amend, modify as necessary all relevant laws, regulations, policies and practices regarding rights-based fisheries to ensure they are in line with the UNDRIP;

2. Interim Nation-to-nation agreements using section 4.1 of the Fisheries Act—true shared decision making;

3. Permanent step—introduce new legislation in cooperation with Mi'kmaw Wolastoqiyik and Peskotomuhkati, to create

a new legislative framework that will allow for the full implementation of rights-based fisheries.

The priorities of Mi'kmaw leadership remain the well-being, security, and sustainability of the rights of the nation, as they have for centuries. Honouring the Peace and Friendship Treaties are at the heart of Indigenous and settler relations. The remedy, for many, requires full recognition of Mi'kmaw rights and title, meaningful consultation, and fulfillment of the fiduciary obligations of the Crown. The authority of Indigenous legal principles and practices must be recognized by DFO and supported for all of us to live in our shared futures as a just society.

To conclude, the KMKNO negotiation and consultation processes make significant and meaningful impacts on the relationship between the Mi'kmaq and settler society. By entering into negotiations as equal partners with the governments of Canada and Nova Scotia, the Mi'kmaq are able to work towards the recognition and implementation of their Indigenous and Treaty Rights. The process has been laborious, long, slow, and at times wrought with tension, but it has generated foundations for self-governance. In order to ensure the success of the process, those representing the Mi'kmaq, namely the Assembly and the technical support teams of KMKNO recognize they must address the issues of openness and accountability or risk losing the support of the Mi'kmaq they represent. Only a legitimate negotiation process, built upon meaningful recognition of the rights of the Mi'kmaq, can lead to positive, sustainable change in Nova Scotia. There is much to do in order to address the centuries of colonialism, which the Mi'kmaq have endured, and the work of KMKNO is germinal in rebuilding the nation. It is the foothold for establishing jurisdiction for self-determination in the formation and enforcement of Mi'kmaq laws, self-identification of beneficiaries and infrastructure for self-government.

The province retains accountability for consultation and is responsible for ensuring the proponent engagement with the Mi'kmaq is adequate—the standards for provincial and federal fulfillment of their treaty obligations and responsibilities must be much higher, faster, and stronger. Part of the process involves decolonizing policies and processes through Treaty Rights education, which is currently being undertaken by the province in a wholesale curricular change and in the provision of treaty education courses for civil servants. It is a positive direction, which may shift the discourse from rights recognition as something the Crown and settlers have to give up, to substantive and just treatment of Mi'kmaw nationhood. The federal government has work to do.

Situated within Mi'kmaq legal principles, the Marshall Inquiry recommendations, the KMKNO pillars, the Truth and Reconciliation Commission Calls to Action (Sinclair 2015), and in the UN Declaration on the Rights of Indigenous Peoples, are the tools necessary for refreshing, restructuring, and achieving the treaty implementation and nation-to-nation relationships between Indigenous peoples and the province of Nova Scotia and the Government of Canada. From these principles, a comprehensive action plan that establishes Indigenous laws and governing institutions that enshrine and operationalize Treaty Rights as a regular course of business can be developed and sustained. This will require, from all parties, the careful and transparent maintenance of consultation and consent processes as well as the replacement or elimination of legislation, policies, and practices that perpetuate systemic discrimination, produce inequality, and deny Indigenous Rights, in order to foster an environment of reconciliation that facilitates self-determination. Prime Minister Trudeau in the mandate letters to his ministers stated that, "No relationship is more important to me and to Canada than the one with Indigenous Peoples. It is time for a renewed, nation-to-nation relationship with Indigenous Peoples, based on recognition of rights, respect, co-operation, and partnership" (Trudeau 2017). It is time to make things right.

NOTES

1   McMillan is grateful to the many Mi'kmaw people who shared their insights that informed this chapter, particularly co-authors Janice Maloney and Twila Gaudet and the members of the KMKNO team. Many thanks to Dr. Sherry Pictou, Dr. Albert Marshall, and the wonderful people exploring understandings of *netukulimk*, including Kerry Prosper, Naiomi Metallic, Tuma Young, Justin Martin, Clifford Paul, the Mi'kmaw Conservation Group, Unama'ki Institute of Natural Resources, Atlantic Policy Congress, Dr. Shelley Denny, Melissa Nevin, and StFX and Dalhousie students. Special thanks to Senator Dan Christmas and MP Jaime Battiste. Preliminary historical research on KMKNO was supported the University of Calgary School of Public Policy and Alex Miller. Many thanks for the inspiration and extraordinary patience of editors Jennifer Winter and Brendan Boyd. As ever, I hope this work honours the legacy of Donald Marshall Jr.

2   Positioned between the French colonies along the St. Lawrence River and the American colonies to the south, Mi'kma'ki (or Acadia, as it was known to Europeans at the time) became a battleground between French and British colonial powers. Beginning in the early 1600s and lasting for roughly 150 years, the territory of Acadia was the site

of many violent clashes between the French and English (Paul 2006). Many Mi'kmaq fought alongside the French in conflicts throughout this period. After Port Royal fell to British control in 1710, the French ceded control of mainland Nova Scotia to the British through the Treaty of Utrecht in 1713. The French maintained control of Unama'ki, what is now Cape Breton Island, where they built the Fortress of Louisbourg, which became the stronghold of French military presence on the Atlantic coast (Upton 1979).

3 Tuma Young (2018) notes that this word refers to the treaty diplomacy processes of the Mi'kmaq. *Mawiomi* is a formal gathering for establishing and renewing relationships.

4 For excellent scholarship on Mi'kmaw Peace and Friendship Treaties see William C. Wicken's *The Colonization of Mi'kmaw Memory and History, 1794–1928: The King v. Gabriel Sylliboy* (Toronto: UTP, 2012) and *Mi'kmaq Treaties on Trial: History, Land, and Donald Marshall Junior* (Toronto: UTP, 2002).

5 In 1763, King George III of England issued a Royal Proclamation, which became the basis for the creation of new colonial governments in North America. The Royal Proclamation also decreed that the lands of Indigenous peoples, which had not been purchased or ceded to the Crown, be reserved for use by Indigenous nations.

6 See Arthur Manuel's *The Reconciliation Manifesto: Recovering the Land Rebuilding the Economy* (Toronto: Lorimer, 2017).

7 *R. v. Sparrow* (1990) established that the Crown is legally accountable to Indigenous peoples, which became the foundation of the principle upon which the duty to consult arises. Subsequent cases including *Delgamuukw* (1997), *Haida Nation* (2004), *Taku River* (2004), and *Mikisew Cree* (2005) helped to develop the doctrine further, embedding in case law principles such as the priority of Aboriginal and Treaty Rights in decision-making processes and the inclusion of First Nations in resource development projects (Morellato 2008).

8 The White Paper policy drafted by Minister of Justice Jean Chrétien for the Trudeau government proposed to convert reserves to private property and to eliminate Indian status, thus removing the legal identities of Indigenous peoples and their rights to their lands.

9 The statement of facts presented to the Provincial court in Antigonish read:

> On August 24, 1993, and at or near Pomquet Harbour, Donald Marshall (an aboriginal person, being a status Mi'kmaq Indian registered under provisions of the *Indian Act* and a member of the Membertou Band, an Indian Band under the *Indian Act*) and Leslie Jane McMillan brought their eels from the holding pens ashore at the location where they kept their boats. This location is situated on lands that are part of the Afton Indian Reserve, at Antigonish County. Marshall helped weigh and load his eels onto a truck belonging to South Shore Trading Company, New Brunswick. South Shore is engaged in the purchase and sale of fish. Marshall sold 463 pounds of his eels to South Shore at $1.70 per pound. Marshall did not at any time hold a licence within the meaning of S. 4(1)(a) of the Maritime Provinces Fishery Regulations and S. 35(2) of the Fishery Act with respect to fishing for or selling eels from Pomquet Harbour (*R. v. Marshall* [1999] 3 S.C.R 26014).

10 The charges against Jane McMillan were dismissed early on in the trial as the late Judge Embree understood the case to be a matter of Indigenous Treaty Rights and she is not an Indigenous person.

11   See McMillan (2018), 87–88. The concept of *netukulimk* (responsible harvesting) guided Mi'kmaw resource use and management and lay at the heart of Mi'kmaw legal consciousness and *tplutaquan* (law). To practice *netukulimk* required Mi'kmaq to individually and collectively seek the bounty that *Niskam* (the Creator) had provided to the ancestors but to do so in a way that respected and honoured the places where one hunts, gathers, and fishes, along with the spirits that reside there. Prior to harvesting, Mi'kmaq made offerings and prayers, "enacting a reverence for all things of creation imbued with spirit." *Netukulimk* is about respect, reverence, responsibility, and reciprocity. Its practice and philosophy embrace co-existence, interdependence, and community spirit. Failure to practice *netukulimk* could lead to a failed hunt; a poor harvest; spiritual sanctions; or communal sanctions, shunning, or shaming.

12   The federal government has had a policy to negotiate comprehensive land claims or modern treaties with Indigenous groups and provincial or territorial governments since 1973. There is a great deal of criticism of this policy, and it has undergone revisions (Monchalin 2016). See for example Eyford (2015).

13   Some members of the Mi'kmaw Nation worry that the office acts on its own volition and is selling out sacred Mi'kmaw Treaty Rights by entering into agreements with corporate entities and federal and provincial governments that do not respect Mi'kmaw sacred interconnectedness with the environment. Some people reject the authority of Indian Act Chiefs. Some think negotiation takes too long, dilutes Treaty Rights, and prefer immediate action in order to meet the urgent housing, employment, education, health and justice needs of their families and communities.

14   The process was crafted by the Mi'kmaq legal team lead by Bruce Wildsmith and Eric Zscheile with the late Honourable Jim Prentice for the federal government and the late Michael Baker for the province.

15   Today, the KMKNO's board of directors is composed of the chiefs of the assembly, the national Assembly of First Nations' regional vice-chief, the Mi'kmaw grand chief, the kji keptin, and two district chiefs with ex officio status.

16   Interview October 12, 2017. On file with author.

17   Interview October 12, 2017. On file with author.

18   Interview October 12, 2017. On file with author.

19   Interview October 12, 2017. On file with author.

20   The Main Table is where negotiations between federal, provincial and Mi'kmaw governments take place. A first priority of the Main Table was to negotiate a process to address the Crown's duty to consult on any proposed activities that may impact Aboriginal, title and Treaty Rights. The province of Nova Scotia changed the name of its Office of Aboriginal Affairs to the Office of L'nu Affairs on February 23, 2021 (Office of L'nu Affairs 2021).

21   Interview October 12, 2017. On file with author.

22   Letter dated September 30, 2020, authored by The Hon. Daniel Christmas, The Hon. Brian Francis, Mr. Jaime Battiste.

23   According to the 2006 census, 97.1% identified as White, 1.5% as First Nations and 0.6% as Black. In the 2016 census 5% self-identified as Indigenous.

24   Interview January 27, 2021. On file with author.

References

Asch, M., J. Borrows, & J. Tully, eds. 2018. *Resurgence and Reconciliation: Indigenous-Settler Relations and Earth Teachings*. Toronto: University of Toronto Press.

Augustine, Stephen. 2016. "Negotiating for Life and Survival." In *Living Treaties: Narrating Mi'kmaw Treaty Relations*, ed. Marie Battiste (Sydney: Cape Breton University Press), 16–23.

Battiste, Jaime. 2014. "Wejikesiek: Is it Time to Exercise Our Mi'kmaq Jurisdiction over the Moose Hunt?" https://www.mmnn.ca/2014/06/wejikesiek-is-it-time-to-exercise-our-mikmaq-jurisdiction-over-the-moose-hunt/.

Battiste, Marie, ed. 2016. *Living Treaties: Narrating Mi'kmaw Treaty Relations*. Sydney: Cape Breton University Press.

Borrows, J. 2010. *Canada's Indigenous Constitution*. Toronto: University of Toronto Press.

Borrows, J., L. Chartrand, O. Fitzgerald, R. Schwartz, eds. 2019. *Braiding Legal Orders: Implementing the United Nations Declaration on the Rights of Indigenous Peoples*. Waterloo: Centre for International Governance Innovation.

Borrows, J. and M. Coyle, eds. 2017. *The Right Relationship: Reimagining the Implementation of Historical Treaties*. Toronto: University of Toronto Press.

CBC News. 2016. "For M"kmaq, Hunting Moose is 'The Heart and Soul of What the Creator has Designed.'" *CBC News*, November 29, 2016. http://www.cbc.ca/news/canada/nova-scotia/cape-breton-moose-hunt-mi-kmaq-elder-1.3872837.

Christmas, Senator Daniel. 2021. "Statement by Nova Scotia Senator Dan Christmas on DFO's New path for First Nations to fish in pursuit of a moderate livelihood." Statement released by Senator Christmas, March 4, 2021. https://www.aptnnews.ca/wp-content/uploads/2021/03/Senator-Dan-Christmas.pdf.

Coates, Ken. 2000. *The Marshall Decision and Native Rights*. Montreal: McGill-Queens University Press.

Committee on the Elimination of Racial Discrimination. 2021. CERD/EWUAP/103rd Session/2021/MJ/CS/ks. April 30, 2021. United Nations. Accessed at https://web.archive.org/web/20220126210358/https://tbinternet.ohchr.org/Treaties/CERD/Shared%20Documents/CAN/INT_CERD_ALE_CAN_9398_E.pdf.

Denys, Nicolas. 1908. *The Description and Natural History of the Coasts of North America (Acadia)*. Trans. W. F. Ganong. Toronto: The Champlain Society.

Eyford, Douglas R. 2015. *A New Direction: Advancing Aboriginal and Treaty Rights*. Ottawa: Government of Canada. https://www.rcaanc-cirnac.gc.ca/eng/1426169199009/1529420750631

Fisheries and Oceans Canada. 2021. "Minister Jordan Issues Statement on a New Path for First Nations to Fish in Pursuit of a Moderate Livelihood." Statement by the Office of the Minister of Fisheries, Oceans and the Canadian Coast Guard, Government of Canada. March 3, 2021. https://www.canada.ca/en/fisheries-oceans/news/2021/03/minister-jordan-issues-statement-on-a-new-path-for-first-nations-to-fish-in-pursuit-of-a-moderate-livelihood.html.

Googoo, Chief Rod. 2017. "Remarks Respecting ATRA and Mi'kmaq of Nova Scotia Harvester Identification." Nova Scotia Hunters and Anglers Conference, March 25, 2017. https://web.archive.org/web/20201023005610/http://mikmaqrights.com/wp-content/uploads/2017/03/Chief-Rod_Hunters-and-Anglers_25Mar17.pdf.

Googoo, Maureen. 2016. Millbrook Second NS First Nation to Leave Mi'kmaq Rights Initiative. *Kukukwes News*, May 20, 2016. http://kukukwes.com/2016/05/20/millbrook-second-ns-first-nation-to-leave-mikmaq-rights-initiative/.

Henderson, James. 1997. *The Mi'kmaw Concordant*. Halifax: Fernwood Publishing.

Hickman, T. A. 1989. *Royal Commission on the Donald Marshall, Jr., Prosecution: Digest of Findings and Recommendations*. [Halifax, NS]: Province of Nova Scotia.

Hoffman, Bernard. 1955. *Historical Ethnography of the Micmac of the Sixteenth and Seventeenth Centuries*. PhD. diss., Department of Anthropology, Berkeley.

Howe, Miles. 2013. "Hunger Strike Ends on Day 11, Made in Nova Scotia Process Halted." *Halifax Media Co-op*, March 12, 2013. http://halifax.mediacoop.ca/story/hunger-strike-ends-day-11-made-nova-scotia-process/16720.

Indigenous and Northern Affairs Canada. 2015. *Evaluation of Consultation and Accommodation*. April 2015. Ottawa: Government of Canada. https://www.rcaanc-cirnac.gc.ca/eng/1458737607040/1537894208416.

Isaac, Thomas. 2001. *Aboriginal and Treaty Rights in the Maritimes: The Marshall Decision and Beyond*. Saskatoon: Purich Publishing Ltd.

King, Sarah. 2014. *Fishing in Contested Waters*. Toronto: University of Toronto Press.

Kwilmu'kw Maw-klusuaqn. "We Are Seeking Consensus." *Kwilmu'kw Maw-klusuaqn*. http://mikmaqrights.com.

Kwilmu'kw Maw-klusuaqn: Mi'kmaq Rights Initiative. n.d. *Our History*. https://mikmaqrights.com/?page_id=7.

Made-in-Nova Scotia Framework Agreement. Mi'kmaq, Nova Scotia, Canada. 23 February 2007. https://novascotia.ca/abor/docs/Framework-Agreement.pdf.

Manning, Fabian. *Peace on the Water: Advancing the Full Implementation of Mi'kmaq, Wolastoqiyik and Peskotomuhkati Rights-based Fisheries*. Ottawa: Senate of Canada, 2022.

Manuel, A. 2017. *The Reconciliation Manifesto: Recovering the Land Rebuilding the Economy*. Toronto: Lorimer.

McDonald, Ken. 2021. *Implementation of the Mi'kmaw and Maliseet Treaty Right to Fish in Pursuit of a Moderate Livelihood*. Ottawa: House of Commons, Canada. https://www.ourcommons.ca/Committees/en/FOPO/StudyActivity?studyActivityId=10962295.

McMillan, L. Jane. 2011. "Colonial traditions, Cooptations, and Mi'kmaq Legal Consciousness." *Law and Social Inquiry Journal of the American Bar Foundation* 36, no. 1: 171–200.

————. 2012. "Mu kisi maqumawkik pasik kataw—We Can't Only Eat Eels: Mi'kmaq Contested Histories and Uncontested Silences." *Canadian Journal of Native Studies* 32, no. 1: 119–42.

————. 2016. "Living Legal Traditions: Mi'kmaw Justice in Nova Scotia." *UNB Law Journal* 67: 187–210.

————. 2018. *Truth and Conviction: Donald Marshall Jr. and the Mi'kmaw Quest for Justice.* Vancouver: University of British Columbia Press.

————. 2019. "Committing Anthropology in the Muddy Middle Ground." In *Transcontinental Dialogues: Activist Alliances with Indigenous Peoples of Canada, Mexico, and Australia,* ed. A. Hernández Castillo, S. Hutchings, and B. Noble (Tucson: University of Arizona Press), 65–92.

————. 2021. "Rooted in Mi'kma'ki: Living L'nu Constitutionalism." *Rooted* 1, no. 1: 33–35. https://issuu.com/rootedmcgill/docs/rootedvol1issue1

McMillan, L. Jane, and Kerry Prosper. 2016 "Remobilizing Netukulimk: Indigenous Cultural and Spiritual Connections with Resource Stewardship and Fisheries Management in Atlantic." *Reviews in Fish Biology and Fisheries* 26, no. 4: 629–47.

McMillan, L. Jane and Fred Wien. 2022. "A Mi'kmaq Nation Approach: Conversations with Mi'kmaw Leaders." In *Contested Waters: The Struggle for Rights and Reconciliation in the Atlantic Fishery* ed. Fred Wien and Rick Williams (Halifax: Nimbus Publishing), 182–92.

McMillan, L. Jane, Janelle Young, and Molly Peters. 2013. "The Idle No More Movement in Eastern Canada." *Canadian Journal of Law and Society* 28, no. 3: 429–31.

Metallic, Naiomi and Constance MacIntosh. 2020. "Canada's Actions Around the Mi'kmaq Fisheries Rest on Shaky Legal Ground." *Policy Options,* November 9, 2020. https://policyoptions.irpp.org/magazines/november-2020/canadas-actions-around-the-mikmaq-fisheries-rest-on-shaky-legal-ground/

Monchalin, Lisa. 2016. *The Colonial Problem.* Toronto: University of Toronto Press.

Morellato, Maria. 2008. "The Crown's Constitutional Duty to Consult and Accommodate Aboriginal and Treaty Rights" Research paper for National Centre for First Nations Governance. https://fngovernance.org/wp-content/uploads/2020/06/Crown_Duty_to_Consult__Accommodate.pdf

Nova Scotia. 2017. "Pardon, Apology, for Late Grand Chief Gabriel Sylliboy." News release, Premier's Office, February 16, 2017. https://novascotia.ca/news/release/?id=20170216004.

Office of Aboriginal Affairs. 2012. *Proponent's Guide: The Role of Proponents in Crown Consultation with the Mi'kmaq of Nova Scotia.* Halifax: Office of Aboriginal Affairs.

Office of L'nu Affairs. 2021. *Business Plan 2021–22.* Halifax: Office of L'nu Affairs. https://novascotia.ca/government/accountability/2021-2022/L%27nu-Affairs-2021-2022-Business-Plan.pdf.

Paul, Daniel. 2006. *We Were Not the Savages.* Halifax: Fernwood Publishing.

Pictou, Sherry. 2018. "Mi'kmaq and the Recognition and Implementation of Rights Framework." *Yellowhead Institute* June 5, 2018. https://yellowheadinstitute. org/policybriefs/mikmaq-and-the-recognition-and-implementation-rights-framework/.

Prins, Harald. 1996. *The Mi'kmaq: Resistance, Accommodation and Cultural Survival*. Fort Worth: Harcourt Brace College Publishers.

Prosper, Kerry, L. Jane McMillan, Anthony Davis, and Morgan Moffitt. 2011. "Returning to Netukulimk: Mi'kmaq Cultural and Spiritual Connections with Resource Stewardship and Self-governance." *International Indigenous Policy Journal* 2, no. 4: Article 7.

Royal Commission on Aboriginal Peoples. 1992. "Presentation by Alex Christmas, President of the Union of Nova Scotia Indians." Royal Commission on Aboriginal Peoples, Eskasoni / Prince Edward Island Wednesday, May 6, 1992. 1: 123–66. https://data2.archives.ca/rcap/pdf/rcap-224.pdf

Sinclair, Murray. 2015. *Final Report of the Truth and Reconciliation Commission of Canada, Canada's Residential Schools: The History, Part I*. Winnipeg: Truth and Reconciliation Commission of Canada. McGill-Queen's University Press, for the Truth and Reconciliation Commission of Canada. https://publications.gc.ca/ collections/collection_2015/trc/IR4-9-1-1-2015-eng.pdf.

Surette, Allister. 2021. *Implementing the Right to Fish in Pursuit of a Moderate Livelihood: Rebuilding Trust and Establishing a Constructive Path Forward*. https://www. dfo-mpo.gc.ca/fisheries-peches/aboriginal-autochtones/moderate-livelihood-subsistance-convenable/surette-report-rapport-mar-2021-eng.html.

Trudeau, Justin. 2015. "Minister of Fisheries, Oceans and the Canadian Coast Guard Mandate Letter." November 12, 2015. https://www.pm.gc.ca/en/mandate-letters/2015/11/12/archived-minister-fisheries-oceans-and-canadian-coast-guard-mandate.

———. 2017. "Minister of Crown-Indigenous Relations and Northern Affairs Mandate Letter." October 4, 2017. https://pm.gc.ca/en/mandate-letters/2017/10/04/archived-minister-crown-indigenous-relations-and-northern-affairs.

———. 2019. "Minister of Fisheries, Oceans and the Canadian Coast Guard Mandate Letter." December 13, 2019. https://pm.gc.ca/en/mandate-letters/2019/12/13/ .archived-minister-fisheries-oceans-and-canadian-coast-guard-mandate.

———. 2021. "Minister of Fisheries, Oceans and the Canadian Coast Guard Mandate Letter." December 16, 2021. https://pm.gc.ca/en/mandate-letters/2021/12/16/ minister-fisheries-oceans-and-canadian-coast-guard-mandate-letter.

Umbrella Agreement. Miq'maq, Nova Scotia, Canada. 7 June 2002. https://novascotia.ca/ abor/docs/Umbrella-Agreement.pdf.

UN General Assembly. 2007. *United Nations Declaration on the Rights of Indigenous Peoples: Resolution / Adopted by the General Assembly*. 2 October 2007, A/ RES/61/295. http://www.refworld.org/docid/471355a82.html.

Upton, L. F. S. 1979. *Micmacs and Colonists: Indian–White Relations in the Maritimes, 1713–1867*. Vancouver: University of British Columbia Press.

Whitehead, Ruth Holmes. 1991. *The Old Man Told Us: Excepts from Micmac History 1500–1950*. Halifax: Nimbus Publishing.

Wicken, William C. 2002. *Mi'kmaq Treaties on Trial: History, Land, and Donald Marshall Junior*. Toronto: University of Toronto Press.

———. 2012. *The Colonization of Mi'kmaw Memory and History, 1794–1928: The King V. Gabriel Sylliboy*. Toronto: University of Toronto Press.

Wildsmith, Bruce H. 1992. "Treaty Responsibilities: A Co-Relational Model." Special Edition on Aboriginal Justice, *University of British Columbia Law Review* 26: 324–37.

———. 2001. Vindicating Mi'kmaq Rights: The Struggles Before, During and After Marshall. *Windsor Yearbook of Access to Justice* 19: 203–42.

Young, Janelle. 2015. "Reimagining Mi'kmaq-State Relations: Facing Colonialism at the Mi'kmaq-Nova Scotia-Canada Tripartite Forum." Master's thesis, Dalhousie University.

Young, Tuma. 2016. "L'nuwita'simk: A Foundational Worldview for a L'nuwey Justice System." *Indigenous Law Journal* 13, no. 1: 75–102.

———. 2018. "Kisa'muemkewey." Paper series for Treaty Education curricula. On file with author.

Wolfe, Patrick. 1999. *Settler Colonialism and the Transformation of Anthropology: The Politics and Poetics of an Ethnographic Event*. London: Cassell.

Zimonjic, Peter. 2020. "MPs hold emergency debate on NS lobster fishery dispute." *CBC News*, October 19, 2020. https://www.cbc.ca/news/politics/parliament-debate-nova-scotia-lobster-dispute-1.5768468.

Cases Cited

Calder v. Attorney-General of British Columbia, [1973] S.C.R. 313.

Haida Nation v. British Columbia (Minister of Forests), [2004] 3 S.C.R. 511, 2004 SCC 73.

Isaac v. The Queen [1975] 13 NSR (2nd) 460 (S.C.A.D).

Mikisew Cree First Nation v. Canada (Minister of Canadian Heritage), 2005 SCC 69, [2005] 3 S.C.R. 388.

R. v. Marshall (No.2), [1999] 3 SCR 533.

R. v. Denny, Paul and Sylliboy [1990] 94 NSR (2nd) 253.

R. v. Marshall [1999] 3 S.C.R. 456.

R. v. Sparrow [1990] 1 S.C.R. 1075

Simon v. The Queen [1985] 2 S.C.R. 387.

Taku River Tlingit First Nation v. British Columbia (Project Assessment Director), [2004] 3 S.C.R. 550, 2004 SCC 74.

To Consult or Not to Consult? A Tale of Two Provinces

Victoria A. Bikowski and Gabrielle Slowey

Natural resource development is a central component of Canada's national identity; from fish to fur to timber to minerals to oil and gas, Canada's economic history and ongoing development is and has been intimately tied to resource exploitation. In 2020, Canada was the fourth largest producer and third largest exporter of oil globally and has the fourth largest proven oil reserves (Government of Canada 2022c).[1] It is also the fifth largest producer and sixth largest exporter of natural gas (Government of Canada 2022c). Most oil and gas exploration and production take place in Western Canada, and, in varying degrees, across all provinces.

Canada's provincial and federal governments are traditionally strong proponents of the oil and gas industry, promoting economic benefits for all Canadians from coast to coast to coast. Government officials at multiple levels have argued that oil and gas production has resulted in socio-economic, innovative, and even environmental benefits for many Canadians (Benoit 2014, 3). However, not all people in Canada agree with these claims.

Oil and gas development has been, and continues to be, a highly contentious issue for many people in Canada, but none more so than Indigenous Peoples. Oil and gas development most often occurs on or around traditional territories and lands of Indigenous Peoples. As a result, oil and gas development is more likely to affect Indigenous Peoples directly and adversely when compared to non-Indigenous Canadians. It therefore comes as no surprise that Indigenous Peoples are often at the forefront of opposition to resource development, although this does not mean that all Indigenous Peoples oppose oil and gas development projects in Canada (Slowey 2009).

Many different factors influence whether Indigenous Peoples oppose or support natural resource development, ranging from potential environmental harms or adverse impacts to land to job creation and resource revenue sharing agreements. This chapter endeavours to explore these different factors, while focusing specifically on the role of provincial duty-to-consult policies in shaping First Nations' response to development.[2] We focus on policies emerging from the duty to consult because of the growing importance and influence of this legal doctrine in natural resource development. Resource development frequently triggers the Crown's duty to consult Indigenous Peoples, and these consultation policies guide the form and substance of consultation and engagement activities in light of development projects that affect Aboriginal and Treaty Rights.

This chapter explores how different First Nations respond differently to unconventional oil and gas development that occurs or is proposed in their respective territories and the role provincial consultation policies play. The guiding questions for this chapter are: What factors influence whether a First Nation supports or rejects oil and gas projects? How do consultation policies shape First Nations' responses? We use a case study approach to answer these questions, comparing the experiences of two First Nations that have both challenged and accepted extraction in varying degrees, namely, the Athabasca Chipewyan First Nation and the Fort McKay First Nation, of northern Alberta against that of two other First Nations who have had very different experiences, for different reasons—namely, the Lubicon Lake Band (LLB), also located near Alberta's oil sands and the Elsipogtog First Nation located in proximity to the Frederick Brook Shale play in New Brunswick.

We compare the economic importance of oil and gas development in each province, the impacts of oil and gas development, the operationalization of provincial duty to consult policies, and First Nations' responses to development and consultation. We conclude that where First Nations support development it is clear that the overall impacts include the ability to benefit economically from development, and a sense of having been relatively meaningfully engaged or consulted. The analysis presented below reveals that different approaches to the duty to consult vis-à-vis consultation policies can yield vastly different results. More specifically, poor or inadequate policies can jeopardize major resource development projects, and in turn, undermine the political and economic objectives of provincial governments. The role of consultation policies in aiding natural resource development therefore must not be underestimated, particularly in provinces (or territories) where natural resources are a vital part of the economy.

1   Alberta's Oil Sands

1.1   Oil and Gas Production in Alberta

Alberta is Canada's largest source of oil and gas resources. Historically, oil and gas development has been a key driver of Alberta's provincial economy (Government of Alberta 2022a). Since 1947, the Government of Alberta has exploited its oil and gas resources to meet its economic growth and development objectives, including economic self-sufficiency and global competitiveness. Oil and gas production in Alberta has resulted in significant economic benefits for both the provincial and federal governments (Government of Canada 2022c; Government of Alberta 2023). Production has also enabled Alberta to become a "have" province, which means that the province typically does not receive federal equalization payments from the Government of Canada (2008).[3]

Economic benefits from oil and gas development can be measured in a variety of ways, but royalty revenue provides a good measure of their fiscal value, at least at the provincial level. Between 2015/16 and 2021/22, the Government of Alberta received $5,256 million in natural gas and by-product revenue, $7,107 million in conventional oil revenue, and $26,262 million in oil sands royalty revenue (Government of Alberta 2023). In total, Alberta received $38,625 million in oil and gas royalty revenue during this time, comprising 11% of government revenue. This royalty revenue does not even include revenue from bonuses and sales of Crown leases, rentals and fees, freehold mineral tax, or related sources of income.

Alberta is heavily invested in oil and gas production and the Government of Alberta has facilitated this type of resource development because it has been in the provincial government's economic interest to do so. Oil and gas resources are perceived as a critical component of Alberta's long-term economic success. As such, the Government of Alberta has often ignored, or has justified, the environmental and human costs of development, particularly in the oil sands.

1.2   Impacts of Oil Sands Development

Extractive methods used in the oil sands have had devastating consequences on the regional environment. Negative impacts include mass deforestation, the displacement and death of wildlife, and the destruction of peatlands, which are vital carbon sinks (Rooney, Bayley, and Schindler 2011, 5). These methods have also compromised the integrity of Alberta's freshwater resources by diverting water from rivers and wetlands, polluting key tributaries (e.g., the Athabasca River) and aquifers with toxic runoff from the production process, and by draining freshwater resources for production usage (Thurton 2020). Thus, oil sands development has disrupted the natural environment by altering the landscape and negatively impacting freshwater resources by drawing upon them as part of the production process (Donev 2018). Development has also resulted in high levels of air pollution in the region and contributes to global climate change by reducing Canada's carbon sequestration potential and by producing significant amounts of greenhouse gases (Dyer and Huot 2010).

There are also human costs associated with development. First, oil sands development threatens the overall health and safety of surrounding Indigenous nations, including human and non-human species. For instance, scientists (unaffiliated with either the provincial or federal government) have found evidence suggesting that water pollution has been the leading cause of emerging rare and virulent forms of cancer and disease (e.g., bile ducts cancer, autoimmune diseases) amongst Indigenous Peoples living near the oil sands (Slowey and Stefanick 2015, 201). Second, oil sands activity has been associated with social problems, including higher levels of substance use in surrounding communities, as well as heightened community exposure to transient populations that have played a role in rising levels of criminal activity (e.g., drug trade, rape, sex trafficking, and violent crime) in the region (Ruddell and Ortiz 2014; Vecchio 2022). Thirdly, the destruction of the natural environment and its resources poses a direct threat to Indigenous culture and identities, which are largely derived from Indigenous Peoples' reciprocal relationship with the land. Given the overwhelming evidence of the environmental and human/non-human costs of development, it is understandable why Indigenous Peoples (and environmental groups) choose to oppose the oil sands. The Government of Alberta and the oil industry often dismiss these costs as trade-offs for economic prosperity. The reality is that the provincial government invests a lot of time and effort into promoting oil sands development, and its policy on the duty to consult helps ensure greater predictability around the development process.

1.3   Evolution of Alberta's Consultation Policy

Prior to developing its first policy on the duty to consult, the Government of Alberta initiated studies throughout the 1970s and 1980s to help inform oil sands policy. One government agency, the Alberta Oil Sands Environmental Research Program (AOSERP), was responsible for exploring how communities neighbouring the oil sands would be affected by development. Specifically, AOSERP investigated the economic, environmental, and social impacts of oil sands development. A key objective of the research was to identify how Indigenous Peoples would be impacted, where Indigenous Peoples would have a place in development (i.e., employment and job opportunities), and how the provincial government would establish a baseline for integrating Indigenous Peoples into the government workforce (Paskey, Steward, and Williams 2013, 57). These investigations signalled the beginning of the Government of Alberta's interest in establishing greater predictability around land management and resource development in the oil sands region.

During the late 1980s and 1990s, there were fewer government-led studies on how Indigenous Peoples would be affected by development. However, by the early 2000s, the Government of Alberta's interest in Indigenous Peoples increased again. In September 2000, the provincial government released *The Government of Alberta's Aboriginal Policy Framework*, which sought to address Indigenous-provincial relations (Government of Alberta 2005, 2). Later, in 2004, Canada's legal landscape changed in such a way that Alberta would have to become even more proactive when it came to Indigenous relations, especially within the context of resource development.

A trilogy of landmark cases on the duty to consult arose from the Supreme Court of Canada (SCC) in 2004 and 2005: *Haida Nation v. British Columbia* (2004),[4] *Taku River Tlingit First Nation v. British Columbia* (2004),[5] and *Mikisew Cree First Nation v. Canada* (2005).[6] Taken together, these cases identified and confirmed that the Crown has an obligation to consult and accommodate Indigenous Peoples on matters that may affect their Aboriginal and Treaty Rights. They also helped establish minimum legal expectations around the duty to consult and essentially required federal and provincial governments to devise and implement courses of action to ensure that the duty is fulfilled by the Crown (Newman 2014, 15). Although the Government of Alberta already had its *Aboriginal Policy Framework* in place, these landmark cases pushed the provincial government to take Indigenous-provincial relations more seriously and to enact a new policy. By May 2005, the Government of Alberta released it's First Nations consultation policy on land management and resource development, which represented a commitment from the provincial government to consult First Nations on matters pertaining to land management and resource development that may affect their constitutional or Treaty Rights (Government of Alberta 2005, 2). In 2013, the provincial government revised its consultation policy and released *The Government of Alberta's Policy on Consultation with First Nations on Land and Natural Resource Management* (Government of Alberta 2013).[7] By April 2020, the Government of Alberta amended its policy a second time to make it more comprehensive and streamlined (Government of Alberta 2020). The language used in the policy also changed slightly to focus more specifically on economic development opportunities for First Nations. Key developments and the evolution of Alberta's consultation policy (and guidelines) are noted below (table 5.1).

The Government of Alberta's approach to consultation has not only evolved in response to landmark cases concerning Aboriginal and Treaty Rights, such as *Haida*, *Taku*, and *Mikisew*, amongst others, but also in response to political and legal events concerning Indigenous Rights.[8] These events include the United Nation's adoption of the *United Nations Declaration on the Rights of Indigenous Peoples* (UNDRIP) on September 13, 2007 (UN General Assembly 2007); the Government of Canada's endorsement of UNDRIP on November 12, 2010 (Government of Canada 2010); and Canada's adoption of UNDRIP on May 10, 2016 (Government of Canada 2016a).[9] All of these events had an important role to play in encouraging the Government of Alberta to produce a comprehensive consultation policy and corresponding guidelines.

Alberta's 2005 policy on consultation with First Nations explains the purpose of the policy and consultation model, as well as outlines general expectations around consultation and the roles and responsibilities of key parties involved (the Crown, First Nations, and project proponents). The amended 2013 policy provides a more detailed overview of the consultation process and expectations around consultation. The policy covers important topics like Treaty Rights, traditional uses of land, matters subject (and not subject) to the policy, elements of consultation (i.e., content of the duty, scope

Table 5.1: Key Developments and the Evolution of Alberta's Consultation Policy and Guidelines.*

YEAR(S)	KEY DEVELOPMENTS
2000	*The Government of Alberta's Aboriginal Policy Framework* is released in September 2000.
2005	**Alberta releases *The Government of Alberta's First Nations Consultation Policy on Land Management and Resource Development* in May 2005;** The Oil Sands Consultation Group is formed by the ministers of energy, environment, and sustainable resource development.
2006	The *Oil Sands Consultation Group Final Report and Recommendations* is released on March 31, 2006.
2007	The Aboriginal Consultation Interdepartmental Committee (ACIC) is commissioned by the Government of Alberta in January 2007; *Alberta's First Nations Consultation Guidelines on Land Management and Resource Development* is released on November 14, 2007.
2009	The *Responsible Actions: A Plan for Alberta's Oil Sands* is released.
2012	Alberta releases its *Discussion Paper on First Nation Consultation*.
2013	**Alberta releases *The Government of Alberta's Policy on Consultation with First Nations on Land and Natural Resource Management* on August 16, 2013;** The Aboriginal Consultation Office (ACO) is established; Alberta releases the draft *Government of Alberta's Corporate Guidelines for First Nations Consultation Activities*.
2014	A draft version of *The Government of Alberta's Guidelines on Consultation with First Nations on Land and Natural Resources Management (Guidelines)* is released on May 9, 2014; *The Government of Alberta's Guidelines on Consultation with First Nations on Land and Natural Resources Management* is released on July 28, 2014.
2015	*The Government of Alberta's Proponent Guide to First Nations Consultation Procedures for Land Dispositions* is released on February 3, 2015.
2019	*The Government of Alberta's Proponent Guide to First Nations and Métis Settlements Consultation Procedures* is released on December 1, 2019.
2020	**Alberta amends its 2013 *Policy on Consultation with First Nations* on April 1, 2020.**

*This table is not a comprehensive list of key developments. Developments related to consultation with Métis Settlements, for example, are not included in the table. External developments, such as landmark cases on the duty to consult, the federal government's endorsement of the United Nations Declaration on the Rights of Indigenous Peoples (UNDRIP), and other events that may have played a role in influencing or shaping Alberta's approach to consultation with Indigenous Peoples are also not listed here.

of consultation, depth of consultation), direct consultation by the Crown, delegated consultation, and key steps in the consultation process (and other considerations) in greater detail than its predecessor. Overall, the new policy is more comprehensive and covers specific topics that are of concern to First Nations and project proponents (industry). The new policy also focuses more on accommodation and reconciliation than its predecessor (Government of Alberta 2013, 1–2; 4; 7), which was mainly focused on establishing a practical consultation process that would create greater certainty (Government of Alberta 2005, 2). Additionally, Alberta's consultation guidelines effectively clarify the expectations around consultation, the consultation process, and its procedures, as well as provide direction on meeting the administrative requirements of consultation (Government of Alberta 2019).

On balance, the Government of Alberta's policy and guidelines on consultation with First Nations are comprehensive. They specify the roles, responsibilities, and rights of all rights holders and stakeholders engaged in, and affected by, development; provide a detailed account of how consultation protocols may be approached, which includes information on direct Crown consultation and delegated consultation; describe how consultation processes can be co-ordinated across jurisdictions, agencies, departments, and quasi-judicial bodies; and include a step-by-step process for consultation, which provides details on consultation triggers, stages of the consultation process, and processing timelines. Moreover, successive provincial governments continue to expand the consultation policy, guidelines, and corresponding protocols. Overall, the Government of Alberta has produced a consultation policy and guidelines that effectively lay out what is required and expected for all parties involved in terms of consultation with First Nations in Alberta.

1.4   First Nations Impacted by Oil Sands Development

Most oil sands projects are located within Treaty 8 territory, meaning that twenty-four First Nations are directly or indirectly affected by development, including twenty-three Treaty 8 First Nations in Alberta (Treaty 8 Tribal Association 2021) and the LLB. Some of these First Nations strongly oppose oil sands development, while others do not. The reasons for their support or opposition largely depends on whether their overall experience with oil sands development has been positive or negative. The experiences of three affected First Nations are described below.

ATHABASCA CHIPEWYAN FIRST NATION

The Athabasca Chipewyan First Nation (ACFN) is an Indigenous (Dene) nation located immediately north of the Athabasca oil sands development, approximately 200 kilometres (km) north of Fort McMurray. ACFN has a total registered membership population of 1,396 people (Government of Canada 2022b) and is a signatory of Treaty 8.[10] As a signatory, ACFN has "surrendered" title to lands except for those set aside as reserves (Huseman & Short 2012, 219–20). However, whether land has been surrendered remains a contested issue, particularly in light of oil sands development.

ACFN contends that Treaty 8 obligations have not been met. ACFN leaders claim that their people signed the treaty to have their traditional way of life recognized and maintained without restriction, so long as "the sun shines, the grass grows and the water flows" (Turner 2017, 31–32). One of the guarantees that Treaty 8 made to the ancestors of present-day ACFN members was the "right to pursue their usual vocations of hunting, trapping and fishing throughout the tract surrendered" (Treaty 8 First Nations of Alberta 2023). However, since the oil sands have transformed the ecological integrity of the Athabasca region in a significant way, these vocations can no longer be easily carried out, if at all. Successive Canadian governments have not honoured the promises made in signing Treaty 8 (e.g., land set aside for hunting, trapping, and fishing; agricultural supplies; etc.), and because of oil sands operations and accompanying environmental degradation and change in the region, ACFN members are no longer able to exercise their Treaty Rights. These broken promises and losses have spurred ACFN leadership to legally challenge both the notion of surrendered lands as well as any further expansion of the oil sands. Recent challenges include a 2011 constitutional challenge over five oil and gas leases that Alberta's minister of energy granted to Shell Canada Ltd. (*Athabasca Chipewyan First Nation v. Alberta [Minister of Energy]*, 2011), a notice of question of constitutional law regarding Shell's Jackpine Mine Expansion Project in 2012 (*Cold Lake First Nations v. Alberta [Energy Resources Conservation Board]*, 2012),[11] and an application for review of a pipeline project that was proposed and approved in Treaty 8 territory in 2018 (*Athabasca Chipewyan First Nation v. Alberta*, 2018). In all three cases, ACFN argued that the duty to consult and accommodate was not adequately discharged.

Overall, ACFN has argued that Alberta's consultation process undermines its members' constitutional rights and Indigenous Rights defined under UNDRIP (Athabasca Chipewyan First Nation 2020). ACFN further claims that the consultation process does not value partnership between First Nations and the Crown, and that most oil sands projects are approved despite First Nations' objections (Lavoie 2018). However, ACFN is not entirely opposed to development because of the value and economic opportunities it creates for its membership.

To clarify, ACFN is one of the few First Nations in Canada that is able to refuse federal government funding (and the accompanying rules and regulations associated with it) (Sterritt 2014). ACFN has signed several impact benefit agreements (IBAs) with oil and gas companies operating in the oil sands and within its traditional territory. Although the provisions of the IBAs are confidential, ACFN leadership has indicated that these agreements have provided enough funding to enable the First Nation to not accept money from the federal government (Sterritt 2014).[12] ACFN has also established twenty companies through its umbrella corporation, Acden (formerly ACFN Business Group), which offers industrial and commercial services to the oil sands industry. The companies generate approximately $250 million in revenue annually for the First Nation (Sterritt 2014). The revenue generated through IBAs and oil sands-related companies has empowered ACFN to improve standards of living for its membership by providing them with much-needed community infrastructure and social services. Additionally, ACFN leaders have contended that industry partnerships help the First Nation improve its capacity to self-govern (Richards 2020).

It is evident that ACFN does not oppose development per se. Rather, ACFN is opposed to not being treated equally or fairly when it comes to decisions made around resource development. ACFN appears to be more supportive of development when its members can benefit from development, and more importantly, when it is included in major development plans and important decision-making processes. The latter point is particularly evident in ACFN's more recent engagements with Teck Resources Ltd. and the Government of Alberta, where Chief Allan Adam described the consultation process around Teck's Frontier Oil Sands Project as "fresh and positive" and a "'model' for how companies planning major projects should move forward in the future" (Bench 2020).

FORT MCKAY FIRST NATION

The Fort McKay First Nation (FMFN) is an Indigenous nation with mixed ancestry (Cree, Dene, and Métis) and a total registered population of 967 people (Government of Canada 2022b). It is a signatory of Treaty 8 and is located in the Regional Municipality of Wood Buffalo, approximately 60 km north of Fort McMurray. FMFN was one of the first Indigenous nations to experience the devastating effects of development given its close proximity to oil sands operations. In the early 1980s, oil sands mining effluent from Suncor Energy Inc.'s mining operations polluted FMFN's water resources. Members had unknowingly been drinking and bathing in this water for up to three weeks (Turner 2017, 198–99). In response, FMFN erected a blockade on the main road through its community to send a message to the Government of Alberta, the Government of Canada, and the oil industry. Shortly afterwards, FMFN engaged in negotiations with the provincial and federal governments to explore business opportunities for the First Nation and to establish the Fort McKay Industry Relations Corporation (Turner 2017, 200–1). Leadership at the time understood that development was going to proceed, regardless of whether FMFN supported or opposed it. FMFN was also struggling economically and saw the oil sands as a way to develop new economic opportunities for the First Nation (Lavoie 2018).

With the expansion of the oil sands, FMFN has raised concerns pertaining to community health and cultural identity. For example, some FMFN members have blamed the oil sands for the rise in cases of asthma, rashes, cancer, and premature births amongst its membership (McCarthy 2015). FMFN has also communicated concerns over the rapid pace of development and how it undermines the ecological integrity of the region, which in turn exacerbates hunting, trapping, and fishing rights infringements and adversely affects cultural identity (Pederson 2007, 38). Additionally, FMFN has expressed its concerns about a lack of consultation over oil and gas projects, particularly consultation over cumulative effects (Pederson 2007, 32). The frequent dismissal of Treaty Rights, a lack of respect or support for individual First Nations' consultation protocols, and inadequate information-sharing are also key concerns (Pederson 2007, 61; 32; 64).

Despite FMFN's concerns, the First Nation has not been as staunchly opposed to development as some other First Nations in Alberta have been, even in light of the ecological and social changes that have occurred. FMFN has taken the stance that change is inevitable, and that change can result in "cultural evolution and improvement" when mutually beneficial partnerships are formed with industry and the Crown (Fort McKay First Nation 2021). FMFN concedes that its traditional ways of life can be preserved alongside continuous and responsible development (Fort McKay First Nation 2018, 3). FMFN does not shy away from oil sands development and seldom opposes it.

FMFN has used oil sands development to its advantage, wherever possible. In 1986, FMFN established the Fort McKay Group of Companies, which offers a variety of services to oil and gas companies and is wholly owned and operated by the First Nation. By 2016, the Group of Companies was participating in several joint ventures that generated more than $150 million dollars in revenue annually (Government of Canada 2016b). Through its Group of Companies and other oil sands-related endeavours, FMFN has been able to generate over $700 million in revenue annually for the First Nation (Hussain 2014) and has over $2 billion in financial holdings (Tasker 2016). This income has enabled FMFN to buy equity stakes in oil sands projects, such as Suncor Energy Inc.'s East Tank Farm Development,[13] which help FMFN generate even more revenue (Suncor Energy 2016).

The economic benefits and opportunities generated through FMFN's partnerships with industry have significantly improved its members' overall standards of living by providing them with better health services, employment opportunities, social programs, and more (Murphy 2008, 88). Former Chief Jim Boucher has also pointed out that FMFN has zero unemployment and its members have an average annual income of $120,000 (Bird 2017). Given the socio-economic benefits associated with oil sands development, FMFN has contemplated developing resources on its traditional territory one day. For this First Nation, oil sands development and related activities are a means to secure long-term financial stability for future generations and to increase its independence overall.

LUBICON LAKE BAND

The Lubicon Lake Band of Little Buffalo is an Indigenous (Cree) nation with a total registered population of 533 people (Government of Canada 2017). LLB is situated west of the oil sands, approximately 450 km north of Edmonton, and is geographically located within Treaty 8 territory. However, this First Nation is not party to Treaty 8 because it was by-passed by Treaty Commissioners in 1899 (Ferreira 1992, 27). This error resulted in LLB not being recognized as a First Nation by the Government of Canada for decades (Government of Canada 2014a).[14]

Historically, LLB has strongly opposed oil and gas development in Alberta. This opposition began in the early 1970s when the Government of Alberta constructed roads that facilitated oil and gas exploration through LLB's traditional territory. In 1976, LLB tried to file a caveat against the provincial government to halt construction.[15] Through the caveat, LLB claimed title to approximately 85,470 km², based upon its unextinguished Aboriginal title (Ferreira 1992, 12).[16] However, the claim failed because LLB did not possess a certificate of title, which barred it from filing a caveat (Ferreira 1992, 13).

Between the 1970s and early 1980s, oil production increased and approximately 400 wells existed within a 24 km radius of LLB's territory by 1982 (Ferreira 1992, 12). Expansion was alarming for LLB because rapid development was accompanied by a noticeable decline in wildlife in the area, which its members relied upon for sustenance and maintaining cultural practices (Ferreira 1992, 18–19). These changes compelled LLB to oppose further development. The Nation took action by building a national support network, uniting with other Indigenous nations who shared similar experiences, launching petitions, filing an injunction to halt oil and gas activities, boycotting the Calgary 1988 Winter Olympics, and creating blockades around its territory (Ferreira 1992, 16–18; 24–25).[17] While other Indigenous nations have tried to address their development concerns by asking for buffer zones or a review of development applications, LLB has waged a very public and action-oriented campaign designed to raise maximum awareness to their plight. Yet, despite all their efforts, LLB has not been able to bring development to a halt.

Since 2011, over 70 percent of LLB's traditional territory has been leased for resource development, including oil sands development (Alberta Native News 2018). LLB has pressed the provincial and federal governments for a land claims settlement. An agreement was eventually reached in October 2018, resulting in a $113 million settlement and the setting aside of 246 km² of land in Little Buffalo (CBC News 2018). LLB is now considered to be a First Nation that is entitled to similar land and treaty benefits that Treaty 8 First Nations are entitled to (Alberta Native News 2018). Whether the settlement changes the First Nation's stance on resource development is unclear, but Chief Billy Joe Laboucan has said the following:

I know there have been a lot of resource extraction in our area … but it's no use lamenting the past. We're moving forward. We always look seven generations ahead. That's what we've been taught. We're speaking and preparing for the unborn and hopefully that they will have a better future, better homes, good livelihood, good peace of mind and still be able to look after our land and our resources (Bennett 2019).

This sentiment reflects LLB's pragmatism towards oil and gas development within their traditional territory.

1.5   Summary of Development in the Alberta Oil Sands

Alberta has valuable oil and gas resources that have yielded considerable economic benefits for the province. However, there are environmental and human costs of development that the provincial government has had to become more attuned to. The Government of Alberta has also been pressured into taking Aboriginal and Treaty Rights more seriously in the context of land management and resource development and has responded accordingly by developing a consultation policy and guidelines. This has been a critical step for establishing greater certainty around oil sands development.

2   New Brunswick's Frederick Brook Shale Play

2.1   Oil and Gas in New Brunswick

The Province of New Brunswick has a long history of natural resource development, including oil and gas development. In the early 1850s, mining for oil shale and albertite took place in Albert County and the province's first oil well was drilled in 1859 (Park 2012, 14). The Stoney Creek Field and McCully Gas Fields were discovered in 1909 and 2000, respectively (Government of New Brunswick n.d.).[18] Both fields have produced a considerable amount of oil and gas resources (CBC News 2011),[19] but despite having these producing fields, the province has never been a leading oil and gas producer in Canada.

New Brunswick has historically struggled economically. It has been labelled as a poor, "have-not" province (Government of Canada 2011),[20] and assumed the title of Canada's poorest province in 2019 (Jones 2019). New Brunswick's economic struggle is in part due to its historically resource-based economy, troubled by boom-and-bust cycles and sunset industries, as well as its inability to diversify economically. In response to these shortcomings, the Government of New Brunswick, under the leadership of Premier Shawn Graham, released an action plan in 2007, *Our Action Plan to be Self-Sufficient in New Brunswick*, which outlined how the province would become self-sufficient by 2026 (Hodd 2009, 197). As part of this initiative, the provincial government also sought to turn New Brunswick into an energy hub in the Maritimes (CBC News 2007). Succeeding governments, namely Progressive Conservative (PC) governments, sought to turn this goal into a reality by tapping into the Frederick Brook Shale (FBS) play, including the McCully Field.

The FBS development area spans approximately 150,000 acres across southern New Brunswick (Corridor Resources Inc. 2015). Early estimates suggested that there is over 65 trillion cubic feet (tcf) of gas reserves in the play (Alexander, Qian, Ryan, and Herron 2011, 4–5). A former premier of New Brunswick also estimated that over $7 billion in royalties and tax revenue could be generated by developing New Brunswick's shale gas industry; however, the timeline for this estimate was not specified (CBC News 2013c). If this evaluation is correct, then this is a significant amount of money for a historically poor province.

2.2   Potential Impacts of Shale Gas Development

The FBS play consists mainly of shale gas resources, which means hydraulic fracturing ("fracking") is required for extraction. Fracking involves drilling down and horizontally into layers of rock and injecting fracking fluid (i.e., water, sand, and various chemicals) at pressures great enough to fracture the rock and release the oil and gas resources within (Williams, Macnaghten, and Davies 2017).

Fracking is a controversial form of unconventional resource extraction because it requires large amounts of water and chemicals to successfully extract oil and gas from rock formations. A single well requires about 1.5 to 16 million gallons of water, meaning that local freshwater (i.e., surface, groundwater) resources can easily be depleted in the process (U.S. Geological Survey 2020). The chemicals used in fracking fluids can also contaminate water resources, and some forms of contamination can have long-lasting effects (United States Environmental Protection Agency 2016, 37). Fracking may induce earthquakes as well (Grebe 2019), which can cause property damage and bodily harm or injuries.

New Brunswick residents have expressed their concerns about fracking. In Kent County, residents communicated that they were concerned that fracking would result in irreparable harm to the environment (Fast 2016). More specifically, they were concerned about water contamination. First Nations in the county were also worried about how contamination would turn their territories into hazardous and unsafe places to live, fish, and hunt, and subsequently, negatively impact their Aboriginal and Treaty Rights (Howe 2015, at 2352 of 5224).

2.3　New Brunswick's Duty to Consult Policy

In November 2011, the Government of New Brunswick released its first consultation policy, *Government of New Brunswick Duty to Consult Policy*, to help protect Aboriginal and Treaty Rights and to improve its relationship with First Nations in the province. The policy explains what the duty to consult is and what the Government of New Brunswick's role is in fulfilling this duty. The policy sets out what triggers consultation and the roles and responsibilities of government (federal and provincial) and First Nations (Government of New Brunswick 2011, 1). A section on the duty to consult policy outlines the policy statement and goal, key objectives of the policy, and guiding principles, while a section on the duty to consult delineates the policy's application, matters subject to the policy, triggers, and roles and responsibilities (Government of New Brunswick 2011). Overall, the policy is brief and does not provide a step-by-step process for consultation.

New Brunswick's consultation policy has not been changed or altered since 2011, but in August 2019, the Department of Aboriginal Affairs released a guide to support industry on consultation and engagement with Indigenous Peoples titled, *Interim Proponent Guide: A Guide for Proponents on Engaging with Aboriginal Peoples in New Brunswick*. This guide provides practical and specific advice on the consultation, engagement, and accommodation process. It differentiates the roles and responsibilities of project proponents and the provincial government in consultation activities, provides advice on determining which Indigenous Peoples to engage with and how to engage with them, clarifies information that is relevant to the duty to consult and accommodate, provides advice on how to document consultation efforts, and clarifies how the provincial government will use relevant information provided to support its duty to consult and accommodate (Department of Aboriginal Affairs 2019). In effect, the *Interim Proponent Guide* provides more guidance

Table 5.2: Key Developments and the Evolution of New Brunswick's Duty to Consult Policy and Guidelines

YEAR(S)	KEY DEVELOPMENTS
2011	*The Government of New Brunswick Duty to Consult Policy* is released.
2014	The Government of New Brunswick announces a moratorium on fracking (comes into effect March 2015).
2019	Moratorium partially lifted.
2019	**The Department of Aboriginal Affairs releases industry guide:** *Interim Proponent Guide: A Guide for Proponents on Engaging with Aboriginal Peoples in New Brunswick.*

on the consultation process in New Brunswick. However, it is merely a guide and therefore is second in order of authority to the consultation policy.

The development of New Brunswick's consultation policy and proponent guide corresponds with key events that took place at the time of their releases. The consultation policy emerged at a time when a natural gas and exploration and production companies began seismic testing in Kent County, while the guide was released shortly after a province-wide moratorium on fracking was partially lifted by the provincial government. These events are discussed in the following sections.

2.4 *Communities Impacted by Shale Gas Development*

Little to no public consultation has taken place over potential shale gas development in New Brunswick. In 2009, for example, Premier Shawn Graham and his Liberal government did not release a public notice or engage with the public when the Department of Natural Resources put land up for tenders for shale gas. Nor did his government consult the public on the awarding of leases to Southwestern Energy Resources Canada Inc. (SWN) in 2010 for shale gas exploration (Howe 2015, at 1403 of 5224).[21] Consultation did not improve when Premier David Alward was elected in 2010 and the PCs came into power. Two key developments are worth noting here: (1) Alward appointed himself as the minister responsible for Aboriginal Affairs, enabling him to have the power to determine whether the duty to consult was triggered or not by shale gas exploration activities, such as seismic testing (Government of New Brunswick 2010); and (2) Alward later determined that seismic testing would *not* adversely affect Indigenous Peoples and their use of lands and resources for rights-bearing activities, and therefore consultation was not required under these circumstances (Howe, 2015 at 1742–65; 1768–69 of 5224). Alward's actions meant that consultation with Indigenous Peoples over shale gas activities would be kept to a minimum.[22]

It was not until 2011, when SWN began seismic testing, that New Brunswick residents became increasingly aware of potential fracking in Kent County. Concerns around environmental and human costs associated with shale gas development prompted residents to protest fracking in the province (Howe 2015, at 1641 of 5224; 1485 of 5224). The anti-fracking movement in New Brunswick began with non-Indigenous Canadians (i.e., Anglophones, Francophones or Acadians), but quickly became a united front for both non-Indigenous and Indigenous peoples. Indigenous Peoples recognized that their Aboriginal and Treaty Rights could be adversely impacted by development. One First Nation that was at the centre of the movement was Elsipogtog First Nation.

ELSIPOGTOG FIRST NATION

Elsipogtog First Nation (EFN) is an Indigenous (Mi'kmaq) nation located in Kent County, New Brunswick. It is the largest First Nation in the province, with a total population of 3,423 people (Government of Canada 2019a). It has also been labelled as one of the poorest communities in Canada (CBC News 2010). EFN's traditional territory once consisted of millions of hectares, but now the First Nation resides on about two thousand acres on the Richibucto Indian Reserve No. 15, just southwest of Rexton (Elsipogtog First Nation 2021). EFN is a signatory of the Peace and Friendship Treaties (1725–1779) (Government of Canada 2014b), which means that EFN has never ceded or surrendered lands and resources to the Crown (Government of Canada 2019).[23]

EFN led the anti-fracking movement in the province between 2011 and 2013. Like other New Brunswick residents, EFN members were concerned about the environmental risks associated with fracking, but more importantly, they were concerned about Aboriginal and Treaty Rights infringements associated with development. EFN conveyed their concerns to the provincial government through in-person meetings and interlocutory orders. EFN explained to government officials that they were never consulted on shale gas development activities, despite these activities taking place on its unceded territory. However, EFN's concerns went unaddressed because it was a member of the Assembly of First Nations Chiefs in New Brunswick (AFNCNB), which meant that the First Nation technically delegated consultation activities to this regional organization (Howe 2015, at 4281 of 5224).

In 2013, EFN withdrew from AFNCNB (CBC News 2013b), because it felt that this organization was insufficiently representing its interests (CBC News 2015). Withdrawing from AFNCNB also enabled EFN to pursue a court injunction to suspend all of SWN's exploratory activities in its territory (CBC News 2013a). However, the New Brunswick Court of Queen's Bench did not grant the injunction to EFN, because there was no evidence that SWN's activities would amount to a degree of harm to the First Nation (CBC News 2013a). The Court reminded EFN that it delegated consultation responsibilities to AFNCNB, so any disputes over how this organization participated in the consultation process should be resolved at trial (CBC News 2013a). Upon failing to secure an injunction, EFN leaders and community members took direct action.

EFN members engaged in protest and erected blockades around SWN's seismic testing zones and equipment and storage facilities. EFN's direct action resulted in standoffs with the Royal Canadian Mounted Police (RCMP) in December 2013, which ultimately ended in outbreaks of violence and mass arrests (Galloway and Taber 2013). The conflict garnered national attention, resulting in EFN gaining more support from both Indigenous and non-Indigenous peoples across New Brunswick and Canada (Howe 2015, at 2359 of 5224). The conflict also encouraged SWN to end its exploratory work in 2013 (APTN National News 2013), and a moratorium on fracking was announced in December 2014 by Premier Brian Gallant and his newly elected Liberal government (Bissett 2014). The moratorium came into effect on March 27, 2015 (Southwestern Energy Company 2015).

2.5   Moratorium on Fracking

The Government of New Brunswick's moratorium on fracking stipulated that the development of the province's shale gas resources would not proceed until certain conditions were met. Specifically, the provincial government would not lift the moratorium unless a social licence to operate was in place; the environmental and human impacts of fracking were well understood; a plan to mitigate the impacts was established; a process to respect the duty to consult was created; and a mechanism to maximize the benefits of development was introduced (Government of New Brunswick 2014).

SWN suspended its drilling plans for New Brunswick because of the moratorium. In a letter dated December 16, 2014, SWN's Executive Vice-President of Corporate Development, Jeff Sherrick, communicated to the Government of New Brunswick that SWN would like to continue to work in New Brunswick, but the "moratorium has forced [SWN] to suspend [its] drilling plans and redirect resources to projects to other jurisdictions" (Brown, L. 2015). The letter further pointed to the provincial government's failure to honour its duty to consult obligations as a primary issue for SWN. In effect, SWN argued that because the duty ultimately rests with the Crown, the Government of New Brunswick "needs to do more to advance this file" (Brown, L. 2015). The letter concluded that further investment in the province would require addressing consultation issues, along with other issues outlined in the letter.

In the years following the suspension of SWN's activities, New Brunswick business groups called on the provincial government to reconsider its moratorium on fracking. In response to their requests, the PC government, under the leadership of Premier Blaine Higgs, partially lifted the moratorium on fracking in the province in May 2019. Higgs' cabinet approved an order-in-council to exempt the Sussex area from the province-wide moratorium with the intention of opening the area up for business (Poitras 2019). This decision allowed oil and gas companies like Corridor Resources Inc. to pursue fracking in the FBS play (Intiar 2020).

The partial lifting of the fracking moratorium was not well received by the Liberal opposition, Indigenous groups and peoples, and non-Indigenous peoples of the Sussex area. The opposition described the decision as a "closed-door regulatory change" and criticized the PC government for lifting the ban without consulting New Brunswick residents, including Indigenous Peoples (Brown, S. 2019). Indigenous groups in New Brunswick have described the government's actions as unlawful and warned that this decision may re-ignite conflict between government, First Nations, and industry (Poitras 2019). Leaders of the Tobique First Nation, Pabineau First Nation, and the Wolastoqey Nation in New Brunswick (WNNB) indicated that it is within their legal rights to be consulted on these matters (Mi'gmaq and Wolastoqey Nations 2019), that consultation should take place even before test drilling is underway (Intiar 2019), and that serious dialogue with First Nations needs to occur before any more developments take place (Poitras 2019). As for non-Indigenous residents, concerns about the environmental costs of fracking remain and consequently there has been a lack of support for lifting the ban (Weldon 2018).

The Government of New Brunswick released its proponent guide in August 2019, shortly after it partially lifted the moratorium. In theory, the guide would help reduce uncertainty around the consultation process, but regulatory uncertainty remains a key issue for industry. In 2019, Corridor Resources halted its search for investors to back its plan for fracking in Sussex due to uncertainty around consultation and when (or if) Corridor's assets in the McCully Field would become exempt from the moratorium (Magee 2019). In the following year, Corridor was taken over by new management and changed its name to Headwater Exploration. Headwater plans to consult with First Nations and to pursue the exemption and development in the region (Intiar 2020). It has yet to be determined whether Headwater has been successful with its endeavours; only time will tell if history repeats itself.

2.6   Summary of Potential Shale Gas Development in New Brunswick

New Brunswick possesses valuable shale gas resources that could potentially put the province on a path towards economic self-sufficiency. However, there are significant environmental concerns that need to be taken into consideration before development proceeds. Moreover, New Brunswick residents, but specifically Indigenous Peoples, need to feel adequately consulted in order to ensure that shale gas activities do not reignite conflict between the provincial government, First Nations, and industry. Such conflict will further inhibit the provincial government's political and economic planning priorities.

3   Findings and Conclusions

Alberta and New Brunswick have different economic histories, relationships with Indigenous Peoples, policies on the duty to consult, and experiences with developing oil and gas resources. However, despite their differences, a lot can be learned about oil and gas development and consultation with Indigenous Peoples when juxtaposing their experiences. Comparing their experiences helps elucidate how economic benefits, nation-to-nation relationships, and feelings towards consultation influence how Indigenous Peoples respond to oil and gas development. Additionally, each province's experience provides insight into how policies on the duty to consult shape community response, impact resource development projects, and impact the political and economic agendas of provincial governments.

First Nations that stand to benefit economically from oil and gas development are less likely to oppose development. This is mainly because they can improve the standards of living in their communities through a variety of socio-economic benefits and opportunities for their members. Economic benefits from oil and gas development also have the potential to lift First Nations out of absolute and relative poverty. Both ACFN and FMFN have become more accepting of oil sands development since they have achieved economic benefits and opportunities through agreements with government and industry. ACFN and FMFN have also generated a significant amount of wealth for their nations through their involvement in the oil sands. Conversely, both LLB of Alberta and EFN of New Brunswick have not been awarded similar opportunities and have strongly opposed oil and gas development.

Another factor that influences how First Nations respond to oil and gas development are their nation-to-nation relationships with the Crown, as defined by treaties and agreements between the Government of Canada, First Nations, and provincial (and territorial) governments. This is because the parameters of nation-to-nation relationships largely determine the scope of consultation around resource development. The provisions of Peace and Friendship Treaties, Numbered Treaties, Comprehensive Land Claims Agreements, and other modern agreements all shape the scope of the duty to consult differently, even though the duty is legally independent of these agreements. The impacts of oil and gas development on Indigenous nations like LLB, who were historically excluded from the Numbered Treaties, have been especially adverse, because the Nation did not have a right to be consulted by the Crown. The traditional territory of LLB has been compromised for industry profit, and the First Nation has never had a say in how development should proceed. Unsurprisingly, LLB has strongly opposed development for decades. Signatories of the Peace and Friendship Treaties, such as EFN, have also strongly opposed development. This is because its lands and resources were never surrendered to the Crown in exchange for benefits. Thus, it was inevitable that any development taking place on EFN's lands without consultation, or their consent, would incite conflict. As for signatories of the Numbered Treaties like ACFN and FMFN, the notion of ceded territory is debated. However, these First Nations acknowledge that the nature of Treaty 8 often precludes them from challenging the Crown's ownership of lands and resources. As a result, ACFN and FMFN have taken a pragmatic approach to land management and resource development to try to work in partnership with project proponents and the Crown. Lastly, Comprehensive Land Claims Agreements and other modern agreements can provide Indigenous nations like LLB with opportunities to negotiate the terms of their agreements on more equitable grounds than historic treaties (i.e., Peace and Friendship, Numbered). Indeed, the Peace and Friendship and Numbered Treaties have the shared disadvantage of being tied to a history of the Crown failing in its obligations, which further hinder and impede nation-to-nation negotiations and discussions.

Finally, when First Nations are not adequately or meaningfully consulted, they are more likely to oppose development. This is just common sense. All the First Nations mentioned in this chapter have opposed oil and gas development at some point because they did not feel like they were adequately or meaningfully consulted. However, this review shows that ACFN and FMFN have grown more receptive towards development because they have had more opportunities to engage with project proponents and the provincial government. On the other hand, First Nations like LLB and EFN have opposed development because they were not being treated equitably or fairly and were hardly consulted (if at all) about the developments taking place near their communities and on their traditional lands.

When comparing the overall experiences of both Alberta and New Brunswick, it seems that poorly thought-out and executed policies on the duty to consult can jeopardize resource development projects, and in turn, undermine the political and economic objectives of provincial governments. This has been the case with New Brunswick's inadequate consultation practices that have incited protests and riots, which also inspired the moratorium that was placed on fracking in the province and a company's ire. Although there are *many* factors to consider when evaluating how First Nations, or Indigenous Peoples more broadly, respond to development and the outcomes of resource projects, one cannot help but think that there may be a correlation between comprehensive policies (and guidelines) on the duty to consult and community non-opposition or support for resource projects. More detailed consultation policies clearly delineate expectations around the consultation process and the roles and responsibilities of all key parties involved. Not only do they bring clarity to the consultation process, but there is less room for alternative interpretations. In turn, the process is more direct and predictable, and less likely to incite conflict between engaged parties. Although the Government of Alberta's consultation policy is far from perfect, and the brevity and vagueness of the Government of New Brunswick's duty to consult policy may not have been the sole cause of conflict in 2013, it is worth considering that these policies have played an important role in shaping community response and development more broadly.

As the cases of Alberta and New Brunswick demonstrate, natural resources are a vital part of provincial economies. For any provinces that are interested in developing natural resources, whether it be oil and gas or other resources, the role that duty to consult policies (and guidelines) play in development should not be underestimated. It is in the interest of provincial (and territorial) governments to devise and deliver duty to consult policies that are, ideally, designed in collaboration with Indigenous Peoples and that ultimately enable Indigenous Peoples to benefit from development taking place in a manner that improves their relationship with the Crown (i.e., reconciliation), and ensures they are meaningfully consulted.

NOTES

1   Canada has approximately 172 billion barrels of proven oil reserves, most of which are found in the Alberta oil sands (Government of Canada 2022c).

2   The duty to consult is a constitutional legal doctrine found in section 35(1) of the *Constitution Act, 1982*. The doctrine requires the Crown (i.e., federal and provincial governments) to consult, and where appropriate accommodate, Indigenous Peoples over actions or decisions that may negatively impact their Aboriginal or Treaty Rights (Government of Canada 2021).

3   Equalization payments are transfers of funds from the Government of Canada to the provinces. These payments are meant to compensate poorer provinces for their relatively weak tax bases and/or resource endowments. Alberta was a "have" province for fifty-five years until 2020 when the COVID-19 pandemic negatively impacted the provincial economy, which resulted in the province becoming eligible for equalization payments (Rieger 2020).

4   *Haida Nation v. British Columbia (Minister of Forests)*, [2004] 3 S.C.R. 511, 2004 SCC 73.

5   *Taku River Tlingit First Nation v. British Columbia (Project Assessment Director)*, [2004] 3 S.C.R. 550, 2004 SCC 74.

6   *Mikisew Cree First Nation v. Canada (Minister of Canadian Heritage)*, [2005] 3 S.C.R. 388, 2005 SCC 69.

7   The Government of Alberta also released *The Government of Alberta's Policy on Consultation with Metis Settlements on Land and Natural Resource Management* in

2015, but investigating Alberta's relationship with Métis, or rather Métis Settlements, and corresponding policies and guidelines is beyond the scope of this chapter.

8   Other landmark cases include, but are not limited to: *Beckman v. Little Salmon/ Carmacks First Nation*, 2010 SCC 53, [2010] 3 S.C.R. 103; *Rio Tinto Alcan Inc. v. Carrier Sekani Tribal Council*, 2010 SCC 43, [2010] 2 S.C.R. 650; *Tsilhqot'in Nation v. British Columbia*, 2014 SCC 44, [2014] 2 S.C.R. 256; and *Mikisew Cree First Nation v. Canada (Governor General in Council)*, 2018 SCC 40, [2018] 2 S.C.R. 765.

9   The federal government's endorsement of UNDRIP demonstrated Canada's commitment to promoting and protecting Indigenous rights, whereas the adoption of UNDRIP signalled that Canada was a full supporter, without qualification, of UNDRIP and made a commitment to its implementation. It is also worth noting here that federal legislation on UNDRIP was eventually enacted in 2021. The United Nations Declaration on the Rights of Indigenous Peoples Act (S.C. 2021, c. 14) received Royal Assent and came into force on June 21, 2021 (Government of Canada, 2022a).

10   The ancestors of present day ACFN members signed the treaty at Fort Chipewyan in 1899.

11   A notice of question of constitutional law is when a party raises a question about the constitutional validity or applicability of legislation, a regulation or a by-law made under legislation, or a rule of common law.

12   One notable and non-confidential example is the trust fund (the Community Sustainability Fund) that ACFN was able to create with the assistance of Total Energy in 2011. The trust fund was established to enhance the quality of life of future generations by supporting community infrastructure projects associated with housing, health, social development, culture, and so on. In 2020, the fund was valued at over $60 million.

13   On September 6, 2016, FMFN signed a participation agreement for the purchase and sale of 34.3 percent equity interest in Suncor's East Tank Farm Development. The East Tank Farm serves as a storage facility for bitumen and dilutant, and as a blending and cooling facility.

14   In 1973, LLB was formally granted band status by the federal government, which provided its members with access to annual funding for social assistance, education, and social benefits. LLB was also awarded membership in the North Peace Tribal Council in 1995, which granted it access to a political forum to share and discuss information regarding Aboriginal and treaty rights.

15   According to the Government of Alberta, a caveat is a "warning (in land law) that someone is claiming an interest on a parcel of land." In other words, it is a "notice of a claim of interest on land," and its validity can be disputed in court (Government of Alberta 2022b).

16   According to Ferreira, LLB claimed 33,000 square miles of land in the area.

17   On September 23, 1982, LLB filed for an interim injunction to halt oil and gas activities temporarily until a settlement could be made on its land claims. However, its application was dismissed.

18   The Stoney Creek Field was the province's first long-term oil and gas field. It was discovered approximately 15 km south of Moncton by Contact Exploration Inc.

(Kicking Horse Energy Inc.). The McCully Gas Field, on the other hand, was discovered in 2000 by Corridor Resources Inc. The McCully field is located near Sussex.

19   It has been estimated that the Stoney Creek produced over 800,000 barrels of paraffinic oil and 28 billion cubic feet (bcf) of sweet natural gas. By comparison, the McCully Gas Field has produced over 57 bcf of natural gas to date.

20   In contrast to "have" provinces, "have-not" provinces receive equalization payments from the federal government.

21   SWN Resources Canada Inc. is a subsidiary of SWN Energy Company, which is a leading natural gas and natural gas liquids producer in the United States (Southwestern Energy Company 2022).

22   When consultation did occur, it took the form of organized meetings and group workshops led by SWN representatives who gathered "Indigenous perspectives" from community members. During these meetings, participants were not informed that they were being consulted, even though the meetings would be used as evidence of the company's "neighbourliness" (Howe 2015, at 1885 of 5224).

23   The Peace and Friendship Treaty was signed circa 1760 by Chief Michael Augustine of the Richebuctou (Richibucto) Tribe (Kennedy 2006).

References

Acden. 2020. "Welcome to Acden." Acden. Accessed September 24, 2020. https://www. acden.com/about-acden.

Alberta Native News. 2018. "Lubicon Lake Band, Alberta and Canada Celebrate Historic Land Claim Settlement." *Alberta Native News*. October 30, 2018. https://www. albertanativenews.com/lubicon-lake-band-alberta-and-canada-celebrate-historic-land-claim-settlement/.

Alexander, Matthew D., Lining Qian, Tim A. Ryan, and John Herron. 2011. *Considerations for Responsible Gas Development of the Frederick Brook Shale in New Brunswick.* Saint John: Fundy Engineering and Atlantica Centre for Energy.

APTN National News. 2013. "SWN Ending Exploration Work in NB, Will Be Back in 2015: Elsipogtog War Chief Levi." *APTN National News*. December 6, 2013. https:// www.aptnnews.ca/national-news/swn-ending-exploration-work-nb-back-2015-war-chief-levi/.

Athabasca Chipewyan First Nation v. Alberta (Minister of Energy), 2011 ABCA 29.

Athabasca Chipewyan First Nation v. Alberta, 2018 ABQB 262.

Athabasca Chipewyan First Nation. 2020. "Governance." Athabasca Chipewyan First Nation. Accessed September 15, 2020. https://www.acfn.com/governance.

Bench, Allison. 2020. "Teck Project Environmental Deal Reached Between First Nation and Alberta Government." *Global News*. February 23, 2020. https://globalnews.ca/news/6585803/environmental-deal-athabasca-chipewyan-teck-ab-government/.

Bennett, Dean. 2019. "Alberta Band Settles Long Standing Land Claim for $113 Million and Swath of Land." *The Canadian Press.* Accessed April 13, 2021. https://www.todayville.com/edmonton/alberta-band-settles-long-standing-land-claim-for-113-million-and-swath-of-land/.

Benoit, Leon. 2014. *The Cross-Canada Benefits of the Oil and Gas Industry: Report of the Standing Committee on Natural Resources.* Ottawa: House of Commons, Canada. https://www.ourcommons.ca/Content/Committee/412/RNNR/Reports/RP6644319/rnnrrp07/rnnrrp07-e.pdf.

Bird, Hilary. 2017. "Mikisew Cree and Fort McKay First Nations Close $503M Deal on Oilsands Project." *CBC News.* November 23, 2017. https://www.cbc.ca/news/canada/north/northern-alberta-first-nations-close-oilsands-deal-1.4416534.

Bissett, Kevin. 2014. "New Brunswick Introduces Fracking Moratorium." *The Globe and Mail.* December 18, 2014. http://www.theglobeandmail.com/news/politics/new-brunswick-introduces-fracking-moratorium/article22139797/.

Brown, Laura. 2015. "SWN Suspends Drilling Program in N.B., Applies for Long-term License." *Global News.* March 9, 2015. https://globalnews.ca/news/1871861/swn-suspends-drilling-program-applies-for-long-term-license/.

Brown, Silas. 2019. "New Brunswick Indigenous Chiefs Left 'Blindsided' by Decision to Lift Fracking Moratorium." *Global News.* June 5, 2019. https://globalnews.ca/news/5356115/indigenous-chiefs-issue-warning-gas-fracking/.

CBC News. 2007. "N.B. Releases its 2026 Self-sufficiency plan." *CBC News.* November 23, 2007. http://www.cbc.ca/news/canada/new-brunswick/n-b-releases-its-2026-self-sufficiency-plan-1.642089.

———. 2010. "7 N.B. Communities Among Canada's Poorest." *CBC News.* February 23, 2010. https://www.cbc.ca/news/canada/new-brunswick/7-n-b-communities-among-canada-s-poorest-1.901847.

———. 2011. "IN DEPTH: N.B. Shale Gas Industry." *CBC News.* November 26, 2011. https://www.cbc.ca/news/canada/new-brunswick/in-depth-n-b-shale-gas-industry-1.1041598.

———. 2013a. "Elsipogtog Seeks Shale Injunction, Warns of 'Radical Elements.'" *CBC News.* November 14, 2013. https://www.cbc.ca/news/canada/new-brunswick/elsipogtog-seeks-shale-injunction-warns-of-radical-elements-1.2426414.

———. 2013b. "First Nations Chiefs Divide Approach to Shale Gas." *CBC News.* November 20, 2013. http://www.cbc.ca/news/canada/new-brunswick/first-nations-chiefs-divided-in-approach-to-shale-gas-1.2433118.

———. 2013c. "McKenna Says Shale Gas Could Mean $7B in Royalties, Taxes." *CBC News.* February 11, 2013. https://www.cbc.ca/news/canada/new-brunswick/mckenna-says-shale-gas-could-mean-7b-in-royalties-taxes-1.1329931.

———. 2015. "Maliseet Chiefs Split from Assembly of First Nations Chiefs in New Brunswick." *CBC News.* October 21, 2015. http://www.cbc.ca/news/canada/new-brunswick/maliseet-mi-kmaq-assembly-split-1.3282437.

———. 2018. "Lubicon Lake Band, Government Officials Sign Historic Land-claim Settlement." *CBC News.* November 13, 2018. https://www.cbc.ca/news/canada/edmonton/lubicon-lake-band-government-officials-sign-historic-land-claim-settlement-1.4903322.

Cold Lake First Nations v. Alberta (Energy Resources Conservation Board), 2012 ABCA 304.

Corridor Resources Inc. 2015. "2012 Joint Venture Opportunity, Frederick Brook Shale Transaction Highlights." Corridor Resources Inc., August 12, 2015. https://web.archive.org/web/20201101014410/https://www.nbchf-cnbfh.ca/submission/submission-from-corridor-resources-inc/

Department of Aboriginal Affairs. 2019. *Interim Proponent Guide—A Guide for Proponents on Engaging with Aboriginal Peoples in New Brunswick.* Fredericton: Government of New Brunswick, Department of Aboriginal Affairs. https://leglibbibcat.legnb.ca/e-repository/monographs/31000000051530/31000000051530.pdf.

Donev, Jason. 2018. "Water Impacts of the Oil Sands." Energy Education. Accessed January 12, 2021. https://energyeducation.ca/encyclopedia/Water_impacts_of_oil_sands.

Dyer, Simon, and Marc Huot. 2010. "Mining vs. In Situ: What is the Highest Environmental Impact Oil?" Pembina Institute. May 27, 2010. https://www.pembina.org/pub/2017.

Elsipogtog First Nation. 2021. *Community.* Accessed June 11, 2021. https://web.archive.org/web/20210615044133/https://elsipogtog.ca/.

Fast, Stewart. 2016. "A Matter of Trust: The Role of Communities in Energy Decision-Making." University of Ottawa. November. Accessed May 1, 2021. https://www.uottawa.ca/positive-energy/sites/www.uottawa.ca.positive-energy/files/nrp_mattertrust_casestudy_kentcounty_24nov2016.pdf.

Ferreira, Darlene Abreu. 1992. "Oil and Lubicons Don't Mix: A Land Claim in Northern Alberta in Historical Perspective." *Canadian Journal of Native Studies* 12, no. 1: 1–35.

Fort McKay First Nation. 2018. "Annual Report 2018." Fort McKay First Nation. Accessed April 13, 2021. https://www.fortmckay.com/app/uploads/2020/01/FMFN_2018AnnualReport.pdf.

Fort McKay First Nation. 2021. "History and Traditional Lands." Fort McKay First Nation. Accessed April 13, 2021. https://www.fortmckay.com/our-story/history-traditional-lands/.

Galloway, Gloria, and Jane Taber. 2013. "N.B. Protesters Plan More Protests after Violent Clash with RCMP over Shale-gas Project." *Globe and Mail.* October 17, 2013. https://www.theglobeandmail.com/news/national/rcmp-move-in-on-first-nation-protesting-shale-gas-development/article14904344/.

Government of Alberta. 2005. *The Government of Alberta's First Nations Consultation Policy on Land Management and Resource Development.* Edmonton: The Government of Alberta. https://open.alberta.ca/dataset/1006f6ce-400c-4c5a-a21e-dcb511da66b4/resource/be9f23c6-cb3c-4abc-aeeb-5f8f82106b1c/

download/3118589-2005-first-nations-consultation-policy-on-land-management. pdf.

———. 2013. "The Government of Alberta's Policy on Consultation with First Nations on Land and Natural Resource Management, 2013." *Alberta Government*. Accessed April 12, 2021. https://open.alberta.ca/publications/6713979.

———. 2014. "The Government of Alberta's Guidelines on Consultation with First Nations on Land and Natural Resource Management." July 28, 2014. https://open.alberta. ca/dataset/f1eb5282-5784-45f7-a35a-f03bf206de0e/resource/263300f3-5ca9-4477-98d4-d30d505aa694/download/3775118-2014-guidelines-consultation-first-nations-land-natural-resource-management.pdf.

———. 2015. "Government of Alberta's Proponent Guide to First Nations Consultation Procedures for Land Dispositions." Edmonton: Government of Alberta. https://open.alberta.ca/dataset/747deb1f-4fa4-4357-85fa-eca52ec2079b/resource/029d7911-2904-4d9d-95dd-19b122e31ad9/download/proponentguide-firstnationsconsultation-procedureslanddispositions.pdf.

———. 2016. "The Government of Alberta's Proponent Guide to First Nations and Metis Settlements Consultation Procedures." June 6, 2016. https://open.alberta.ca/dataset/40499ce0-dd05-4e7a-b7f5-42a02e71b8ec/resource/c0adf205-ac7d-4901-b825-6f0dfaad6d9d/download/2016-proponent-guide-to-first-nations-and-metis-settlements-consultation-procedures-2016-06-06.pdf.

———. 2019. "The Government of Alberta's Proponent Guide to First Nations and Metis Settlements Consultation Procedures." Alberta Government. Accessed September 3, 2020. https://open.alberta.ca/dataset/27af23c5-e71a-482d-9d49-afdb0ec8064e/resource/73b6152a-d449-4bf6-9b67-4093b8dc9f63/download/ir-goa-proponent-guide-to-first-nations-and-metis-settlements-consultation-procedures-2019.pdf.

———. 2020. "The Government of Alberta's Policy on Consultation with First Nations on Land and Natural Resource Management, 2013 [Amended 2020]." Alberta Government. April 1, 2020. https://open.alberta.ca/dataset/801cf837-4364-4ff2-b2f9-a37bd949bd83/resource/8fa6a92a-3523-457a-b3b0-1e72f3cb79b8/download/ir-policy-consultation-first-nations-land-resources-2013-amended-2020.pdf.

———. 2022a. "Oil Sands Facts and Statistics." Government of Alberta. Accessed May 26, 2022. https://www.alberta.ca/oil-sands-facts-and-statistics.aspx#:~:text=Contact-,Overview,infrastructure %20projects %20we %20rely %20on.

———. 2022b. "Register a Land Title Document or Plan." Government of Alberta. May 30, 2022. https://www.alberta.ca/register-land-title-document-plan.aspx.

———. 2023. *Royalty Summary Revenue Workbook 2021/22*. Edmonton: Government of Alberta. https://open.alberta.ca/dataset/historical-royalty-revenue/resource/7e7dd029-e61c-4b7f-866f-0ed1b74488d5.

Government of Canada. 2008. *Canada's Equalization Formula*. Ottawa: Government of Canda, Parliamentary Information and Research Service.

———. 2010. *Canada Endorses the United Nations Declaration on the Rights of Indigenous Peoples*. Ottawa: Government of Canada. November 12, 2010. https://www.canada.

ca/en/news/archive/2010/11/canada-endorses-united-nations-declaration-rights-indigenous-peoples.html.

———. 2011. "Equalization Program." Government of Canada. Updated December 19, 2011. https://www.canada.ca/en/department-finance/programs/federal-transfers/equalization.html.

———. 2014a. "Backgrounder: Lubicon Claim Negotiations." Government of Canada. December 1, 2014. https://www.canada.ca/en/news/archive/2014/12/backgrounder-lubicon-claim-negotiations.html.

———. 2014b. "Historic Treaties in Atlantic Map." Government of Canada. Updated August 11, 2022. Accessed June 15, 2023. https://www.rcaanc-cirnac.gc.ca/eng/1371838686166/1611592678600.

———. 2016a. "Canada Becomes a Full Supporter of the United Nations Declaration on the Rights of Indigenous Peoples." Government of Canada. May 10, 2016. https://www.canada.ca/en/indigenous-northern-affairs/news/2016/05/canada-becomes-a-full-supporter-of-the-united-nations-declaration-on-the-rights-of-indigenous-peoples.html.

———. 2016b. "Oil Sands: Indigenous peoples." Government of Canada. Updated July 7, 2016. https://www.nrcan.gc.ca/energy/publications/18736.

———. 2017. "Summary Report on Recipient Audit Performed on Lubicon Lake Band." Government of Canada. Updated September 21, 2017. https://www.sac-isc.gc.ca/eng/1444341876315/1620411469234.

———. 2019. "Negotiations in Atlantic Canada." Government of Canada. Updated February 1, 2019. https://www.rcaanc-cirnac.gc.ca/eng/1100100028583/1529409875394?wbdisable=true.

———. 2021. "Government of Canada and the Duty to Consult." Government of Canada. Updated December 9, 2021. https://www.rcaanc-cirnac.gc.ca/eng/1331832510888/1609421255810.

———. 2022a. "Implementing the United Nations Declaration on the Rights of Indigenous Peoples Act." Government of Canada. Updated April 17, 2023. https://www.justice.gc.ca/eng/declaration/index.html#:~:text=Next %20Steps-,The %20United %20Nations %20Declaration %20on %20the %20Rights %20of %20Indigenous %20Peoples,Assent %20and %20came %20into %20force.

———. 2022b. "Registered Population." Government of Canada. Accessed May 31, 2022. https://fnp-ppn.aadnc-aandc.gc.ca/fnp/Main/Search/FNRegPopulation.aspx?BAND_NUMBER=463&lang=en.

———. 2022c. *Energy Fact Book 2022–23*. Ottawa: Natural Resources Canada. https://publications.gc.ca/collections/collection_2022/rncan-nrcan/M136-1-2022-eng.pdf.

Government of New Brunswick. 2010. "Alward sworn in as 32nd premier of New Brunswick." Government of New Brunswick. October 12, 2010. https://www2.gnb.ca/content/gnb/en/news/news_release.2010.10.1638.html.

———. 2011. *Government of New Brunswick Duty to Consult Policy.* Fredericton: Aboriginal Affairs Secretariat, Province of New Brunswick. https://web.archive. org/web/20220901044747/http://www2.gnb.ca/content/dam/gnb/Departments/aas-saa/pdf/en/DutytoConsultPolicy.pdf.

———. 2014. "Government Introduces Moratorium on Hydraulic Fracturing in New Brunswick." Government of New Brunswick. December 18, 2014. https://www2. gnb.ca/content/gnb/en/news/news_release.2014.12.1404.html.

———. n.d. "New Brunswick Oil and Natural Gas." Government of New Brunswick. Accessed May 26, 2022. https://www2.gnb.ca/content/dam/gnb/Corporate/pdf/ ShaleGas/en/History.pdf.

Grebe, Vanessa. 2019. "New Induced Seismicity Study: Fracking and Earthquakes in Western Canada." Government of Canada. January 10, 2019. https://www.nrcan. gc.ca/simply-science/new-induced-seismicity-study-fracking-and-earthquakes-western-canada/21672.

Hodd, Thomas. 2009. "Let's Get Creative: The Forgotten Role of Culture in New Brunswick's Quest for Self-Sufficiency." In *Exploring the Dimensions of Self-Sufficiency for New Brunswick*, ed. Michael Boudreau, Peter G. Toner and Tony Tremblay (Moncton: New Brunswick and Atlantic Studies Research and Development Centre), 196–209.

Howe, Miles. 2015. *Debriefing Elsipogtog: The Anatomy of a Struggle.* Halifax: Fernwood Publishing.

Huseman, Jennifer, and Damien Short. 2012. "'A Slow Industrial Genocide': Tar Sands and the Indigenous Peoples of Northern Alberta." *The International Journal of Human Rights* 16, no. 1: 216–37.

Hussain, Yadullah. 2014. "Well-entrenched in Oil Sands, Fort McKay First Nation Eyes Even Deeper Ties." *Financial Post.* March 13, 2014. https://financialpost.com/ commodities/energy/fort-mckay-oil-sands.

Intiar, Inda. 2019. "Indigenous Leaders Blindsided, Business Leaders Unsurprised That Shale Gas Moratorium Is Lifted." *Huddle.* June 5, 2019. https://huddle.today/ indigenous-leaders-blindsided-business-leaders-unsurprised-that-shale-gas-moratorium-is-lifted/.

———. 2020. "Corridor Will Revisit Sussex Area Fracking Plan with New Name and Management." *Huddle.* January 16, 2020. https://huddle.today/corridor-will-revisit-sussex-area-fracking-plan-with-new-name-and-management/.

Jones, Robert. 2019. "'Tough to Take': New Brunswick Grabs Unwanted Title as Canada's Poorest Province." *CBC News.* December 18, 2019. https://www.cbc.ca/news/ canada/new-brunswick/new-brunswick-poorest-province-equalization-payments-1.5400170.

Kennedy, Patricia. 2006. "Treaties, Surrenders and Agreements." Library and Archives Canada. Updated June 20, 2006. Accessed June 15, 2023. https://www. collectionscanada.gc.ca/aboriginal-heritage/020016-3012-e.html.

Lavoie, Judith. 2018. "'Nowhere Else to Turn': First Nations Inundated by Oilsands Projects Face Impossible Choices." *The Narwhal*. June 30, 2018. https://thenarwhal.ca/nowhere-else-turn-first-nations-inundated-oilsands-face-impossible-choices/.

Magee, Shane. 2019. "Sussex-area Fracking Plans Shelved Over Regulatory Uncertainty." *CBC News*. August 13, 2019. https://www.cbc.ca/news/canada/new-brunswick/corridor-fracking-sussex-regulatory-uncertainty-1.5245024.

McCarthy, Shawn. 2015. *Where Oil and Water Mix*. November 6, 2015. http://www.theglobeandmail.com/news/alberta/where-oil-and-water-mix-oil-sands-development-leaves-fort-mckays-indigenous-communitytorn/article27151333/.

Mi'gmaq and Wolastoqey Nations. 2019. "All 15 New Brunswick First Nations Come Together over Consultation Concerns with Higgs Government." New Brunswick Environmental Network. July 25, 2019. https://nben.ca/en/resources/news-from-groups/1984-all-15-new-brunswick-first-nations-come-together.html.

Murphy, Tim. 2008. *Journey to the Tar Sands*. Toronto: James Lorimer & Company Ltd.

Newman, Dwight. 2014. "The Rule and Role of Law: The Duty to Consult, Aboriginal Communities, and the Canadian Natural Resources Sector." MacDonald-Laurier Institute Aboriginal Canada and the Natural Resource Economy Series. Ottawa: MacDonald-Laurier Institute.

Park, Adrian. 2012. "Shale Gas in New Brunswick: Promise, Threat, or Opportunity?" *Journal of New Brunswick Studies* 3: 14–23.

Paskey, J., G. Steward, and A. Williams. 2013. *The Alberta Oil Sands Then and Now: An Investigation of the Economic, Environmental Social Discourses Across Four Decades*. OSRIN Report No. TR-38. Edmonton: University of Alberta.

Pederson, Cole. 2007. *Oil Sands Consultations: Aboriginal Consultation Final Report*. Calgary: Aboriginal Energy & Aboriginal Consultation Interdepartmental Committee.

Poitras, Jacques. 2019. "Indigenous Leaders Warn of Protests, Halting Developments Over Shale Gas Exemption." *CBC News*. June 8, 2019. https://www.cbc.ca/news/canada/new-brunswick/shale-gas-moratorium-exemption-sussex-indigenous-consultation-protests-1.5167450.

Richards, Tadzio. 2020. "Adam's Choice: A First Nation Weighs the Pros and Cons of Buying into the Oil and Gas Industry." *Alberta Views*. May 1, 2020. https://albertaviews.ca/adams-choice/.

Rieger, Sarah. 2020. "Alberta Becoming a 'Have Not' Province Doesn't Change Issues with Federation, Kenney Says." *CBC News*. July 28, 2020. https://www.cbc.ca/news/canada/calgary/alberta-net-receiver-financial-transfers-1.5666387.

Rooney, Rebecca C., Suzanne E. Bayley, and David W. Schindler. 2011. "Oil Sands Mining and Reclamation Cause Massive Loss of Peatland and Store Carbon." *Proceedings of the National Academy of Sciences* 109, vol. 13: 1–5.

Ruddell, Rick, and Natalie R. Ortiz. 2014. "Boomtown Blues: Long-Term Community Perceptions of Crime and Disorder." *American Journal of Criminal Justice* 40: 129–46.

Slowey, Gabrielle. 2009. "A Fine Balance: Aboriginal Peoples in the Canadian North and the Dilemma of Development." In *First Nations First Thoughts: The Impact of Indigenous Thought in Canada*, ed. Annis May Timpson (Vancouver: UBC Press), 229–47.

Slowey, Gabrielle, and Lorna Stefanick. 2015. "Development at What Cost?" In *Alberta Oil and the Decline of Democracy in Canada*, ed. Meenal Shrivastava and Lorna Stefanick (Edmonton: Athabasca University Press), 195–224.

Southwestern Energy Company. 2015. "Annual Report on Form 10-K." *United States Securities Exchange Commission*. December 31, 2015. https://www.sec.gov/Archives/edgar/data/7332/000000733216000038/swn20151231x10k.htm.

Sterritt, Angela. 2014. "Athabasca Chipewyan First Nation Makes the Best of Oil Money." *CBC News*. April 2, 2014. https://www.cbc.ca/news/indigenous/athabasca-chipewyan-first-nation-makes-the-best-of-oil-money-1.2579126.

Suncor Energy. 2016. "Suncor Energy and Fort McKay First Nation Announce Agreement for Equity Partnership in East Tank Farm Development." *Suncor Energy*. September 6, 2016. https://sustainability-prd-cdn.suncor.com/-/media/project/suncor/files/news-releases/2016/2016-09-06-suncor-energy-fort-mckay-first-nation-announce-agreement-for-equity-partnership-en.pdf?modified=20210902050919

Tasker, John Paul. 2016. "Environmentalists Have Impoverished First Nations, Pro-pipeline Chief Says." *CBC News*. December 7, 2016. https://www.cbc.ca/news/politics/pro-pipeline-trans-mountain-first-nations-poverty-1.3886008.

Thurton, David. 2020. "Environmental Watchdog Report Says Alberta Oilsands Tailings Ponds Are Tainting Groundwater." *CBC News*. September 3, 2020. https://www.cbc.ca/news/politics/oilsands-tailings-groundwater-contamination-1.5711471.

Treaty 8 First Nations of Alberta. 2023. Articles of Treaty No. 8. Accessed June 15, 2023. https://treaty8.ca/articles-of-treaty-no-8/#:~:text=And %20Her %20Majesty %20 the %20Queen,of %20the %20country %2C %20acting %20under.

Treaty 8 Tribal Association. 2021. *Treaty 8 Agreement*. Accessed April 12, 2021. http://treaty8.bc.ca/treaty-8-accord/.

Turner, Chris. 2017. *The Patch*. Toronto: Simon & Schuster Canada.

U.S. Geological Survey. 2020." How Much Water Does the Typical Hydraulically Fractured Well Require?" UCGS. Accessed June 13, 2021. https://www.usgs.gov/faqs/how-much-water-does-typical-hydraulically-fractured-well-require?qt-news_science_products=0#qt-news_science_products.

UN General Assembly. 2007. *United Nations Declaration on the Rights of Indigenous Peoples: Resolution / Adopted by the General Assembly*. October 2, 2007. A/RES/61/295 United Nations. Accessed May 26, 2022. https://social.desa.un.org/sites/default/files/migrated/19/2018/11/UNDRIP_E_web.pdf.

United States Environmental Protection Agency. 2016. *Hydraulic Fracturing for Oil and Gas: Impacts from the Hydraulic Fracturing Water Cycle on Drinking Water Resources in the United States (Final Report)*. Washington: United States Environmental Protection Agency. https://cfpub.epa.gov/ncea/hfstudy/recordisplay.cfm?deid=332990.

Vecchio, Karen. 2022. *Responding to the Calls for Justice: Addressing Violence Against Indigenous Women and Girls in the Context of Resource Development Projects*. Report of the Standing Committee on the Status of Women, House of Commons, Canada. Ottawa: Government of Canada. https://www.ourcommons.ca/Committees/en/FEWO/StudyActivity?studyActivityId=11620568.

Weldon, Tori. 2018. "Nobody Asked Us if We Want Fracking, Sussex LSD Chair Says." *CBC News*. December 4, 2018. https://www.cbc.ca/news/canada/new-brunswick/sussex-area-lsd-fracking-moratorium-1.4930621.

Williams, Laurence, Phil Macnaghten, and Richard Davies. 2017. "Framing 'Fracking': Exploring Public Perceptions of Hydraulic Fracturing in the United Kingdom." *Public Understanding of Science* 26, no. 1: 89–104.

Meadow Lake: Looking Back on 30 Years of Aboriginal Forest Management and Manufacturing

Stephen Wyatt and Jonah Dumoe

Since 1988, the nine First Nations of the Meadow Lake Tribal Council (MLTC) in Saskatchewan have been engaged in forest management, harvesting and forest product manufacturing to an extent not equalled by any other First Nation in Canada. This model is centred around the action of Mistik Management Ltd. (Mistik, a forest management company), NorSask Forest Products Inc. (NorSask, a sawmill) and Meadow Lake Mechanical Pulp (MLMP, a pulp mill), but has expanded to include a range of other businesses and operations. It has enabled the MLTC nations to exercise self-determination and accrue economic benefits from forestry operations occurring in their traditional territories. Their success has been the subject of several studies (Anderson and Bone 1995; Beckley and Korber 1996; Chambers 1999; Anderson 2002), and is often used as an example of Indigenous engagement in forestry.

The success of MLTC needs to be seen against the backdrop of First Nations engagement in Canada's forests. Historically, First Nations have inhabited forest lands in Canada, and have used a variety of knowledge and practices to utilize and manage these lands and resources to meet their cultural, spiritual, and material needs. In most cases, this close connection with lands and resources has been maintained (e.g., Berkes 1998). The same lands provide the basis of Canada's forest industry, a vital sector in the national economy, with 94% of forest lands being vested in governments (provincial, territorial, and federal), and approximately 80% of First Nation communities are located in areas of importance to the forest industry.[1] While the majority of forestry activities occur on traditional lands, studies typically find that control of these lands and resources remains with government agencies or private companies, while Indigenous communities receive relatively few tangible benefits (Parkins et al. 2006). Legal challenges by First Nations have led to landmark court rulings that have established the rights of First Nations regarding resource development occurring in traditional territories, including the *Haida* (2004), *Taku River* (2004) and *Mikisew Cree* (2005) cases (Newman 2009). As Tindall and Trosper (2013) note, the history of Indigenous/non-Indigenous relations in relation to natural resources is characterized by both conflict and collaboration, reflecting differing visions about rights, knowledge, appropriate use and, indeed, whether the land should be used or not.

Unsurprisingly, the diversity of Indigenous Peoples and land issues across Canada has given rise to an extensive literature of case studies, with a variety of disciplinary perspectives illuminating these complex relationships in different ways. Anthropological and historical analyses help us to understand the reciprocal relationship between Indigenous Peoples and their lands (Feit 2000), and how traditional institutions may apply in contemporary contexts (Nadasdy 2003). Collaborative management approaches have received much attention, highlighting both the potential benefits and the challenges and barriers that may prevent a more balanced relationship (Feit and Spaeder 2005; Natcher, Davis, and Hickey 2005). Research on economic arrangements, such as that at Meadow Lake, has explored how to promote economic development in an Indigenous context and particularly the importance of distinguishing between ownership and management roles (Hickey and Nelson 2005; Trosper et al. 2008). The colonial structures that underlie land and resource management in Canada are being increasingly questioned, especially by Indigenous scholars who stress the importance of responsibilities and relationships as a means of enabling Indigenous Peoples exercise their rights in ways that they choose (Alfred and Corntassel 2005; McGregor 2011; Corntassel 2012). The Meadow Lake experience brings together all these themes, and the success of the MLTC First Nations could serve as a model to inspire other First Nations and provincial authorities to encourage the participation of First Nations in resource development, as well as practical examples of how these complex issues and relationships can be managed. This case study examines the Meadow Lake model of forest sector development, focusing on three elements: governance, community engagement, and economic development. This approach is relevant for two reasons: to understand how First Nations can improve the socio-economic well-being of their communities through entrepreneurship and by participating in decision-making pertaining to local resource development; and to understand the elements that are critical to resolving resource development disputes in traditional territories. To do so, we review documents and annual reports from MLTC, its forestry businesses and from member First Nations. We also interviewed key people who have played critical roles in MLTC forest sector development at tribal, corporate and community levels.[2] Finally, we use a range of business and statistical data to consider the economic impacts of the Meadow Lake forestry model, including the Community Well-Being Index developed by Aboriginal Affairs and Northern Development Canada (AANDC 2015).

We begin by summarizing the development of forestry activities at Meadow Lake from the 1980s to the current day, providing a backdrop that helps understand the key elements of the Meadow Lake forestry model. We then dig deeper into this experience by focusing on three key elements: the governance and organizational structures that help to balance relations between political and economic interests, and between Indigenous and non-Indigenous parties; the mechanisms that have been established to support community engagement in forest management and to overcome challenges; and the results obtained by MLTC's economic development strategy in relation to promoting business and employment and to enhancing community well-being. These themes are all interconnected, and so our conclusion seeks to identify a number of lessons that could be of use to other Indigenous nations, to government policy making and to private enterprises who seek to collaborate with Indigenous nations.

Chronology of Meadow Lake Forest Sector Development

The Meadow Lake Sawmill was built in 1971 by Parsons and Whittemore, a U.S. firm. Although working as a sawmill, the primary function of the mill was to supply softwood chips to the Prince Albert Pulp Mill, owned by the same company. However, poor design, operational difficulties and low production led to Parsons and Whittemore abandoning the mill for several years before selling it to the provincial government in 1986 (Anderson and Bone 1995). This was an interim measure and in 1988 the Saskatchewan government sold equal parts of the mill to MLTC and to TechFor Services Ltd (a company formed by mill employees). Soon after acquisition, the company was renamed NorSask Forest Products Ltd.

Negotiations around the purchase of the mill involved conditions from both MLTC and the Saskatchewan government. In addition to the employment created by the mill, MLTC was seeking a Forest Management Licence Agreement (FMLA) that would give them forest management responsibilities over much of the traditional territories of MLTC member nations (Interview ex-MLTC, March 23, 2017). The 3.3 million hectares of Crown land covered by this FMLA included both softwood and hardwood. As the NorSask mill used only softwoods (i.e., spruce and pine), the Saskatchewan government required that MLTC agree to seek other partners to use the hardwood resource (Anderson and Bone 1995). Finally, the government required that NorSask establish forest management partnerships with all First Nations whose traditional territories could potentially be impacted by forestry development activities within the FMLA area.

In 1990, Millar Western Pulp (MWP), a forestry company located in neighbouring Alberta, agreed to establish a pulp mill at Meadow Lake as a joint venture with the Crown Investment Corporation of the Province of Saskatchewan to use the hardwoods (Anderson and Bone 1995). MWP purchased a 20% stake in NorSask, with the remainder being held by MLTC (40%) and the employees (40%). The mill began operations in 1992 with a production capacity of 240,000 air-dry-metric-tons (ADMT), but this has been increased to reach nearly 400,000 ADMT (about 1 million m^3 of logs) in 2016. With the establishment of the pulp mill, NorSask and MWP created a not-for-profit operating company called Mistik Management Ltd., each with a 50% shareholding (Mistik is a Cree word for wood). In 1998, Mistik took over responsibility for all forestry-related operations including harvesting, hauling, road construction and community engagement (Mistik 2007). Employees remained shareholders in NorSask until 1998, when MLTC bought out its partners to become sole owners. MWP also bought out the government share of the pulp mill to become the sole owner. However, in 2006, Millar Western chose to refocus its activities and the pulp mill was placed under bankruptcy protection. The following year, it was acquired by Paper Excellence, a Vancouver-based forestry company that is owned by an Asian conglomerate, and the mill is now named Meadow Lake Mechanical Pulp (MLMP) (Interview MLMP, February 15, 2018; SJRS 2016). The current ownership structure is presented in figure 6.2.

Mistik's forest management processes were challenged in 1992–93 during the Canoe Lake crisis. Following this, Mistik established a range of community engagement processes for both MLTC member communities, and other communities in the FMLA area. A comprehensive twenty-year management plan (totalling nine volumes) was approved in 1997, with subsequent updates being adopted in 2007 and 2018. Changes to provincial forestry legislation in 2002 lead to part of the original FMLA being transferred to support the establishment of a new fiberboard mill (Meadow Lake OSB) with Mistik retaining management of 1.8 million ha (see figure 6.1; Mistik 2007). The management plans paved the way for certification of Mistik operations according to sustainable forest management standards, notably the international Forest Stewardship Council standard in 2007. Finally, it should be noted that Mistik has actively supported forest-related research by collaborating in projects with a variety of university and government research institutions and a Science Advisory Board, although the latter is no longer active (Mistik 2007).

Canada's forestry economy is cyclic by nature, and NorSask and Mistik are not exempt from the rises and falls of other businesses in the forest sector. The Canadian recession of 1980–82 almost certainly affected the profitability of Parsons and Whittemore, with the establishment of NorSask coinciding with a stronger economy. Another recession in 1989–92 was followed by a relatively long period of high demand and profitability (strong U.S. demand, a weak Canadian dollar and duty-free access to the U.S. all contributed to this), during which MLTC, communities and partners were all able to enhance ongoing operations and invest in new initiatives. However, this period ended in 2004 when Canada's forest sector fell into crisis with the imposition of U.S. duties on Canadian timber (2001), the bursting of the housing bubble in the USA (2006) and the 2007–09 global financial crisis (Barriault et al. 2017). This caused great disruption across Canada, with many sawmill and paper mills closing, either temporarily or permanently. Although NorSask reduced production and employment during this period, the mill remained operational and MLMP maintained pulp production, thereby providing stability for Mistik and its contractors (see table 6.2). Since 2012, the economic viability of forestry businesses has gradually improved, but a major fire at NorSask in January 2017 and a renewal of U.S. duties on Canadian timber provide future challenges.

Formal ownership and governance structures have also changed over the years. Initially, MLTC held its NorSask shares through MLDC Investments.

Table 6.1 Timeline of MLTC Forest Sector Development

YEAR	EVENTS
1971	Parsons and Whittemore build the first sawmill in Meadow Lake.
1981	The Province of Saskatchewan acquired all mill assets from Parsons and Whittemore.
1988	NorSask Forest Product Ltd. established and the first FMLA signed (3.3 million ha).
1990	Millar Western Pulp mill built and Mistik Management Ltd. created.
1992	Canoe Lake Crisis erupted.
1993	Co-management boards established.
1994	MLTC transferred its business holdings to MLTC RDI.
1997	NorSask twenty-Year Forest Management Plan (1997–2017).
1998	MLTC acquired 100% ownership of NorSask Forest Product Ltd.
2002	Forest legislation changes, FMLA changed to a Forest Management Agreement for 1.8 million ha.
2004–12	Canada-wide forest sector crisis.
2004–07	Forest certifications—ISO 2004, CSA 2005, FSC 2007.
2007	Mistik's twenty-year Forest Management Plan (2007–2027).
2007	Paper Excellence buys pulp mill, now named Meadow Lake Mechanical Pulp (MLMP).
2013	MLTC RDI launched MLTC II.
2017	Major fire at NorSask Sawmill, subsequent rebuilding. Renewal of U.S. duties on timber.

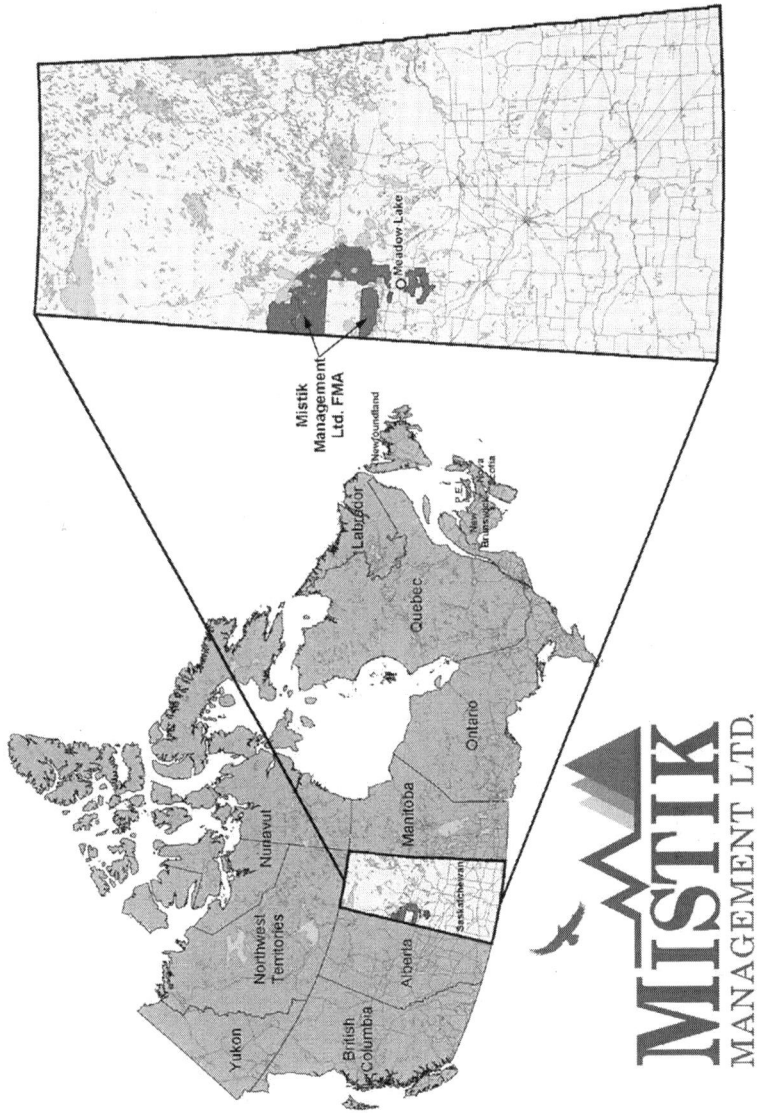

Figure 6.1:
The Mistik Forest
Management Area

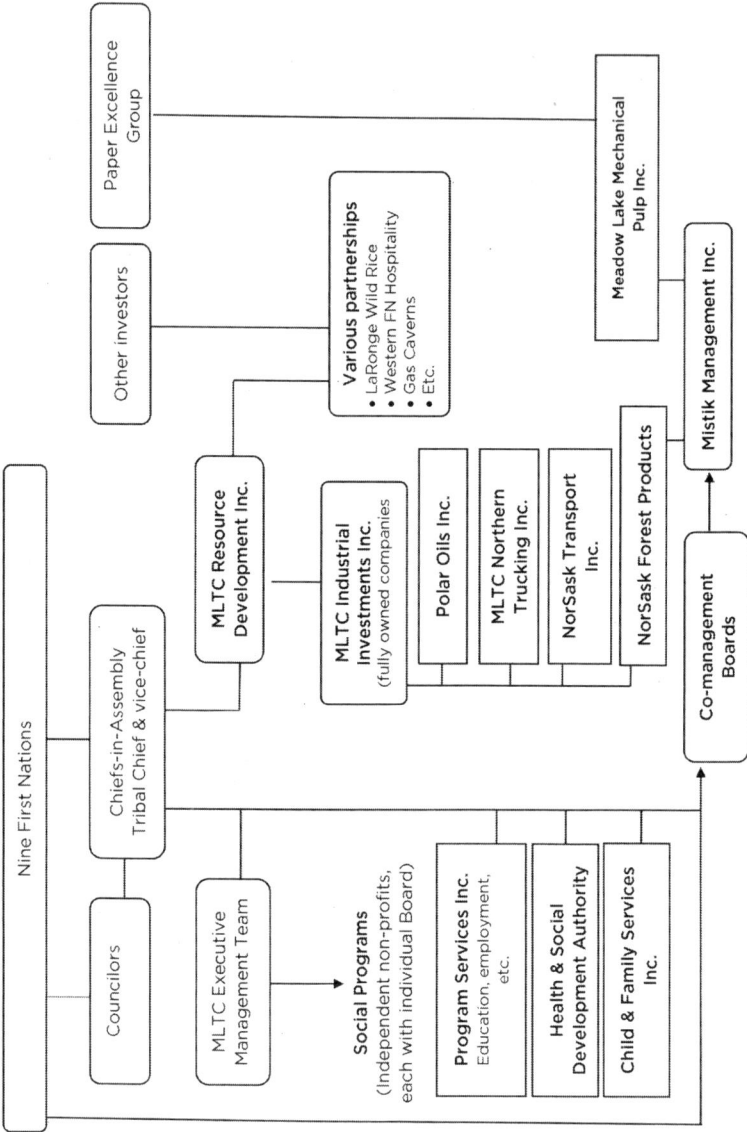

Figure 6.2:
MLTC
Governance
Structure.

Table 6.2 Key Economic indicators of Meadow Lake Forestry Businesses (1997-2016).

	1997	1998	1999	2000	2001	2002	2003	2004	2005	2006	2007	2008	2009	2010	2011	2012	2013	2014	2015	2016
EMPLOYMENT																				
NorSask	194	161	161	173	163	152	152	144	144	144	149	101	84	55	103	115	191	251	205	145
MLMP	207	206	204	202	200	173	174	171	171	171	153	164	168	169	161	164	175	184	195	195
Mistik	45	45	45	45	35	30	25	25	25	25	17	12	11	11	11	11	11	11	11	11
L&M									86	80	88	89	91	37	70	86	80	82	81	78
Harvesting	240	240	240	240	240	240	240	228	228	228	228	210	210	210	210	210	210	210	210	210
L&M Harv									41	41	38	38	36	30	32	28	26	26		
Renewal	21	21	21	21	21	21	21	17	17	17	17	17	10	10	20	20	17	17		
Total	707	673	671	681	659	616	612	585	712	706	690	631	610	522	607	634	710	781	702	639
QUANTITY OF WOOD PRODUCTS																				
MLMP Pulp	242	244	269	278	256	293	299	321	316	312	325	328	343	364	346	261	371	348	362	398
NorSask Lumber	101	101	101	107	108	109	109	76	105	76	100	85	53	24	20	57	71	95	122	106
NorSask Chip	76	76	76	74	77	71	50	49	65	50	56	51	23	11	9	27	37	50	69	57
Dillon Lumber	0	0	0	0	3	3	8	3	3	3										
L&M Lumber											12	13	16	5	17	20	21	19	17	16

Data on employment provided by MLMP and NorSask to Mistik Management and included in 10-year management plans for 1997-2006 and 2007-2016. See https://mistik.ca/forest-management/2019-fmp/. Wood product quantity is pulp, thousand air-dry-metric-tonnes; lumber, million foot-board-measure; chip, thousand oven-dry-tonnes.

Subsequently, a holding company, MLTC Resource Development LP (referred to as MLTC RDI), was formed and by 1994 all MLTC business holdings were transferred to this company (Interview MLTC II, March 23, 2017). In 1998, MLTC RDI became full owner of NorSask and the FMLA was transferred to Mistik, in which NorSask and MLMP continued to hold equal shares. In 2013, MLTC RDI formed another holding company called MLTC Industrial Investments LP (MLTC II) to manage all companies fully owned by MLTC.

Governance of Meadow Lake Forest Sector Development

Over the last thirty years, Meadow Lake has developed a fairly sophisticated governance structure for the political and commercial aspects of forest management, as well as for its other activities, as illustrated in figure 6.2. In this context, "governance" does not simply mean the actions of a government, but instead refers to the different types of relationships between governments and non-government parties as they decide on a set of rules and to operate a set of institutions that determine who gets what, where, when, and how in society (Howlett, Rayner, and Tollefson 2009).[3] In Meadow Lake, the interlocking roles of MLTC, of individual bands, of corporations owned by MLTC and bands, and of private companies all contribute to "governance."

Political Governance—The Meadow Lake Tribal Council

Meadow Lake Tribal Council has its origins in 1981 when six Cree First Nations and four Dene First Nations in Northwest Saskatchewan united to form the Meadow Lake District Chiefs joint venture. Big Island Lake Cree Nation (originally known as Joseph Bighead) subsequently withdrew from this arrangement in 1988. An agreement was signed in 1986 and the joint venture was renamed as Meadow Lake Tribal Council (MLTC) in 1996. The agreement set the basic goal of MLTC—to "continue our ancestors' mission to join and unite in a common front to protect and preserve our Indian way of life." Promoting economic development to benefit all nine nations has been a key role of all the organizations (Anderson 1997). MLTC is responsible for the common affairs of the nine nations and for the provision of a range of social programs.[4] However, the members of each nation elect their own Band Council (usually under the process established by the Indian Act), which is responsible for community affairs, and for political negotiations with provincial and federal governments.

Three groups, each with distinct functions, contribute to MLTC governance.[5] Firstly, a quasi-legislative body, referred to as the chiefs-in-assembly, is comprised of the chief of each of the nine member Nations. The chiefs-in-assembly are responsible for approving the bylaws and policies that govern MLTC. Secondly, two members of the chiefs-in-assembly are elected to four-year terms as tribal chief and tribal vice-chief, and are responsible for overall leadership of MLTC. Both positions are elected by 49 voting delegates from all nine First Nations, and if a Cree chief is elected to one post, a Dene chief will customarily be elected to the other. Finally, 47 councillors are elected by the memberships of all nine First Nations to advise the chiefs-in-assembly in making policies that will be responsive to specific needs in each First Nation community. The chiefs-in-assembly and the 47 councillors meet periodically to review operational results against planned priorities.

Rather than managing social programs from within the political structure, MLTC has chosen to establish three incorporated non-profit organizations dedicated to: health and social development; child and family services; and program services (education, employment, etc.). Each of these is wholly owned by MLTC, but with a board of directors appointed by MLTC and by each of the member nations. These boards provide oversight and help ensure that program delivery is effective and responsive to community needs, but also separates daily management from political processes. This separation of operational and political roles was a key lesson from the Harvard project on American Indian Economic Development (Cornell and Kalt 1992), and MLTC business activities have also been delegated to a separate for-profit organization. Nevertheless, some MLTC management staff consider that strict separation is not effective, as programs need to be responsive to community concerns as expressed through elections and political leaders also need to lobby governments for funding (Interviews MLTC & ex-MLTC, March 23, 2017). Balancing the advantages of each role has resulted in some changes as trends towards too much separation have been followed by moves back to increased political oversight.

Commercial Governance—MLTC RDI and MLTC II

While NorSask was a particularly important early investment for MLTC, it is not the only business owned by the council. In 1994, the council decided to transfer their shares in NorSask and other businesses to a holding corporation—Meadow Lake Tribal Council Resource Development LP (MLTC

RDI[6]). As an independent development corporation, it was intended that this would improve opportunities for joint ventures and help attract external investors. The MLTC RDI board is comprised of the elected Chiefs from each of the nine MLTC First Nations, the MLTC Tribal Chief and two independent directors with extensive business experience in the resource sector. While the presence of elected Chiefs is important from a community perspective, it can also lead to tension related to political influence and differences between business and community priorities, particularly if logging is scheduled in certain areas or if members of one community are more successful in obtaining contracts than members of another (Interviews MLTCII & ex-MLTC, March 23, 2017). Strong separation of operational management from band governance has been identified as a key factor in determining the success of Aboriginal forestry (and other) businesses in Canada (Trosper et al. 2008).

The economic growth strategy of MLTC has nevertheless been remarkably successful (section 5 below), with steady expansion in the MLTC business portfolio. As a result, in 2013, MLTC RDI launched a new holding corporation—Meadow Lake Tribal Council Industrial Investments (MLTCII[7])—which became responsible for managing all businesses that are wholly owned by MTLC. While MLTC RDI is the sole shareholder of MLTCII, the latter company is managed by an independent board of directors that cannot include elected officials from any of the member First Nations (Interview MLTCII, March 23, 2017). This arrangement limits the exposure of the First Nations to corporate and legal risks associated with the businesses. While the chiefs on the MLTC RDI board are able to set broad directions for commercial development, the fully owned MLTC businesses are also shielded from direct political influence.

Forest Sector Governance—NorSask and Mistik Management

As described previously, MLTC initially bought a 50% stake in NorSask in 1988, subsequently increasing this to full ownership in 1998. Prior to 1998, company operations were overseen by a board comprising representatives of both shareholders (MLTC and employees). With full MLTC ownership, corporate direction was set by the MLTC RDI board until 2013, and subsequently by the MLTCII board. Throughout these changes, the NorSask management team has comprised both Indigenous and non-Indigenous staff, with an increasing proportion of the former.

Governance arrangements for Mistik Management are more complex than those of NorSask. Commercial forestry in Canada is often characterized by a separation between operations in the forest and those in the mill (factories), with further separation of mills based on the principal products or wood types. In Meadow Lake, NorSask uses softwood (mainly spruce and jack pine) to produce building lumber; Meadow Lake Mechanical Pulp (MLMP) uses hardwoods (mainly aspen and poplar) to produce pulp for paper making; and Mistik Management is responsible for managing forests and timber harvesting for both mills. Mistik was established in December 1989 as a not-for-profit joint venture, with each partner owning equal shares. The pulp mill has been through several ownership structures but has been wholly owned by Paper Excellence (an Asian-owned company based in Vancouver) since 2007. As a result, the Mistik board is comprised of four directors representing NorSask and MLTC along with four directors representing MLMP and Paper Excellence (Interview Mistik, March 24, 2017). The chair of the board is a non-Indigenous person based in Meadow Lake, and decision-making is based on unanimity, rather than a majority or consensus approach. Co-management boards are also invited to one of Mistik's four board meetings each year, providing an opportunity for all groups to better appreciate wider issues and the concerns of others.

Both Mistik and NorSask have recruited qualified and experienced managers, both Indigenous and non-Indigenous. The Mistik team is responsible for planning forestry operations, harvesting, transport, and reforestation activities and ensuring community engagement while the NorSask team has maintained the viability of the sawmill in a highly competitive forest sector, including during an economic crisis that saw the closure of mills throughout Canada. Forestry operations such as harvesting, road construction, and transport are undertaken by independent contractors, often companies owned by MLTC member nations, families or individuals, but also including non-Indigenous companies. While creation of employment opportunities for individuals from MLTC communities is a central goal of the forestry program, the companies have also recruited non-Indigenous professionals with the expertise necessary to provide effective management. Several non-Indigenous staff members have been with the companies for more than a decade, providing stability and leadership both within the companies and in relationships with non-Indigenous partners. This helps ensure that the companies attain their commercial objectives and implement high quality forest management as expected by MTLC communities, while also providing training and career opportunities for members of MLTC communities.

MLTC's actions in becoming the proprietor of a sawmill and co-owner of a company holding a Forest Management Agreement issued by the provincial government can be seen as an acknowledgement of state authority over their traditional forest and of Treaties 6 and 10 signed in 1876 and 1906. However, it can also be seen as an assertion of Indigenous rights to occupy, to manage, and to benefit from their presence on the land, making the most of existing opportunities to promote economic, social, and political governance. First Nations across Canada have been faced by this dilemma of how to assert rights within a colonial governance system, with Rynard (2000), Nadasdy (2003) and McGregor (2011), among others, considering how efforts to respect and recognize Indigenous rights in forestry provide some benefits, while also falling short of what is expected or needed. It is likely that each First Nation will need to find its own response to this dilemma—"There is no concise neat model of resurgence in this way of approaching decolonization and the regeneration of our peoples" (Alfred and Corntassel 2005, 612).

Community Engagement and Forest Management

The Meadow Lake forestry model establishes a critical role for MLTC member communities in forest management in a way that complements the governance structure presented above. While the Harvard project stressed the importance of separating business and political roles, events at Canoe Lake in 1992 also showed the risks if business management becomes too separated from public concerns. Studies across Canada have described models and presented lessons on how to engage communities (both Indigenous and non-Indigenous) in forest management (McGregor 2011; Tindall and Trosper 2013; Wyatt et al. 2013; Teitelbaum 2017), but it is rare that the Indigenous community itself has such a strong position in management. Mistik and MLTC have developed a series of mechanisms to encourage community engagement in forestry.

MLTC Member Nations

Meadow Lake Tribal Council comprises five Cree Nations and four Dene Nations, all of which are located in Northwestern Saskatchewan. The head offices of MLTC are located on Flying Dust First Nation reserve, adjoining the City of Meadow Lake. In 2020, the total First Nation population of the nine member communities was nearly 16,000, including members living both on-reserve and off-reserve (see table 6.3). A tenth community, Big Island Lake Cree Nation, was part of MLTC but chose to withdraw in 1988. While Big Island Lake collaborates with MLTC on some issues, there have also been tensions.

Table 6.3 Population of MLTC Member First Nations in 2020

CREE FIRST NATIONS	ON-RESERVE	OFF-RESERVE	DENE FIRST NATIONS	ON-RESERVE	OFF-RESERVE
Canoe Lake	1,166	1,492	Birch Narrows	481	373
Flying Dust	591	906	Buffalo River	835	683
Makwa Sahgaiehcan	1,281	491	Clearwater River	1,064	1,516
Ministikwan	1,098	259	English River	827	830
Waterhen Lake	993	1,092			
Total population	5,129	4,240		3,207	3,402

Data from the Indian Register maintained by Indigenous Services Canada (ISC 2021).

While all MLTC communities share in governance arrangements, some communities are clearly closer to sites of forestry activities. MLTC head-quarters is located on Flying Dust First Nation while NorSask Sawmill, Mistik Management and MLPP are all nearby. Three other member nations (Ministikwan, Waterhen, and Makwa) are less than one hour's drive from MLTC headquarters and both mills, and so benefit more readily from direct employment opportunities. Nevertheless, communities that are further away (e.g., Clearwater River is over three hours drive) can benefit from harvesting and transport contracts provided by Mistik.

The Canoe Lake Crisis

In early 1992, Mistik commenced logging activities on the traditional territories of the Canoe Lake First Nation (the largest MLTC member nation), leading to dissatisfaction among community members (Anderson and Bone 1995; Beckley and Korber 1996; Anderson 2000). Anderson (2000) identified three main concerns among community members: 1) that clear-cut mechanical harvesting was having adverse impacts on the land and on traditional practices, including trapping and hunting; 2) that community members were unable to contribute to Mistik plans about the size of cut blocks or the rate of harvesting; and 3) that mechanical harvesting provided fewer employment opportunities and economic benefits than more traditional techniques.[8] Beginning in May 1992, protestors, led by Elders from Canoe Lake and including people from other communities, blockaded a provincial highway 65 km north of Meadow Lake, effectively preventing access to Mistik's northern logging operations (O'Meara 1993; Smith 1993). It is important to note that the protestors were not demanding an end to harvesting, but rather changes that would provide them with a more significant role in decision-making and a greater share of the benefits.

After failed attempts to negotiate the removal of the blockade, Mistik requested NorSask (legally responsible for the FMLA) to act, with the provincial government subsequently threatening to charge protestors with illegal occupation of Crown land (Beckley and Korber 1996; Anderson 2000). The protestors then filed a complaint with the Saskatchewan Human Rights Commission, alleging that the provincial government had repeatedly ignored the rights of First Nations under the treaties, under the Natural Resources Transfer Agreement and under the constitution (Smith 1993). In May 1993, the Court found in favour of the government, ordering the protestors to leave and authorizing eviction if this did not happen (Smith 1993). When the protestors vowed to stay, Mistik, with the support of NorSask and MLTC Chiefs, decided to continue negotiations rather than proceed with a court-authorized eviction. The crisis was finally resolved in October 1993 with the signature, by representatives of Canoe Lake First Nation and Mistik Management, of an interim agreement to establish co-management boards (Windspeaker Staff 1993; Anderson 2000).

Conflicts between Indigenous communities and forestry companies are common in Canada (Booth and Skelton 2011), and the Canoe Lake crisis demonstrates that Indigenous ownership alone is insufficient to ensure close relations with communities. Other activities are also needed to seek and obtain community engagement, while conflict is increasingly recognized as a factor that contributes to transformative change in relations between Indigenous and non-Indigenous peoples (Wyatt et al. 2019).

Community Engagement—Co-management and Consultation

Following the Canoe Lake crisis, Mistik and other MLTC partners have developed a range of mechanisms to engage communities, to facilitate dialogue, and to provide Mistik with better information about the land base and the ways in which it is being used. Most importantly, the 1993 co-management agreement with Canoe Lake was followed by a series of similar arrangements with other communities, although not all are referred to as "co-management boards." Most co-management arrangements in Canada are a formal arrangement between a government and local groups (Feit and Spaeder 2005), but the Mistik boards are actually company-community arrangements (Beckley and Korber 1996; Chambers 1999). By 1995, nine such boards had been established, several representing a number of communities—First Nation, Métis and non-Indigenous. These boards allow Mistik to get information about the land base, its people, culture and concerns, while also enabling communities to voice their opinions and concerns about forest management, thereby reducing the risk of protests (Beckley and Korber 1996). Since the beginning, Mistik has provided financial support to these boards, initially as a fixed amount for each board ($10,000, according to Beckley and Korber [1996]), but as an amount based on harvest volume since 1994 (Mistik email, February 6, 2018). Communities also receive dividends from forestry operations through MLTC RDI. A detailed review of two co-management boards by Chambers (1999) not only identified a number of benefits, especially in relation to greater trust, stronger relationships, and the incorporation of local knowledge, but also acknowledged barriers and recommended that efforts be made to further develop the role and capacity of the boards. Currently, eight boards provide input to Mistik's planning processes (Mistik 2015), but future work to review the advantages and barriers identified by Chambers (1999) would be useful.

In addition to the co-management boards, Mistik also has a range of other ways of engaging with communities (Mistik 2015). Firstly, a Public Advisory Group (PAG) was established in 2004 to provide a common forum for all stakeholders, including non-Indigenous communities, trappers and outfitters, municipalities, employees of NorSask, MLMP and other companies, and non-government organizations, in addition to the co-management boards. The PAG typically meets for a full day twice each year, but also facilitates information mail-outs and individual meetings between parties and Mistik. Secondly, as some of Mistik staff are members of MLTC nations, there are extensive informal contacts between them and chiefs and other members of communities, especially in advance of and during operations in particular areas. Thirdly, community members appear to be more willing to visit or contact the Mistik office to voice concerns or to obtain information than would be the case with a non-Indigenous forest manager (interview Mistik, March 24, 2017). Fourthly, preparation of the twenty-year management plan in 2015–17 included a lengthy series of consultations, public meetings and open-houses. Finally, Mistik also works with communities (both MLTC member communities and others) to support traditional practices on the land, water quality after fires and floods, and education.

Although the community engagement initiatives introduced since the Canoe Lake crisis appear to have widespread support from MLTC communities, certain challenges remain. In particular, Big Island Lake Cree Nation (not a member of MLTC) has had more limited exchanges with Mistik and has challenged certain elements of management plans and operations (KPMG 2017, 45–46). Nevertheless, recent changes in leadership and more contact appear to be helping resolve this dispute (MLTC II email February 5, 2018; Interview MLMP, February 15, 2018). These community engagement actions also need to be considered in conjunction with MLTC's role in economic development and in distributing benefits to communities.

Economic Development

Economic development has been one of the primary objectives of MLTC since 1986, aiming to "stimulate economic growth for First Nations and to encourage an entrepreneurial spirit among our people" (MLTC 1991 in Anderson 1997, 1495). This is a common theme in Indigenous forestry, leading to benefits such as employment, skills, income and autonomy, but also associated with challenges, especially in reconciling traditional values and non-Indigenous business models (Hickey and Nelson 2005; Trosper et al. 2008; Booth and Skelton 2011). In 1991, MLTC reported that 106 business projects had been undertaken during the past six years, including the establishment of NorSask, Mistik and other forest-related businesses. In 1994, MLTC decided that promoting economic development would best be achieved by adopting a strategy to "develop and establish 'anchor' businesses around which smaller enterprises can flourish bringing long lasting economic activities and benefits" (MLTC 1994 in Anderson 1997, 1495). The goal of the strategy was "to achieve parity with the province in terms of employment rate and income level [and] to create and maintain 3,240 good paying jobs in the next 20 years" (MLTC 1994 in Anderson 1997, 1495). NorSask and Mistik have since become the focal point of a network of businesses that spread through the various communities of MLTC and further afield in Saskatchewan, while also diversifying into a variety of sectors. Here, we briefly present the outcomes of this strategy using data obtained from websites of First Nations and individual businesses (see also table 6.2).

Business Development, Employment, and Revenue

THE ANCHOR BUSINESSES

While the original anchor business was the NorSask Sawmill, it is now appropriate to include Mistik and MLMP in this group. These businesses have consistently provided between 250 and 460 jobs within the region (table 6.2). Mistik itself is a relatively small employer (currently about fourteen staff), but it creates additional employment opportunities through contract activities, and these are predominately held by First Nation people. The 2015 certification report calculated that "63% of Mistik person days of employment in 2013 were performed by persons of Aboriginal descent" (KPMG 2015, 19). Table 6.4 summarizes the economic contribution of these three anchor businesses, although a breakdown of jobs held by Indigenous and non-Indigenous people is not available. Table 6.2 details direct employment and production for NorSask, MLMP and Mistik during the twenty-year period 1997 to 2016. In particular, these statistics illustrate the complementarity of the different companies. For example, sawmills in Canada tend to be cyclic, as evidenced by the fluctuation in NorSask employment between a low of 55 in 2010 (during Canada's forest sector crisis) and a high of 251 only four years later. In contrast, MLMP is more stable, with annual employment ranging from 153 to 207 throughout the whole period.

Revenue and profitability in the Canadian forest sector is highly variable. Nevertheless, MLTC financial reports indicate that in 2014–15, NorSask had an operating revenue of $56.4 million with a net income of $3.9 million. These financial records also indicate that NorSask contributed $14.1 million in dividend and related payouts to MLTC member communities over the five years 2002 to 2007. Mistik Management operates on a cost-recovery basis, with the partners contributing funds to cover operating costs, but with no dividends being declared. Nevertheless, Mistik paid a total of approximately $14.2 million in royalty (or stumpage) to the Saskatchewan government for timber harvested between 1997 and 2006, and another $8.7 million during the following ten years. Financial information for MLMP is not available.

OTHER FORESTRY-RELATED ACTIVITIES

MLTC has expanded its forestry value chain beyond NorSask and Mistik Management to include transport and fuel sales to logging trucks and equipment. This forestry value chain has created additional employment and generated additional revenues for the tribal council. Of particular importance are harvesting and log transport operations who generally work as contractors to Mistik. MLTC Logging and Reforestation Ltd was created in 1990 under contract to Mistik to supply logs to NorSask and MLMP, and by 1994 it employed 140 people and was one of the top ten logging companies in Canada (Anderson 1997). In 1996, this company was declared bankrupt following difficulties over payments by MLTC member communities (email ex-MLTC, January 30, 2018). The company was broken up in order to establish a number of smaller logging businesses owned by MLTC member communities and individuals. The largest of these is now Waterhen Forestry Products, fully owned by Waterhen First Nation, which harvests and transports 180,000 m^3 of logs per year for Mistik and employs approximately fifty people (Interview MLTCII, March 23, 2017). A number of other forestry contractors exist in other MLTC member communities, both as band-owned and private businesses, but more detailed information is not available. MLTCII is full owner of NorSask Transport and MLTC Northern Trucking, operating a combined fleet of about fifteen trucks hauling logs and woodchip to NorSask, MLMP and to other purchasers in Saskatchewan and Alberta. Not all business start-ups are successful—production of wood pellets for home heating was begun in 2011, but failed because of technical problems (Ambroziak 2017).

MLTC is also applying its forestry experience outside the original FMLA area. A small sawmill was established by NorSask in the village of Dillon (adjoining Buffalo River FN) and supplied with logs by Mistik between 2001 and 2006 (Mistik 2007), although the mill is no longer operational. Mistik is currently responsible for forest management planning for the L&M Forest Products FMLA, which covers a smaller area to the south of Meadow Lake. MLTC also contributed to the establishment of an oriented strand board (OSB) mill in Meadow Lake in 2001, with a minority shareholding in a project managed by Tolko Inc. (who took over full ownership in 2013). Most recently, in 2010, NorSask became a partner in Sakâw Askiy Management Inc. which manages the 3.3-million-hectare Prince Albert FMLA, adjoining the eastern side of the Mistik FMA.[9] Other partners in Sakâw Askiy include the Agency Chiefs Tribal Council and Montreal Lake Cree Nation, MLMP and five other

Table 6.4 Businesses Owned by MLTC and Member Communities.

NAME OF BUSINESS	PRINCIPAL ACTIVITY	OWNERSHIP	EMPLOYEES (APPROX.)*	ANNUAL REVENUE (APPROX.)*
FOREST SECTOR ANCHOR BUSINESSES				
NorSask	Softwood lumber	MLTCII 100%	100	$50-60 million
Meadow Lake Mechanical Pulp	Hardwood pulp	Papers Excellence 100%	180	n/a
Mistik Management Ltd	Forest management	NorSask 50% MLMP 50%	14	n/a
OTHER FOREST SECTOR BUSINESSES				
MLTC Northern Trucking	Transport of chips	MLTCII 100%	14	$3 million
NorSask Transport	Transport of logs	MLTCII 100%	16	$2.5 million
Polar Oil	Fuel sales, distribution	MLTCII 100%	4	$8 million
Waterhen Forestry Products	Harvesting & transport	Waterhen 100%	50	n/a
Sakâw Askiy Management	Forest management	NorSask 9.45%	n/a	n/a
Meadow Lake Bioenergy	Power Plant	n/a		Under development
BUSINESSES NOT IN THE FOREST SECTOR				
Prud'homme Gas Cavern	Gas storage	MLTC RDI 75%	n/a	$670,000
Western FN Hospitality	Super 8 Hotels	MLTC RDI 20.9%	85	$6.4 million
Lac LaRonge Wild Rice	Wild rice packaging	MLTC RDI 21%	n/a	$1 million
Ceres MLTC Fertilizer	Bulk fertilizer sales	MLTC RDI 50%	n/a	$7.3 million
RobWel Constructors	Fabrication, equipment	Clearwater 100%	n/a	n/a
Saskatoon FastPrint	Printing	Birch Narrows 70%	n/a	n/a
Tron	Mining services	English River 100%	n/a	n/a
Mudhajtik & Mintec	Mining services	English River % n/a	n/a	n/a
JNE Welding, Saskatoon	Steel fabrication	English River 30%	n/a	n/a
FDB Gravel	Gravel pit	Flying Dust % n/a	n/a	n/a
FDB Fuel	Fuel station	Flying Dust 100%	n/a	n/a
Flying Energy	Oil and gas holding co.	Flying Dust % n/a	n/a	n/a

* Employment and revenue figures are for 2016-17, or the most recent available. n/a" indicates data not available.

forestry companies. NorSask also holds an allocation of 175,000 m^3 of softwood timber from this FMLA.

NON-FOREST BUSINESSES

MLTC, member communities and private individuals have all invested in a variety of businesses that are not directly related to forestry, which are also included in table 6.4 (although we have not been able to obtain data on all businesses). Among the earliest such businesses was a partnership in 1996 with TransGas (a natural gas distributor) to construct an underground gas storage in the village of Prud'homme (250 km south-east of Meadow Lake and outside MLTC traditional lands). TransGas was seeking a First Nation partner for the project, with MLTC finally taking a 75% shareholding.[10] This project, now renewed through to 2046, provides a stable revenue of $670,000 annually, which contributes to financing other MLTC investments. Partly as a result of this revenue, MLTC has been able to take a 20.9% share of Western First Nation Hospitality, who own and operate eight Super 8 hotels in various parts of Saskatchewan. MLTC is also a shareholder in a variety of other businesses, both in their traditional lands and elsewhere in Saskatchewan, including fuel distribution, wild rice packaging and marketing.

A number of communities have also established their own businesses and shareholdings, often after having created their own holding company (following the MLTC RDI example). In 1990, Clearwater River Dene Nation purchased RobWel Constructions (located in Meadow Lake rather than in their own community), fabricating metal parts and equipment for resource industries. English River First Nation bought Tron, a mining infrastructure company, in 1997 and has since expanded into variety of other businesses in the mining sector. In 2013, Birch Narrows First Nation took a majority share in Saskatoon Fastprint, a printer in Saskatoon. Flying Energy was established in 2014 by the Flying Dust First Nation in order to establish a role in the oil and gas sector, especially in the Bakken field in southern Saskatchewan where the nation obtained lands under the Treaty land entitlement program.

COMBINED EFFECTS

MLTC RDI and MLTCII have provided information on financial benefits of their investments for member communities, but we do not have employment or revenue data for all businesses. During the five-year period April 2002 to March 2007, MLTC paid over $15 million in dividends to member communities, representing nearly $1.7 million per community.[11] Dividend payments are usually made several times each year, with individual payments to each community during this period ranging from $7,000 to $300,000. It should be noted that this period included the beginning of Canada's forest sector crisis (2004–12). MLTC has determined that dividends should be distributed with an equal share to each community, rather than being adjusted to reflect the population of the community. Communities may use these payments for community services or may choose to establish their own businesses or purchase shares in other businesses.

While table 6.4 is not a full list of businesses and investments and much data is missing, it does illustrate the extent and diversity of economic development of the MLTC communities since the early 1990s. We are not able to provide a clear history of all businesses or to determine whether or not these are a result of the anchor strategy outlined by MLTC in 1994. For example, to our knowledge, only Waterhen Forestry Products was established as a direct result of NorSask Forest Products Limited. However, a number of businesses have been created with financial resources and experience made available as a result of profitable forest sector businesses, and others have been established in response to needs or opportunities linked to the forest sector. Anderson (2002) identified 243 direct jobs related to forestry and estimated a further 730 indirect jobs. At the time of writing, the MLTC RDI website notes that their portfolio of eight companies employs more than 2,400 people. Employment data for the forestry businesses (table 6.2) shows an average of 657 direct jobs per year for the period 1997 to 2016. Hence it does appear that MLTC and member communities have been able to leverage their success as owner/manager of NorSask to obtain investment funds and partners, to take advantage of business opportunities and to expand cash flow, without necessarily using profits from NorSask.

Partnerships and Relationships

The number and variety of agreements, joint ventures and partial shareholdings described above and in figure 6.2 and table 6.4 illustrate the importance of partnerships in the Meadow Lake model. NorSask began as a joint venture in the sawmill between MLTC and non-Indigenous workers, successfully creating a profitable business where previous individual efforts by Parsons and Whittemore and by the Saskatchewan government had failed. However, the financial viability of NorSask was conditional upon the establishment of a pulp mill to use the hardwood from the licence area, and this required that NorSask find a suitable industrial partner who was willing to work with MLTC and NorSask in managing and harvesting the forest. The industrial partners, initially Millar Western and then Papers Excellence, have been prepared to work with Norsask and MLTC in a situation where neither party has a majority shareholding in Mistik. This is different to many other joint ventures between First Nations and non-Indigenous forest companies where one partner holds more shares than the other (even if only a few percent).

Successful partnerships are not simply the outcome of formal arrangements, and representatives from both MLTC and non-Indigenous businesses stress the importance of building relationships through these partnerships. This has required building trust and long-term relationships between MLTC and industry partners. Nevertheless, both parties mentioned the presence of conflicts over issues including priority harvesting areas; scheduling; costs of wood delivered to mills; harvesting practices and clear-felling (Interviews ex-MLTC, Mistik & MLMP, March 23–24, 2017, February 15, 2018). Nevertheless, an emphasis on people, on communicating and listening, and on having a consistent vision (which helps focus on beneficial outcomes) has proven useful. According to one senior Mistik representative, the corporate management framework with unanimous decisions and equal shares "should not work." However, instead of causing gridlock, this obliges board members to respect and appreciate the perspectives of others, knowing that neither party can override the other and that they have to find a solution. This has been a source of innovation and has helped to build trust (Interview Mistik, March 24, 2017). Industry representatives also appear to appreciate the professionalism and expertise of MLTC and of its forestry operations, noting that political changes in MLTC or the individual band councils rarely lead to changes in management direction or in the underlying relationships (Interview MLMP, February 15, 2018). However, they did note that there are a number of cultural differences between Papers Excellence and the Dene and Cree peoples of MLTC, and that it was necessary to ensure that these differences did not develop into conflicts.

Joint ventures such as Mistik, or partial shareholdings such as Sakâw Askiy Management, are not the only forms of partnerships. Businesses that are fully owned by MLTC or by individual First Nations, such as MLTC Northern Trucking and Waterhen Forestry Products, are in contractual arrangements with Mistik and also with MLMP (among others). Managers of these businesses need to establish their own relationships, addressing issues similar to those mentioned above. Furthermore, these contractors are also in competition with non-Indigenous contractors within the region and from elsewhere. Hence they need to respond to expectations and needs within their communities while also ensuring economic viability in their commercial operations. As such, Mistik has acted as an incubator for small business, providing contract opportunities, financial assistance, and management support to member nations and to individuals seeking to engage in forestry (Interview ex-MLTC, March 23, 2017).

Income, Employment, and Community Well-being

An important goal of MLTC's economic development strategy was to improve the quality of life for members by providing employment and revenue opportunities. While some previous studies have compared revenue and employment data (e.g., Anderson 2002), we have chosen to use the Community Well-Being Index (CWBI), developed by researchers at Aboriginal Affairs and Northern Development Canada (AANDC 2015). The CWBI integrates census data for four factors—education (high school and university), housing (quantity and quality), labour force (participation and employment), and income—to produce a unified index value that ranges from 0 to 100, in addition to individual indices for each factor. This provides a more complete view than simply comparing employment or revenue figures and also facilitates comparison between Indigenous and non-Indigenous communities. We accessed the CWB scores for each of the nine MLTC First Nations, covering the period from 1981 to 2016. We also compared average CWBI for the MLTC communities to averages for First Nation and non-Indigenous communities in Saskatchewan and across Canada. Figures 6.3 to 6.7 present several key indicators, using the 1 to 100 index, although data was not available for all communities in each census year.

All MLTC member nations experienced improvement in community well-being, except for Mistikwan Lake, which had the same CBWI in 2016 as in 1981. A significant slump in 2006 was compensated for by stronger growth to 2011 in some communities, but levels in 2016 are still below those of 2001 for other communities. We note that four communities—Flying Dust, Canoe Lake, Buffalo River, and English River—are to be found fairly consistently among the highest CBWI scores. We do not know why this should be so, other than noting that the MLTC offices are to be found on Flying Dust reserve, just outside of Meadow Lake. Nor can we explain why Mistikwan Lake

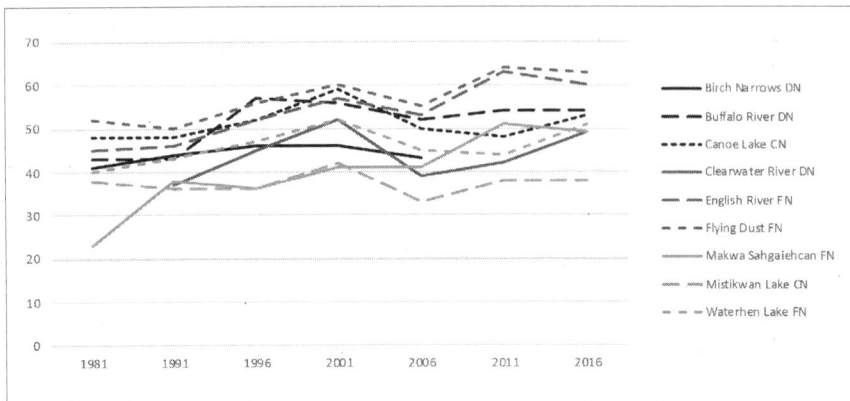

Figure 6.3: Community Well-Being Index (1-100) for the MLTC Nations (1981–2011).
Note: Data source is ISC (2023). CN is Cree Nation, DN is Dene Nation, and FN is First Nation.

has not increased it's CBWI. Finally, we note that Makwa Sahgaihcan First Nation (in the southwestern part of the MLTC area) has made the biggest gains in CBWI, progressing from 23 in 1981 to 51 in 2011, but falling back to 49 in 2016.

The slump in CBWI in 2006 is unfortunately consistent with a broader trend. In their analysis of CBWI across the country, AANDC (2015) notes that average CBWI for First Nations fell in both Saskatchewan and Manitoba in 2006, even though it rose in most other provinces. This appears to be related to housing—the AANDC report noted that housing quality had dropped even though the number of houses had increased, resulting in an overall decline in the housing index in 2006. The 2006 census also coincided with a downturn in Canada's forest sector, which would likely have impacted employment and income in communities engaged in timber harvesting and working for NorSask (see table 6.2). This would almost certainly have affected labour activity in some communities, with a roll-on effect on income (which depends mainly upon employment and government transfers). Hence it appears likely that the 2006 slump is due principally to falling housing quality across Saskatchewan as a whole, with a lesser impact from the forest sector downturn.

Figure 6.4 compares CBWI against provincial and national averages and shows the extent of the gap between First Nations and non-Indigenous

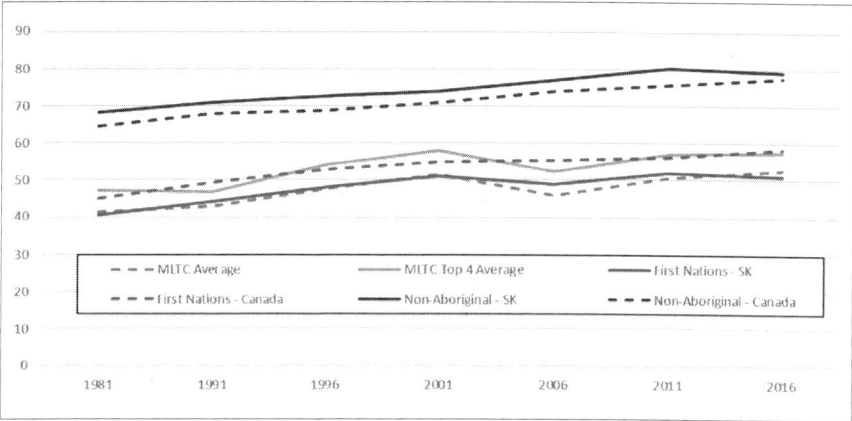

Figure 6.4: Comparing Community Well-Being Index (1-100) for the MLTC Nations Against Other Groups (1981–2016).
Note: Data source is ISC (2023).

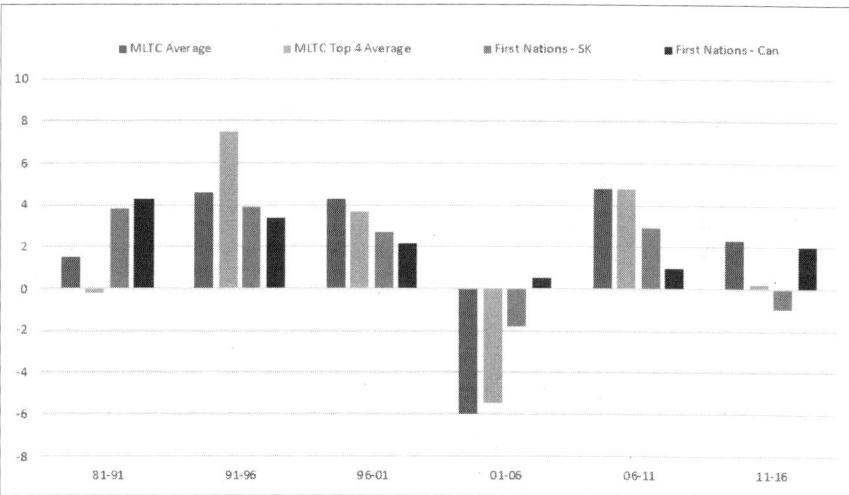

Figure 6.5: Comparing Change in Community Well-Being Index (1-100) Across Five-year Periods (1981-2016).
Note: Data source is ISC (2023).

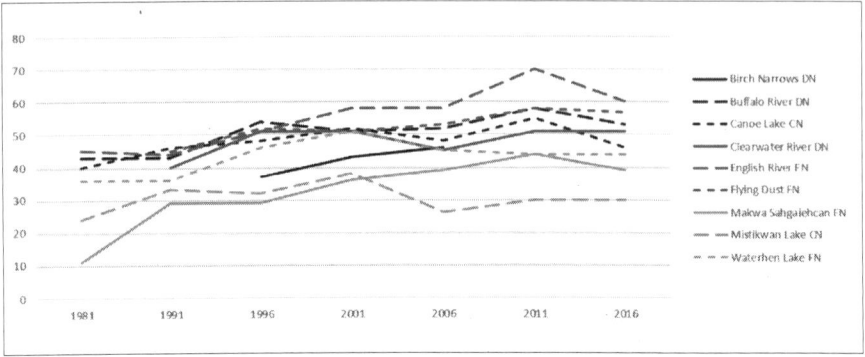

Figure 6.6: Income Component of the CBWI (1-100) for the MLTC Nations (1981–2016).
Note: Data source is ISC (2023). CN is Cree Nation, DN is Dene Nation, and FN is First Nation.

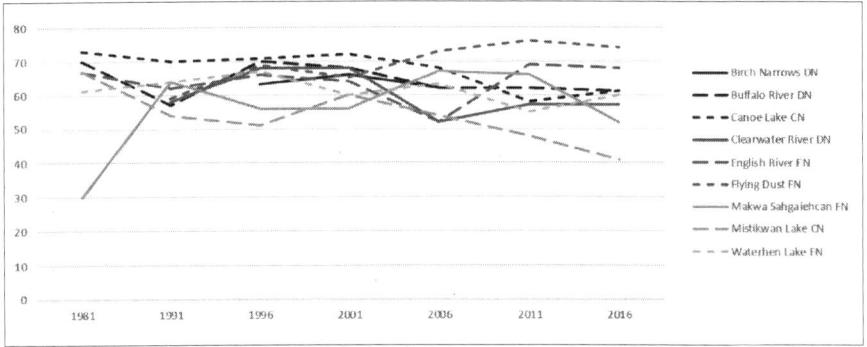

Figure 6.7: Labour Force Component of the CBWI (1-100) for the MLTC Nations (1981–2016).
Note: Data source is ISC (2023). CN is Cree Nation, DN is Dene Nation, and FN is First Nation.

communities at both national and provincial levels.[12] The average CBWI for the nine MLTC communities is consistent with the provincial average for First Nations up until 2001, before falling below in 2006 and 2011 and then moving higher in 2016. However, the average for the top four MLTC communities has remained consistently above the provincial average and exceeded the national average on several occassions. An examination of the rate of change (figure 6.5) shows that the MLTC communities have improved at a faster rate than the provincial and national averages except for the slump in 2006.

Results for income and labour are broadly consistent with those presented by Anderson (2002) who examined changes in employment rates and family income between 1986 and 1996, but the CBW indices provide a more nuanced perspective. Overall, per capita income in the MLTC member nations increased from 1981 to 2016, although a number of communities experienced drops in 2006 and 2016. Four communities (Waterhen, English River, Canoe Lake and Mistikswan Lake) have all declined from 2001 to 2016 (figure 6.6). Several other communities experienced a temporary drop in 2006, before recovering in 2011. Labour force activity (figure 6.7), representing both the employment rate and the number of people available for work, appears variable with no clear trend.

Discussion and Conclusion

Although Meadow Lake's involvement in forestry has been successful, there have also been a number of events that could have caused its failure—the Canoe Lake protests, the forest sector crisis from 2006, relations with non-Indigenous partners, meeting expectations of member communities and contractors, obtaining forest certification, and so on. Avoiding and overcoming these events and achieving successful outcomes provides a number of lessons for other Indigenous nations, for the private sector, and for policy makers from both federal and provincial governments.

MLTC adopted and maintained a consistent economic development strategy, aimed at establishing anchor businesses in forestry as a key sector. Revenues from these businesses have not simply been returned to community services, but have also been re-invested in other businesses, by both the tribal council and member communities. MLTC and member communities appear to have been fairly successful both in identifying business opportunities and in choosing private sector partners, although there have been some failures. With this economic strategy, employment and community well-being have increased faster than the average for Saskatchewan First Nations, although this remains well behind non-Indigenous communities. This creation of wealth within communities also contributes towards greater autonomy by reducing First Nation's dependence upon government funding. While there are many indicators that this economic development strategy has been a success, we consider that there is still a need for more detailed work on employment, income and other returns, and on factors that have contributed to the creation of successful subsidiary businesses within the anchor strategy.

Partnerships and relationships have been an important characteristic of the Meadow Lake model. Government assistance was essential at the start-up stage in agreeing to transfer the mill and an FMLA, and policy appears to have been generally supportive of First Nations owned businesses (although our data is limited). However, it is the engagement of non-government stakeholders that is particularly remarkable in the Meadow Lake model. The partnership of unionized non-Indigenous workers and nine First Nations to turn around a failing government-owned sawmill is especially noteworthy. Subsequently, private sector partners have included a major pulp mill (now owned by an Asian-based firm) and shareholders in businesses in forestry, oil and gas, hospitality, and other sectors. Recognizing different interests, partners have had to develop trust and confidence in each other.

Strong professional management, by both Indigenous and non-Indigenous staff, has contributed to providing leadership for NorSask and Mistik, to enhancing employment and career opportunities for MLTC member communities, and to ensuring relationships with non-Indigenous partners. Importantly, the companies have recruited non-Indigenous professionals to key positions, recognizing that the long exclusion of First Nations from forestry and other resource sectors has resulted in a shortage of skills and experience among members of the communities. In addition to providing contracting opportunities for small businesses (whether owned by individuals or bands), Mistik and MLTC have provided financial and management support and facilitated access to training.

The governance structure has contributed to the success of the model with strong institutions and clear distinctions between political and business roles. The chiefs-in-assembly, tribal chief and vice-chief, and the roles of councillors all provide accountability back to member communities. As Jorgenson (2007, 24) stated, "When Native Nations back up sovereignty with stable, fair, effective, and reliable governing institutions, they create an environment that is favorable to sustained economic development. In doing so, they increase their chances of improving community well-being." The distinction between the business and political roles of MLTC is consistent with the Harvard project on American Indian Economic Development (Cornell and Kalt 1992), which found that the successful American Indian reservations were those that separated their business operations from the influence of political power. Hence, rather than MLTC chiefs being responsible for managing businesses, this role has been delegated to MLTC RDI and MLTCII. In a similar way, MLTC has delegated social programs to non-profit organizations with independent boards within the MLTC structure, while still maintaining a degree of political oversight.

Community engagement is a critical counterbalance to the separation of political and business roles. As the Canoe Lake crisis demonstrated, business management that does not pay sufficient attention to community concerns risks facing conflict. The co-management boards and other public engagement processes established by Mistik Management provide ways for community members and their chiefs to influence forest management, while reducing opportunities for undesirable political interference in matters that should be left to business managers. The MLTC experience also demonstrates that bilateral agreements between communities and businesses can be effective in ensuring effective consultation on natural resource development, and that government-mandated processes are not always necessary. Nevertheless, it must be acknowledged that this community engagement approach is strongest with Mistik but is not the norm for other businesses. Furthermore, as noted for Big Island Lake Cree Nation, tensions that have continued over many years are only now being resolved, demonstrating equally the usefulness of third-party forest certification systems.

The Meadow Lake model also provides options for sovereignty and autonomy. MLTC's initial engagement in the sawmill partnership was conditional upon being granted an FMLA that delegated responsibility for much of the MLTC traditional lands to Mistik Management—an action of territorial affirmation. Although Mistik is only 50% controlled by MLTC and their practices must respect provincial regulations, its management system and style effectively provide a high degree of autonomy to MLTC. Revenue, employment, and other benefits created through forestry and other businesses contribute to making the MLTC communities less dependent upon government transfers and programs, representing both economic and social autonomy. Furthermore, opportunities created by NorSask, Mistik and other businesses have enabled hundreds (if not thousands) of individuals from MLTC member communities to gain skills and expertise and build their capacity in management of natural resources and in other sectors. The participation of Mistik and NorSask in Sakâw Askiy Management could help to expand the Meadow Lake model, adapting it to the needs of a different set of First Nations and their partners.

This review of MLTC's efforts in forestry, and in other business sectors, since 1988 has sought to understand the critical elements of the process that has enabled the tribal council to effectively use their natural resources to leverage greater autonomy on their traditional lands and provide improved benefits and well-being to their population. Although the available information is incomplete, much of this does indicate that the Meadow Lake model has been successful. There have of course been challenges and failures in implementing this model, but along with successes, these provide valuable lessons for other Indigenous nations who seek to assert a greater role in managing and using the natural resources on their traditional lands. We hope that this story will enable MLTC members and leaders to appreciate the uniqueness of what they have achieved and assist other Indigenous Peoples to adapt these lessons to their own situations.

Acknowledgements

This study would not have been possible without the support of key individuals and organizations involved in the Meadow Lake forestry model. Chief Eric Sylvestre of the Meadow Lake Tribal Council welcomed us to the organization and the community, shared his experience and insights and provided us with access to documents and staff. Al Balisky of MLTCII, and previously manager of Mistik, co-ordinated our visit and meetings with key informants, and provided a wealth of information. We were especially lucky to be able to speak with three people who contributed to establishing the Meadow Lake forestry model and we hope that this study bears witness to the vision, commitment and perseverance of Richard Gladue, Ray Ahenakew, and Vern Bachiu. From Mistik, Roger Nesdoly, Bill Murray, Kevin Gillis and Brenda Nightingale, chair of the board, gave us their time and knowledge in addition to sharing an impressive quantity of documentation. At MLTC, Isabelle Opikokew and Christine Derocher explained the governance and institutional structures that underlie much of the success of MLTC and its economic and social programs. Blaine Holmes guided us around the NorSask Sawmill, Paul Orser of MLMP emphasized the importance of the relationships between the partners, and Erica Gladue and Shayne Gladue of MLTC Northern Trucking helped us to recognize the network of businesses that contribute to the Meadow Lake success. Looking to the past, we believe that it is important to remember the names and contributions of several people who helped lay the foundations of the Meadow Lake forestry model: Percy Durocher and

Jim Dalgleish were MTLC Chief and CEO during the initial years and the Canoe Lake crisis; Allen Brander, manager of the sawmill as it transferred from government ownership to NorSask and first CEO of the company; Ray Cariou, chairman of both NorSask and Mistik; and Ty Rutzki, Bob Stromberg and Brock Folkersen—all of whom helped build the governance and financial structures. Finally, we acknowledge the Dene and Cree people of northwest Saskatchewan and their ancestors who acted as stewards of this land over countless generations, providing the basis for everything described in this study.

NOTES

1   Natural Resource Canada. "Forest land Ownership." Accessed July 25, 2017. http://www.nrcan.gc.ca/forests/canada/ownership/17495.

2   Interviews with key informants are identified as sources in the text. However, in order to protect confidentiality, these are referred to by either an organization or a generic group.

3   See also Institute on Governance (IOG), "Defining Governance." Accessed November 5, 2017, https://iog.ca/what-is-governance/.

4   For the roles and responsibilities of the MLTC, see "Governance & Organizational Structure of MLTC," Meadow Lakes Tribal Council, https://www.mltc.ca/governance.php, accessed August 8, 2023.

5   "Governance & Organizational Structure of MLTC."

6   "About MLTC RDI," MLTC Industrial Investments LP (MLTCII), https://mltcii.com/about/rdi/

7   See "MLTC Industrial Investments LP," MLTC Industrial Investments LP, http://mltcii.com/, accessed August 8, 2023.

8   O'Meara, Diana, "Protesters want Logging Control" *Windspeaker*, 10, no. 5 (1992): 12, http://www.ammsa.com/publications/windspeaker/protesters-want-logging-control-0.

9   "Prince Albert Timber Supply Area," Sakâw Askiy Management Inc. (Sakâw), http://www.sakaw.ca/.

10   Documents provided by MLTC RDI.

11   Documents provided by MLTC RDI.

12   The City of Meadow Lake follows the Saskatchewan average almost exactly.

References

AANDC. 2015. The Community Well-Being Index: Well-Being in First Nations Communities, 1981–2011. Ottawa: Aboriginal Affairs and Northern Development Canada.

Alfred, Taiaiake, and Jeff Corntassel. 2005. "Being Indigenous: Resurgences against Contemporary Colonialism." Government and Opposition vol 40, no. 4: 597–614. Doi: 10.1111/j.1477-7053.2005.00166.x.

Ambroziak, Phil. 2017. "NorSask returning to capacity." *Northern Pride*. August 3, 2017. https://northernprideml.com/2017/08/norsask-returning-to-capacity/.

Anderson, Robert B. 1997. "Corporate/Indigenous Partnerships in Economic Development: The First Nations in Canada." World Development vol. 25, no. 9: 1483–503. doi: https://doi.org/10.1016/S0305-750X(97)00050-8.

———. 2000. "The Case of the Meadow Lake Tribal Council." In This Case was Written by Dr. Robert B. Anderson for the Purpose of Entering the 2000 Aboriginal Management Case Writing Competition. Lethbridge, Alberta: University of Lethbridge.

———. 2002. "Entrepreneurship and Aboriginal Canadians: A Case Study in Economic Development." Journal of Developmental Entrepreneurship 7, no. 1: 45–65.

Anderson, Robert B., and Robert M. Bone. 1995. "First Nations Economic Development: A Contingency Perspective." Canadian Geographer / Le Géographe canadien 39, no. 2: 120–30. doi: 10.1111/j.1541-0064.1995.tb00407.x.

Barriault, Francis, François Bellavance, Julien Dutil-Seguin, Catherine Gagné, Alexandre Gendron, Pierre-Louis Harton, Vincent Robillard-Cogliastro, and Stephen Wyatt. 2017. "The softwood lumber dispute: Is a solution possible?" The Forestry Chronicle 93, no. 01: 9–16. doi: 10.5558/tfc2017-005.

Beckley, Tom, and Dianne Korber. 1996. Clear Cuts, Conflict and Co-management: Experiments in Consensus Forest Management in Northwest Saskatchewan. Edmonton: Natural Resources Canada, Canadian Forest Service, Northern Forestry Centre.

Berkes, Fikret. 1998. "Indigenous Knowledge and Resource Management Systems in the Canadian Subartic." In Linking Social and Ecological Systems: Management Pratcices and Social Mechanisms for Building Resilience, ed. Fikret Berkes and Carl Folke (Cambridge: Cambridge University Press), 414–36.

Booth, Annie L., and Norman W. Skelton. 2011. "'There's a Conflict Right There": Integrating Indigenous Community Values into Commercial Forestry in the Tl'azt'en First Nation." Society & Natural Resources 24, no. 4: 368–83.

Chambers, Fiona. 1999. "Co-management of Forest Resources in the NorSask Forest Management Licence Area, Saskatchewan: A Case Study." Master's thesis, University of Calgary.

Cornell, Stephen, and Joseph P Kalt, eds. 1992. What can Tribes do? Strategies and Institutions in American Indian Economic Development. Los Angeles: University of California.

Corntassel, Jeff. 2012. "Re-envisioning Resurgence: Indigenous Pathways to Decolonization and Sustainable Self-determination." Decolonization: Indigeneity, Education & Society 1, no. 1: 86–101.

Feit, Harvey A., and Joseph J. Spaeder. 2005. "Co-management and Indigenous Communities: Barriers and Bridges to Decentralized Resource Management— Introduction." Anthropologica 47, no. 2: 147–54.

Feit, Harvey. 2000. «Les animaux comme partenaires de chasse; Réciprocité chez les Cris de la baie James.» Terrain 34: 123–42.

Haida Nation v. British Columbia (Minister of Forests), [2004] 3 S.C.R. 511.

Hickey, Cliff, and Mark Nelson. 2005. Partnerships Between First Nations and the Forest Sector: A National Survey. Edmonton, Alberta: Sustainable Forest Management Network.

Howlett, Michael, Jeremy Rayner, and Chris Tollefson. 2009. "From Government to Governance in Forest Planning? Lessons from the Case of the British Columbia Great Bear Rainforest Initiative." Forest Policy and Economics 11, nos. 5–6: 383–91. doi: 10.1016/j.forpol.2009.01.003.

ISC. 2021. Registered Indian Population by Sex and Residence, 2020. Ottawa, Indigenous Services Canada.

———. 2023. Community Well-Being Index. Gatineau: Indigenous Services Canada, Government of Canada. https://open.canada.ca/data/en/dataset/56578f58-a775-44ea-9cc5-9bf7c78410e6.

Jorgenson, Miriam, ed. 2007. Rebuilding Native Nations: Strategies for Governance and Development. Tucson: University of Arizona Press.

KPMG. 2015. Forest Management Surveillance Audit #3 Report for Mistik Management Ltd., Forest Management Agreement area, Meadow Lake, Saskatchewan. Vancouver, BC: KPMG Forest Certification Services Inc.

———. 2017. Forest Re-certification Audit Public Summary report for Mistik Management ltd., Forest Management Agreement area, Meadow Lake, Saskatchewan. Vancouver, BC: KPMG Forest Certification Services Inc.

McGregor, Deborah. 2011. "Aboriginal/non-Aboriginal Relations and Sustainable Forest Management in Canada: The Influence of the Royal Commission on Aboriginal Peoples." Journal of Environmental Management 92, no. 2: 300–10. doi: 10.1016/j.jenvman.2009.09.038.

Mikisew Cree Nation v. Canada (Minister of Canadian Heritage), [2005] 3 S.C.R. 388.

Mistik. 2007. 20-Year Forest Management Plan: Volume I, Background Information Document (1997–2006). Meadow Lake, SK: Mistik Management Ltd.

———. 2015. Public Consultation Plan. Meadow Lake, SK: Mistik Management Ltd.

Nadasdy, Paul. 2003. Hunters and Bureaucrats: Power, Knowledge, and Aboriginal-State Relations in the Southwest Yukon. Vancouver: UBC Press.

Natcher, David, Susan Davis, and Cliff Hickey. 2005. "Co-Management: Managing Relationships, Not Resources." Human Organization 64, no. 3: 240–50.

Newman, Dwight G. 2009. The Duty to Consult: New Relationships with Aboriginal Peoples. Saskatoon: Purich Publishing.

O'Meara, Diana. 1992. "Protesters want Logging Control." *Windspeaker*, 10(5):12. Accessed July 12, 2017. http://www.ammsa.com/publications/windspeaker/ protesters-want-logging-control-0.

Parkins, John R., Richard C. Stedman, Mike N. Patriquin, and Mike Burns. 2006. "Strong Policies, Poor Outcomes: Longitudinal Analysis of Forest Sector Contributions to Aboriginal Communities in Canada." Journal of Aboriginal Economic Development 5, no. 1: 61–73.

Rynard, P. 2000. "'Welcome In, but Check in your Rights at the Door': The James Bay and Nisga'a Agreements in Canada." Canadian Journal of Political Science 33, no. 2: 211–43.

SJRS. 2016. Paper Excellence Current and Future Operations Benefits Foot Print Study. Regina, SK: SJ Research Services inc. and FPInnovations for Paper Excellence.

Smith, D.B. 1993. "Saskatchewan Defy Court-Ordered Eviction." *Windspeaker*, 11 (6):3. Accessed July 12, 2017. http://www.ammsa.com/publications/windspeaker/ saskatchewan-protesters-defy-court-ordered-eviction.

Taku River Tlingit First Nation v. British Columbia (Project Assessment Director), [2004] 3 S.C.R. 550, 2004 SCC 74.

Teitelbaum, Sara, ed. 2017. Community Forestry in Canada: Lessons from Policy and Practice. Vancouver: UBC Press.

Tindall, David, and Ronald L. Trosper. 2013. "The Social Context of Aboriginal Peoples and Forest Land Issues." In Aboriginal Peoples and Forest Lands in Canada, ed. David Tindall, Ronald L. Trosper and Pamela Perreault (Vancouver: UBC Press), 3–11.

Trosper, Ronald, Harry Nelson, George Hoberg, Peggy Smith, and William Nikolakis. 2008. "Institutional Determinants of Successful Commercial Forestry Enterprises Among First Nations in Canada." Canadian Journal of Forest Research 38, 2: 226–38. doi: 10.1139/X07-167.

Windspeaker Staff. 2017. "Meadow Lake Protesters Reach Agreement with NorSask." *Windspeaker*, 11(16): R2. Accessed August 12, 2017. http://www.ammsa.com/ publications/windspeaker/meadow-lake-protesters-reach-agreement-norsask.

Wyatt, Stephen, Jean-François Fortier, David C. Natcher, Margaret A. Smith, and Martin Hébert. 2013. "Collaboration between Aboriginal Peoples and the Canadian Forest Sector: A Typology of Arrangements for Establishing Control and Determining Benefits of Forestlands." Journal of Environmental Management 115, no. 1: 21–31. doi: 10.1016/j.jenvman.2012.10.038.

Wyatt, Stephen, Martin Hébert, Jean-François Fortier, Édouard-Julien Blanchet, and Nathalie Lewis. 2019. "Strategic Approaches to Indigenous Engagement in Natural Resource Management: Use of Collaboration and Conflict to Expand Negotiating Space by three Indigenous Nations in Quebec, Canada." Canadian Journal of Forest Research 49: 375–86. doi: 10.1139/cjfr-2018-0253.

Conclusion

Jennifer Winter and Brendan Boyd

The goal of this edited volume is to advance understanding of the relationship between Indigenous Peoples and resource development in Canada through a series of case studies where Indigenous Peoples had a critical role as partners, as protestors, or somewhere in between. We use the lens of resource governance to explore the mechanisms, processes, and institutions for successful establishment of mutually beneficial partnerships and greater involvement and control by Indigenous Peoples in decision-making. The chapters in this book provide different perspectives on the experiences Indigenous Peoples in Canada have had with resource development. The contributing authors address this important issue by investigating a cross-section of resource development projects—oil and gas, renewable energy, mining, and forestry—in Canada where Indigenous Peoples have played a critical role in the projects. As we discuss in the introduction, political and legal developments in Canada have purportedly empowered Indigenous communities and has given them greater say in resource governance and decision-making. Despite legal advancements, we observe slow and uneven progress in developing equitable and mutually acceptable relationships and outcomes among Indigenous communities, resource development companies, and government. This necessitates a better understanding of *what works* in these relationships. While we do not accept prima facie that resource development on or in Indigenous territories is inevitable or beneficial, our focus is on the institutions, mechanisms, and processes used to consult and engage Indigenous communities. Fine-grained analysis of institutions and processes through case studies addresses an important gap in the literature discussing Indigenous Peoples and resource development in Canada. Specifically, exploring how industry and governments consult and engage with Indigenous communities, and the relationships that exist among these actors, is essential to creating better processes and outcomes. With this conclusion, we summarize each chapter's contribution, then describe key themes from the overall work.

In chapter 1, Boyd, Lorefice, and Winter examine policy statements and guideline documents related to consultation and engagement produced by Indigenous groups, government, and industry, thus providing insight into each actor's perspective on the barriers and challenges to consultation. The actors have different documented approaches to resource development. Indigenous groups' documents revealed that resource development is often thought of in the context of reconciliation. In contrast, the analysis suggests that governments are most concerned with fulfilling legal obligations, and industry with reducing risk. Relatedly, an important place where perspectives and objectives differed is the timing of consultation: Indigenous groups raise concerns that industry and governments dedicate insufficient time to establishing trusting relationships and respectful and meaningful consultation. Moreover, the authors find agreement across the different actors' documents that meaningful consultation requires involving Indigenous Peoples in the design of the consultation process itself. A limitation of the approach of analyzing policy documents is that the documents say nothing about the process of engagement and consultation in practice, and the analysis is point-in-time; the case studies provide more fine-grained detail on institutions, processes, and mechanisms.

In chapter 2, Cameron, Martin, and Sharpe describe the development of modern treaties in Yukon, and the implications for resource governance. They argue that First Nations in Yukon have looked for meaningful partnerships with the Crown, which has driven them to sign modern treaties. This has led them to have more say in decision-making, leading to the Nations operating on a more equal footing with government and industry. The authors argue the institutionalization of co-management and co-relational governance explains why there have been few instances of First Nations-driven protests over resource development. The key conclusion from this chapter is that the creation of mutually beneficial institutional partnerships is a long process, and one that requires patience, compromise, and dedication. Moreover, the authors find a precondition for positive relationships is stable institutions, where the institutional processes are negotiated between equal partners.

In chapter 3, Rodon, Therrien, and Bouchard examine whether impact assessment processes and impact benefit agreements contribute to meaningful consultation, and whether the presence of a land claims agreement facilitates these mechanisms in achieving meaningful consultation. They do this through analyzing Indigenous engagement in the approval processes of two mineral development projects in Inuit Nunangat: the Mary River project in Nunavut and the Voisey's Bay project in Nunatsiavut. The key conclusion from this chapter is that impact assessment and impact benefit agreement processes allow proponents to fulfill their duty to consult and to secure the consent of Indigenous groups, but do not provide assurance that the projects will meet the expectations of affected communities. In particular, the authors argue free, prior, and informed consent (FPIC) principles are emerging as a new norm for engagement with Indigenous Peoples, but there is a lack of clarity around the objectives of consultation and the definition of FPIC in Canadian projects.

In chapter 4, McMillan, Maloney, and Gaudet review the history of the Mi'kmaq Rights Initiative and the Kwilmu'lw Maw-klusuaqn Negotiation Office (KMKNO). The Mi'kmaq did not participate in the federal claims commission program, instead establishing their own course of action for consultation and negotiation methods. The chapter highlights the tension between creating a process and organization that pools the collective power of individual communities, while continuing to respect their unique interests and autonomy. The key conclusion from this chapter is that a process that ensures the rights of the Mi'kmaq are respected and acknowledged does not alone ensure the success of negotiations and consultations. Openness and accountability on the part of those representing the Mi'kmaq is required to maintain the support of those they represent.

In chapter 5, Bikowski and Slowey explore what factors influence whether an Indigenous community chooses to support or reject oil and gas projects. They answer this question by using an analytical framework to compare the experiences of Indigenous communities affected by development of the Athabasca oil sands in Alberta with those of the Frederick Brook shale play in New Brunswick. They argue the vastly different outcomes—development in Alberta and its lack in New Brunswick—are a direct result of each province's approach to the duty to consult. The key conclusion from this chapter is that it is in governments' best interest to devise clear plans and policies that will help Indigenous communities feel invested and secure in development projects. Specifically, the same characteristics of modern treaties that ameliorate differences between the Crown and Indigenous communities on the subject of resource development can be applied to consultation processes, and provide legal, political, economic, and cultural certainty to Indigenous communities.

In chapter 6, Wyatt and Dumoe examine the Meadow Lake model of forest sector development, focusing on three elements: governance, community engagement, and economic development. The chapter demonstrates how First Nations can improve the socio-economic status of their communities through entrepreneurship and participation in decision-making regarding local resource development and describes elements that are critical to resolving resource disputes in traditional territories. The authors note that while Meadow Lake's involvement in forestry is and has been successful, it was not without challenges. The key conclusion from this chapter is that a governance structure that maintains clear distinctions between political and business roles, along with community engagement to allow community members to influence resource management, leads to improved economic outcomes and increased autonomy and sovereignty for Indigenous communities. The Meadow Lake example demonstrates that bilateral agreements between communities and businesses can be an effective mechanism for meaningful consultation, and that government-mandated processes are not always necessary.

The case studies in this volume demonstrate how Indigenous communities work within and outside frameworks and processes established by governments and industry to assert their rights and self-determination in resource development. Borrows (2016) notes that there is weak policy or legislative support for Indigenous economic self-determination or control over Indigenous-driven economic and natural resource development outside of government- or business-initiated projects. This often leaves Indigenous communities with little actual power to drive decisions about development. Moreover, the fact that consultation and engagement processes are imposed on Indigenous communities rather than co-developed reflects the fact that institutions and processes are still defined and controlled by the state, limiting the involvement of Indigenous Peoples in decision-making. A common thread through the case studies is the persistent failure of Canadian governments to recognize and respect Treaty Rights, despite the emphasis on procedural duty to consult in policy documents analyzed in chapter 1. And yet, the case studies show that despite the imperfect and biased nature of Canadian institutions—and governments' failures to uphold Indigenous rights—communities are able to engage in self-determined development.

This volume offers four broad lessons. First, the importance of co-management or co-governance arrangements in respecting Indigenous rights and maintaining the autonomy of Indigenous Peoples, particularly through the examples of Yukon (chapter 2), Mi'kmaq (chapter 4), and Meadow Lake (chapter 6). These arrangements support ongoing community engagement, and result in relationships characterized by respect and consent between self-determining partners. Developing governance arrangements was a complex and decades-long process for the Indigenous communities involved. The Yukon and Mi'kmaq experiences demonstrate that establishing self-determination and rights-based governance is a lengthy and adversarial process that remains imperfect, in part because of the fraught nation-to-nation relationship with the Crown. A key failure of governments in these processes was failure to treat the Indigenous communities as equal partners and recognize their rights. In contrast, the Meadow Lake example shows that despite an adversarial situation with protests, private proponents can develop respectful co-management relationships with Indigenous communities. The lesson from all three case studies is that a precondition of positive relationships is accepted institutional spaces for decision-making processes, where Indigenous rights are recognized and upheld, and Indigenous communities are equal partners.

In contrast to the above examples, chapter 3 shows that implementation matters as much as process. The example of Inuit engagement in mining projects governed by the Nunavut Land Claims Agreement demonstrates that engagement processes under land claim agreements can be insufficient and superficial even with co-management agreements in place. This shows that while process is important, implementation is also crucial. The Voisey's Bay case study offers a similar conclusion through a different mechanism. There was no formal agreement in place, but community members and Inuit nation representatives were highly involved in negotiations and the deliberative processes, in the end giving their consent to the project. These five examples speak to the importance of Indigenous communities' assertion of their Treaty Rights and equal footing in negotiations, and recognition of these rights by project proponents and governments.

Second, and relatedly, is the importance of transparency and accountability within Indigenous nations, between representatives and the community members they represent, as part of the stable institutions underpinning effective partnerships and resource governance. This is exemplified by the experiences of the Mi'kmaq (chapter 4), Meadow Lake (chapter 6), and communities participating in the impact assessment of the Voisey's Bay and Mary River mines (chapter 3). The Mi'kmaq developed a unique self-governance model with the KMKNO co-ordinating consultation on behalf of member nations, balancing collective negotiations and communities' individual needs. As McMillan, Maloney, and Gaudet note, the scope and breadth of KMKNO activities mean communication and accountability is paramount in KMKNO fulfilling its mandate and defending Treaty Rights.

Meadow Lake deliberately separated business operations from the influence of political power, and the political governance structures prioritize accountability. The Meadow Lake example also emphasizes that Indigenous-led businesses must also engage with its communities to manage concerns and Treaty Rights. With Voisey's Bay, communities were fully informed about the content of the impact benefit agreement (IBA) and voted in favour of the mine and the IBA. In the Mary River mine case, the land claims agreement process channelled Inuit communities' concerns through local and regional representatives. Divergent views between community concerns and representatives' views, alongside a secretive negotiation process, led to substantial opposition and a superficial engagement process.

Third, economic benefits of development can be closely tied to self-determination, sovereignty, and autonomy, but are not necessarily. The experiences of Fort McKay First Nation (chapter 5) and Meadow Lake (chapter 6) show how strategic investments enable less dependence on government transfers and programs, creating economic autonomy that leads to greater social autonomy. The Mary River project (chapter 3), in contrast, created tension between community members and local and regional representatives, exacerbated by the secretive nature of the Inuit Impact and Benefit Agreement negotiations and the fact that the agreement was signed before the impact assessment process. In this instance, the economic benefits stymied self-determination and undermined the governance process.

Fourth, it is imperative to improve implementation of meaningful consultation and engagement. This is a theme reflected in all chapters, but most poignantly in the discussion of expectations and impact benefit agreements in mining (chapter 3), the long and drawn-out process to recognize Mi'kmaq rights (chapter 4), the comparison of support for oil and gas development in Alberta and New Brunswick (chapter 5), and the analysis of documents related to consultation and engagement (chapter 1). Canadian governments and businesses struggle with the concept of effective and meaningful consultation. Whether this is deliberate—relying on existing institutions to advance development over Indigenous rights—or comes from uncertainty about the application of often-narrow legal guidance to a specific project, current norms can and should change. Several court cases provide guidance, which is slowly changing processes and procedures, but the legal system is a time-consuming and financially costly avenue for dispute resolution. Protest is an effective means for Indigenous communities to uphold their rights, but it is systemic institutional failures that lead to this outcome. Fundamentally, Canadian institutions need to change. A more productive approach is suggested by the case studies presented above: co-develop principles and processes where Indigenous communities are equal partners.

We also note some areas of future research we have identified through developing this edited volume. First, there is much more that can be shared regarding Indigenous Peoples' experiences with resource development and consultation and engagement processes; the chapters presented in this book are a small subset of these experiences. We hope that more Indigenous communities will consider sharing their perspectives and experiences so that self-determination and rights-based governance becomes the norm rather than the exception. Second, and relatedly, there is much scope for research identifying and quantifying the failures of current institutions in upholding Indigenous rights. This goes beyond analysis of court cases and requires co-operative research on large and small injustices related to resource development. Third, as noted by Rodon, Therrien, and Bouchard, the ambiguity inherent in current consultation and approval processes with regard to addressing or considering Indigenous Peoples' concerns appears to require the implementation of a real process reflecting FPIC. The case studies presented in this volume further highlight the need to clarify the objectives of consultation and the definition of FPIC in Canada.

References

Borrows, John. 2016. *Freedom and Indigenous Constitutionalism*. Toronto: University of Toronto Press.

Contributors

VICTORIA A. BIKOWSKI is a PhD candidate in the Department of Politics at York University, Toronto. Her research is focused on how Crown policies on the duty to consult affect Indigenous Peoples and natural resource development in Canada. She has served as a lecturer in the Faculty of Business Administration at Lakehead University, where she taught a course on governance, ethics, and Indigenous business. Victoria is currently a consultant at Suslop Inc., where she works with Indigenous nations and organizations on various development projects at the local, regional, and national level.

KAREN BOUCHARD is a doctoral student in political science at Université Laval. Her research, entitled "Can Modern Treaties Reverse the Resource Curse? A Case Study on the Effects of the Nunavut Land Claims Agreement on Mining and Inuit Socioeconomic Development," examines how the institutions established through Modern Treaties may enhance the positive effects and mitigate the negative repercussions of mining in Nunavut. Her research is part of the Modern Treaties Implementation Research Project co-directed by Thierry Rodon, Professor of Political Science at Université Laval, and Alastair Campbell, Senior Policy Advisor at Nunavut Tunngavik Inc, the Nunavut Inuit land claim organization. Her PhD also contributes to the Knowledge Network on Mining Encounters and Indigenous Sustainable Livelihoods: Cross-Perspectives from the Circumpolar North and Melanesia/Australia (MinErAL Network). Karen has additionally collaborated on research projects with the Nisga'a Lisims Government on the impact of Modern Treaties on Indigenous well-being. Karen is a recipient of a Joseph-Armand Bombardier Canada Graduate Scholarship (SSHRC), the doctoral scholarship of the *Chaire de recherche Sentinelle Nord sur les relations avec les sociétés Inuit* and Northern Scientific Training Program awards. She works part-time as a research analyst in the Strategic Research and Data Innovation Branch at the Departments of Indigenous Services and Crown-Aboriginal Relations and Northern Affairs Canada.

BRENDAN BOYD is an Assistant Professor at MacEwan University in Edmonton, Alberta. He investigates why, how, and with what effect governments learn from each other when developing solutions to critical policy issues. In particular, he studies the role of learning and other cross-jurisdictional influences among Canadian provinces responding to climate change. He is the co-editor of *Provincial Policy Laboratories: Policy Diffusion and Transfer in Canada's Federal System* published by University of Toronto Press.

KIRK CAMERON was born in Whitehorse. He has 20 years of experience in public service at all levels of government, including as Deputy Minister with the Yukon government. In 2003 Kirk moved to consulting, and started his own company in 2009—the Northern Governance Institute. As a public servant, consultant, or elected official, he has worked with all Yukon First Nations, the Yukon government, the Province of British Columbia, the Government of Canada, and the City of Whitehorse. He is co-author of two books, *The Yukon's Constitutional Foundations* (1991) and *Northern Governments in Transition* (1995), as well as many articles on governance and renewable and non-renewable resources topics relating to the territories in Canada. Kirk was first elected to Whitehorse City Council in 2011 and served to March 2015. He was re-elected in October 2021. Other roles have included Justice of the Peace, Acting Chair of the Yukon Environmental and Socio-economic Assessment Board, and Vice-Chair of the Whitehorse Chamber of Commerce. Kirk has three amazing sons pursuing their careers at university and in the private sector. In semi-retirement he enjoys spending time on the deck in the sun with his wife, Vickie Cameron (who loves her deck plants!).

JONAH S. DUMOE (BComm, MAES, MPP, PMP) is an exertive and high-impact professional with experiences in business, economic development, public policy, research, and technology. In previous roles, Jonah served as economic development officer working in First Nation communities in Canada, and graduate research assistant (under the supervision of Dr. Stephen Wyatt) in resource development and forest management in First Nation communities. Jonah also has experience in technology and business operations including serving as project manager for Morgan Stanley Strategic Portfolio globally responsible for technology project lifecycle management policy development, compliance, and oversight. Jonah holds a Bachelor of Commerce degree from MacEwan University in Edmonton, Alberta, a Master in Applied

Environmental Studies (MAES) degree in local economic development from the University of Waterloo, in Waterloo, Ontario, and a Master of Public Policy (MPP) degree from the University of Calgary, in Calgary, Alberta. He is also a certified project management professional (PMP) by the project management Institute of the United States (PMI). Jonah and his family reside in Maryland, in the United States.

TWILA GAUDET (BA, LLB) is a member of Glooscap Mi'kmaw Nation and the Director of Consultation for Kwilmu'kw Maw-klusaqn Negotiation Office.

SOPHIE LOREFICE is an associate in the Litigation and Dispute Resolution Group at Denton's. Her practice area includes commercial and general civil litigation, contract disputes, insurance, estates, privacy and class actions. Sophie takes a client centered approach and works diligently to solve client's legal problems and achieve their goals. Prior to joining the Firm as an associate, Sophie completed her articles with Dentons and served as a summer student in 2019. She also worked in house in commercial real estate in 2018. Prior to her legal studies, Sophie was a Research Associate at the School of Public Policy, University of Calgary.

JANICE MARIE MALONEY (BA, LLB, LLM, KC) is originally from Sipekne'katik Mi'kmaw Nation and is the Executive Director of Kwilmu'kw Maw-klusaqn Negotiation Office, the Mi'kmaq Rights Initiative.

EMILY MARTIN (MA) has Swiss-Alsatian heritage and was raised on the Haldimand Tract, in the territory of the Six Nations. Her career has been deeply focused on free, prior, and informed consent (FPIC) and the duty to consult and accommodate in the context of resource development and land/ water relationships. She completed her MA in partnership with the Little Salmon/Carmacks First Nation (LS/CFN) on the topic of FPIC in the context of mining in LS/CFN Territory and the Yukon more generally. Emily has served as a consultation advisor to a Crown regulator, worked as an independent consultant for First Nation and Crown government clients, and as a Manager of both development and conservation files for the Saugeen Ojibway Nation. Today Emily works as a consultant, researcher, and negotiator.

L. JANE MCMILLAN is Chair and Professor, Department of Anthropology at St. Francis Xavier University in Antigonish, Nova Scotia. Her PhD is from the University of British Columbia (2003). From 2006–2016, Professor McMillan held the Canada Research Chair for Indigenous Peoples and Sustainable Communities. She served as President of the Canadian Law and Society Association from 2012–2014. As a legal anthropologist, she has had the privilege of working with Indigenous communities for more than 25 years, conducting community-driven participatory research and applied policy analysis, and advocating for justice, self-determination and Indigenous treaty and livelihood rights. A former eel fisher and one of the original defendants in the Supreme Court of Canada's *Marshall* decision (1999), she keenly studies the progress of rights implementation in Mi'kma'ki. Professor McMillan is the author of the award-winning *Truth and Conviction: Donald Marshall Jr. and the Mi'kmaw Quest for Justice* (UBC Press 2018) and received the Outreach Award from StFX University in 2021. She is a member of the Mi'kmaq / Nova Scotia / Canada Tripartite Forum Justice Committee, the Atlantic Policy Congress First Nations Chief Secretariat's steering and research subcommittees, and the advisory committee of the Indigenous Justice Strategy. She served on the Research Advisory Board of the Nova Scotia Mass Casualty Commission and, more recently, an "Expert" Advisory Panel to Corrections Service Canada. Dr. McMillan was appointed *Special Advisor, Indigenous Research and Learning Partnerships* at St. Francis Xavier University in 2022. She is a member of the Board of Directors of Innocence Canada.

THIERRY RODON is a professor in the Department of Political Science at Université Laval and holds the INQ Research Chair in Northern Sustainable Development. He currently leads MinErAL, an international and interdisciplinary research project focused on extractive industries and Indigenous livelihood. The project involves researchers and Indigenous partners from Canada, Australia, New Caledonia, and Fennoscandia. He has authored three books: *En partenariat avec l'État* in 1998, *Nested Federalism and Inuit Governance in the Canadian Arctic*, with G. Wilson et C. Alcantara, published by UBC Press in 2020, and *Les apories des politiques autochtones au Canada* published by Presses de l'université du Québec in 2019. He has also co-edited with M. Papillon, *Peuples autochtones et ressources naturelles: regards croisés sur les défis de la mise en oeuvre du consentement libre préalable et éclairée*, published in 2023 by L'Harmattan.

CODY SHARPE holds a Doctor of Philosophy degree from the Johnson-Shoyama Graduate School of Public Policy. He has worked in the public, private, and non-profit sectors and has over fifteen years of experience developing policy advice for organizational leaders, managing programs while directly engaging stakeholders, and educating adult learners in post-secondary and public contexts. Cody has also served as a facilitator and consensus-builder for organizations looking to improve their communications and develop shared strategic priorities. Cody is currently a board member with the Canadian Evaluation Society Education Fund.

GABRIELLE SLOWEY is an Associate Professor in the Department of Politics at York University and is a member of the graduate programs in Politics and Socio-Legal Studies. She is also the former Director of the Robarts Centre for Canadian Studies at York (2015–2021). She was the inaugural Fulbright Chair in Arctic Studies at Dartmouth College (USA) and a York-Massey Fellow. Her research focuses on the political economy of land claims, treaties and self-government, especially across the north/Arctic and in areas where resource extraction takes place. Her work considers questions of community health, environmental security, climate change and Indigenous rights in these contexts. Her approach is very much community-based and community-driven research. It draws upon broader theoretical concerns of colonialism, reconciliation, staples and democracy. In 2018 she was co-PI on a SSHRC Indigenous Research Capacity and Reconciliation Connection Grant for a project titled "Spirit and Intent: The Yukon Umbrella Final Agreement Today and Tomorrow: Supporting the Transfer of Knowledge and Promoting an Understanding of What the Agreements Mean to Improve Future Governance opportunities and relationships." She is the author of numerous publications including Navigating Neoliberalism: Self-Determination and the Mikisew Cree First Nation.

AUDE THERRIEN holds a Master in Political Science from Laval University. Her master's thesis dealt with the social housing politics in Nunavik. She is interested in Indigenous and northern policies and in the participation of Indigenous communities in public management. She has worked for the Quebec housing corporation where she was involved in the evaluation of the social housing programs in Nunavik. She also worked for seven years as coordinator for the Northern Sustainable Development Research Chair.

JENNIFER WINTER is an Associate Professor in the Department of Economics and the School of Public Policy, University of Calgary, and the Departmental Science Advisor at Environment and Climate Change Canada. Her research evaluates climate policies, and examines the effects of government regulation and policy on energy development and the associated consequences and trade-offs. Dr. Winter is an expert in the analysis of policy options for mitigating greenhouse gas emissions and carbon pricing, with experience in advising governments and translating knowledge into formats that are accessible to non-expert audiences. She has testified to the Senate of Canada and House of Commons on emissions pricing policies based on her work in this area, and has advised governments in Canada in several capacities. Dr. Winter is actively engaged in increasing public understanding of energy and environmental policy issues, and serves on several boards and advisory committees.

STEPHEN WYATT is Professor for social forestry and forest policy at the School of Forestry, Université de Moncton at Edmundston, New Brunswick. He holds a PhD and a Masters in Forest Science from Université Laval in Québec and a Bachelors degree in Forestry from the Australian National University. Dr. Wyatt worked in forest management, community development and research positions in Australia, the South Pacific and Quebec before moving to New Brunswick in 2004. He takes his inspiration from Jack Westoby (former head of the FAO Forestry Division), who said "Forestry is not about trees, it is about people. And it is about trees only insofar as trees can serve the needs of people." Most of his research over the last twenty years has been with Indigenous communities in Canada, who are reasserting their rights and knowledge on their traditional lands to develop new models of engagement. He also works on social and community forestry, public participation, forest policy and for equity, diversity, and inclusion in forestry.

Index

mining projects: in British Columbia, 23; in Nunavut, 9, 23. *See also* Mary River project; Voisey's Bay project
Ministikwan Lake Cree Nation, community of, 203, 213, 217
Ministry of Fisheries and Oceans, 135
Mistik Management: community engagement processes, 193, 219; creation of, 192; and forest sector, 193, 200; governance of, 201; location of, 203; management team, 201; and Meadow Lake forestry model, 189; and Meadow Lake Tribal Council (MLTC), 208, 219; and non-Indigenous staff, 200, 207, 218; and opportunities for MLTC communities, 218–19; partnerships, 212, 219
MLMP. *See* Meadow Lake Mechanical Pulp (MLMP)
MLTC. *See* Meadow Lake Tribal Council (MLTC)
MLTC RDI. *See* Meadow Lake Tribal Council Resource Development LP (MLTC RDI)
MLTCII. *See* Meadow Lake Tribal Council Industrial Investments (MLTCII)
modern treaties, 16n4, 63–64; and co-management, 11, 79; development of, 60; and environmental monitoring by Indigenous groups, 12; importance of, 63; pros and cons, 11–12; and reconciliation, 70–71; view of treaty-making process as illegitimate, 11
Montreal Lake Cree Nation, 208
MOU. *See* Tripartite Memorandum of Understanding (MOU)
MWP. *See* Millar Western Pulp (MWP)

National Centre for First Nations Governance, 31
National Energy Board, 8. *See* Canada Energy Regulator
Native Council of Nova Scotia, 129
netukulimk, 132, 144; concept of, 117, 119, 149n11; as guiding principle, 121, 131; and livelihood fishing, 144; as Mi'kmaw traditional law, 139; and sustainability, 144
New Brunswick: Government of, 170–71; oil and gas development in, 168, 172; residents of, 170, 172, 174–75
Newfoundland and Labrador, 13, 129; Government of, 46n7, 90

NIRB. *See* Nunavut Impact Review Board (NIRB)
Nisga'a Final Agreement, 11
Nisga'a Tribal Council, 87
NLCA. *See* Nunavut Land Claim Agreement (NLCA)
non-settlement lands, 64, 68. *See also* settlement lands
NorSask Forest Products: and forest sector, 193, 214; governance of, 201; management team, 200–1; and Meadow Lake forestry model, 189; and Meadow Lake Tribal Council (MLTC), 192, 199; and Millar Western Pulp (MWP), 192; and non-Indigenous staff, 200–201, 207, 218; opportunities for MLTC communities, 218–19; partnerships, 208, 211–12, 219
Northern Gateway pipeline, 35
Northwest Territories (NWT), 3, 12, 26
Nova Scotia, 116, 129; Government of, 30, 121–22; Made-in-Nova Scotia Process, 112, 119, 121–23, 132; Mi'kmaq of, 4, 111–12, 122–25, 127; Native Council of, 129; Treaty Rights in, 119-20, 122
NPC. *See* Nunavut Planning Commission (NPC)
NTI. *See* Nunavut Tunngavik Inc. (NTI)
Numbered Treaties, 16n3, 62–63, 176–77. *See also* Treaty 8
Nunavut Impact Review Board (NIRB), 94–97, 99–100
Nunavut Land Claim Agreement (NLCA), 83, 93, 103n5, 229
Nunavut Planning Commission (NPC), 93
Nunavut Tunngavik Inc. (NTI), 96, 98, 102, 103n11
NWT. *See* Northwest Territories (NWT)

Office of L'nu Affairs, 128, 134
oil and gas activities, 155–57; in Alberta, 157; Indigenous Peoples' opposition to, 155–56; in New Brunswick, 23; in Nova Scotia, 23; in Saskatchewan, 210, 218
oil and gas industry, 155, 158–59, 164–65
oil sands, 158–59; companies, 164–65; development in Alberta, 15, 158–59, 163–64, 168; and Fort McKay First Nation (FMFN), 165–66; impacts from development, 157–58, 162–63, 165; and Lubicon Lake Band (LLB), 156, 166–67; opposed by First Nations, 158, 162, 164;

FSC
www.fsc.org

MIX
Paper
FSC® C100212

Printed by Imprimerie Gauvin
Gatineau, Québec